PENGUIN BOOKS

THE FOURTH HORSEMAN

Andrew Nikiforuk has been writing about people, dismal economies and the environment for more than a decade. His work has won National Magazine Awards in 1989, 1990 and 1993 and top honours for investigative reporting from the Association of Canadian Journalists. In 1991, under the auspices of the Atkinson Fellowship in Public Policy, he wrote a critically acclaimed series on AIDS and the failure of public health policy. He currently writes for a variety of magazines and newspapers and is working on a collection of historical tales about kidnapped Indians and whites. He and his family live in Alberta.

The FOURTH HORSEMAN

*A short history
of plagues, scourges
and emerging viruses*

Andrew Nikiforuk

Penguin Books

PENGUIN BOOKS
Published by the Penguin Group
Penguin Books Canada Ltd, 10 Alcorn Avenue, Toronto, Ontario, Canada M4V 3B2
Penguin Books Ltd, 27 Wrights Lane, London W8 5TZ, England
Penguin Books USA Inc., 375 Hudson Street, New York, New York 10014, U.S.A.
Penguin Books Australia Ltd, Ringwood, Victoria, Australia
Penguin Books (NZ) Ltd, 182–190 Wairau Road, Auckland 10, New Zealand

Penguin Books Ltd, Registered Offices: Harmondsworth, Middlesex, England

First published in Viking by Penguin Books Canada Limited, 1991

Published in Penguin Books, 1992

Published in this edition, 1996

10 9 8 7 6 5 4 3 2 1

Manufactured in Canada

Canadian Cataloguing in Publication Data

Nikiforuk, Andrew, 1955–
The fourth horseman: a short history of plagues, scourges and emerging viruses

Rev. ed.
Includes bibliographical references and index.
ISBN 0-14-025610-5

1. Epidemics – History. 2. Famines – History. 3. Plague – History.
4. Environmentally induced diseases.
I. Title.

RA649.N54 1996   614.4'9   C95-932314-7

DEDICATION

For Doreen and Aidan,
life partners

Contents

The FOURTH HORSEMAN

And I looked, and behold a pale horse: and his name
that sat on him was Death, and Hell followed with him.
And power was given unto them over the fourth part of
the earth, to kill with sword, and with hunger, and
with death, and with the beasts of the earth.

Revelation 6:8

PREFACE

Since this book was first published, a lot of spectacular dying has taken place. Always obliging, the Fourth Horseman has galloped across Africa slaying poor and hungry peasants with cholera, Ebola and tuberculosis. He has delivered HIV to the slums of Asia and hantavirus to the margins of North America. He has used measles to kill seals and dolphins in the great seas. He has infiltrated industrial hospitals and institutions for the elderly and the young with bacteria that no drug will kill. He has, in short, done his appointed job: that of reminding the species of its biological vulnerability when it no longer keeps its household tidy.

As a consequence, a whole shelf of books (and movies) has recently appeared on the awesome work of microbes in ravaged lands and among unhealthy peoples. The best of them include Richard Preston's riveting ode to Ebola, *The Hot Zone*, Robin Henig's measured account of emerging viruses, *A Dancing Matrix*, and Laurie Garrett's microbial encyclopedia, *The Coming Plague*. All are highly readable and important accounts, yet none encompasses the longer story told here. Nor do they share this book's tragic sense of the limits of human knowledge or, for that matter, its admittedly black humour. Consider it, then, a sort of mischievous elder among these page-turners, one with a deep memory and even deeper concerns about the species' descent into a technological chaos blind to Nature and its avenging angels: microbes.

Humankind has now arrived at a spooky crossroads. Death

5

from disease, death on an ever greater scale, is probably inevitable. Our mirage of sustainable health has evaporated in the post-antibiotic era. Neither our bodies nor our communities are particularly well. Our lands ooze like suppurating ulcers; our waters smell of foul things. God and Creation have been defiled and humiliated. Death's handmaiden, disease, couldn't have hoped for a more inviting terrain than this unbalanced and wounded world.

Given recent developments, I have revised and updated this book to include a discussion of emerging and newly transcendent microbes. The hyperactive state of today's flesh eaters, organ bleeders and lung hackers merely reflects the hectic course and increasing instability of technological society. Make one change and you bring about another, introducing new environmental disharmony along the way.

In adding these new, headline-grabbing stories, I hope to provoke readers into leading healthier lives and fighting for greener communities free of technological illusions. The next great plague will not wipe the slate clean but may very well reduce our arrogant numbers to a humble remnant. Once summoned, the Fourth Horseman cannot and will not rest.

Andrew Nikiforuk, Calgary, 1995

INTRODUCTION

Once upon a time a Russian peasant sat under a larch tree minding his own business. As he listened to the birds and the bees, he suddenly spied a large woman in billowing white robes approaching him. Before he could flee the apparition, the Pest Maiden had grabbed him by the neck. "Do you know the Pest?" she hissed. "I am she. Carry me through all Russia. Miss no village for I must visit all. Only you will be safe amid the dying." The peasant did as he was told and the Pest climbed on his back.

Every time they came to a village, the dogs howled, the Maiden waved her robes and hundreds of peasants fell dead before her. After a visit from the Pest, funeral processions clogged the streets. From village to village the peasant carried the Maiden, as commanded, until he could see his own town on top of a hill where his wife, children and aged parents lived. In horror, he threw off the Maiden into a river and plunged her beneath the water. They struggled and the peasant drowned. But shaken by her carrier's fearlessness, the Pest Maiden retreated to the forest to wait for another day and another peasant.

Pestilence used to be a big character in folk tales and an even bigger one in everyday life. People gossiped about Pest Maidens the way they now talk about the weather, and it wasn't idle chatter: most people died—of rashes, boils or bumps in one epidemic or another—before the age of thirty. Peasants never knew when or how the next epidemic might change their lives. Because plagues were such powerful and invisible creatures, story-tellers regularly recreated them as men in black, women in white and rampaging horsemen. With so much disease on the loose in ancient times, our ancestors prayed throughout the day. Before working, travelling or eating they asked God for help "so that neither the pestilence of this year nor the vanity of the world" would suck them under. Prayer seemed to have more meaning when cholera and plague stalked our neighbourhoods.

The biblical authors of the Book of Revelation understood the nature of pestilence in human affairs when they created the Fourth Horseman. Although many people regard the short book as a piece of trumpet-blaring prophecy, it's actually about the presence of history in everyday life. With much fanfare, chapter six of Revelation identifies history's most colourful forces as the four riders of the Apocalypse. Each Horseman has his own fantastic mission. The first rider sits on a white horse, wears a crown and represents the world of God, life and hope. War, the Second Horseman, commands a blood-red steed and carries a huge sword. He also symbolizes the power of government and uncivil politics. The Third Horseman travels on a black horse and holds a scale to measure prosperity and Famine. He is the original dismal economist. The Fourth Horseman, the subject of this book, commands a pale and anemic mount. He is both Pestilence and Death (ancients couldn't tell the two apart) and has the power to kill a "fourth part of the earth" with hunger, sickness and "beasts of the earth" in all shapes and sizes. Together, the Four Horsemen have made and unmade history with revolutions, crop failures and an ever-changing assortment of epidemics.

According to the great Christian philosopher Jacques Ellul, the Four Horsemen surge and disappear like the seasons. The only thing regular about their chaotic galloping is their cyclical appearance. They often canter alone or, like Famine and War, carefully scout the trail for Pestilence. "They pass by, overturning our lives and our comprehension of society and history," says Ellul. "All history depends on them and there are only these forces in history."

Of all the riders of the Apocalypse, the Fourth Horseman has been the busiest. By killing millions in a single month or year, epidemics have crumbled empires, defeated armies and forever changed the way we live and love. Smallpox conquered the New World with such force that the political wounds have hardly healed on the face of Indian culture. Plague defeated feudalism, fertilized the seeds of capitalism and inspired a distrust of nature that still motivates economists and doctors. Malaria extended the viability of the slave trade and coloured the future of the Caribbean. Syphilis introduced menace to sex and people to the wig. Although we may have forgotten our plague-ridden past, the Fourth Horseman still rides into our lives at his convenience. AIDS offers more proof that Pestilence never rests.

Today we don't like to think that we are part of history anymore, or that we are walking memories of past plagues. We believe that clean streets, cotton clothes, garbage trucks and food inspectors have tamed and silenced pestilence. We don't talk about Pest Maidens and Horsemen, and we believe that AIDS is an aberration, a temporary throwback. Along with these assumptions, we also support one of the great lies of the twentieth century: that antibiotics, vaccines and doctors have saved us from pestilence. We entertain this fiction even when history has repeatedly unmasked the youngest science as a bumbling trade that has never stopped a major epidemic. The Fourth Horseman has always galloped out of the picture of his own volition.

The history-making plagues documented in this book began in healthy colonies of bacteria, fungi, viruses or protozoa. These microbes are only some of "the beasts of the earth" that the Book of Revelation identifies as the Fourth Horseman's accomplices. (Rats, lice and fleas also belong to this club.) It takes strong provocation to send germs on a killing spree, and an even stronger effort to stop them once the dying has begun. But when microbes have come aflying, they have usually responded to upheavals in civilization. Wars, overcrowding, farming, tourism, homelessness and pollution can all arouse one or more beasts. Germs have merrily joined in the riots of human history as professional looters. With our ever-changing engines of progress we have always started the riots and blindly summoned the Horseman. The Russians knew this instinctively: the peasant carried the Pest Maiden on his back, and not vice versa.

Forgetting or ignoring the history-making power of pestilence is an act of gross negligence. As the human "population avalanche" continues, people are uprooting or disturbing more microbes and beasts than in all recorded history. The great medical ecologist René Dubos never tired of reminding disbelievers of the unpredictable ways in which microbes and the Fourth Horseman set the boundaries of our history. Dubos didn't buy the modern idea that humans control their own "biological and cultural destiny" and called our relatively plague-free existence a "mirage." He knew that life without Pestilence was a grand illusion. This book, with all of its blood, guts and sex, is a reminder that no matter how pervasive the illusion, the Fourth Horseman always takes his quarter.

1

BEASTS, GERMS AND THE SUPERORGANISM

Guess who this powerful creature is
Who lived before the flood,
Without flesh and blood
Without bones and veins,
Without head and foot.
It becomes neither older nor younger
Than it was in the beginning.
Taliesin

One of the most popular books ever written about germs reads like a war manual. *Microbe Hunters* has more invading, killing and conquering in it than all of *War and Peace*. The title refers to a group of pioneering nineteenth-century scientists, including Louis Pasteur and Robert Koch; the book lionizes these men as a band of warrior-saints intent on saving humankind from demonic germs. In every chapter the brave "Tsars of science" rush from lab to lab ambushing anthrax, attacking tubercles or hunting down cholera bacilli, "the terrible little murderers from the Orient." Without "the Super Napoleonic" skills of the "Death Fighters," microbes might have marched all over the earth, brutally murdering women and children. Caught in the urgency of war, assistants to the great microbe hunters obey search-and-destroy instructions: "Find the microbe, kill the microbe." The great struggle against microbial "assassins" and "sub-visible invaders" also had a secret weapon: "the magic bullet" or the antibiotic. Since its publication in 1926, *Microbe Hunters* has sold millions of copies; new doctors still read it like a boot camp manual.

Not much has changed in the public imagination since *Microbe Hunters* made germs as popular as sharks. Humans don't like *Escherichia coli* or adenoviruses any more than they have liked wolves, auks or passenger pigeons. If a creature doesn't walk upright or look like a baby seal, humans will probably exterminate it. Ever since Pasteur first declared that "microbes are a menace" in the 1880s, scientists have been hunting germs like buffalo with one magic bullet after another. Pasteur didn't intend this kind of hostility but his discoveries put biologists on the war-path. The famous French scientist also didn't really believe that "germ theory," the idea that one germ equals one disease, answered all the great questions about infection. From his experiments with silkworms, he knew that the health and even the body temperature of the host, whether worm or human, had as much to do with a microbe's killing ability as the microbe itself. This kind of laborious ecological analysis has never appealed to twentieth-century doctors and scientists on the move. They have preferred the battlefield approach and have wholeheartedly adopted the "germ theory," giving it a more warlike title: "the doctrine of specific etiology." If one germ equals one disease, then one drug should take care of it. Mention the word bacteria and doctors still run for antibiotics as quickly as duck hunters dive for shotguns. To this day modern medicine is largely based on the training of pill pushers and germ slayers. They have a narrow view of illness and an incredibly distorted view of germs.

The real truth about bacteria reads like science fiction and is a lot more exotic than warfare. Bacteria are not only our ancestors but our number one life-support system. They clean our

water, prime the atmosphere and take care of the dead. Instead
of killing and invading life, they nurture and protect it. As the
planet's oldest, brightest and most numerous life-forms, bacteria
work in teams as one big superorganism. The art of successful
living and planet regulating has taken bacteria two and a half
billion years to learn. Relatives, no matter how distant, don't
generally go out of their way to murder other relatives unless
they have a good reason, and this is also true of the superorganism. It has become a killing machine only when people have
kicked or trampled its frontiers, violating unwritten bacterial
codes. No other offspring or dependent species has disturbed
and challenged the superorganism as much as we have.

Bacteria are not like any other living creature: scientists
even put them in their own class. Unlike plants, fungi and animals they are primarily one-celled beings. As such, they remain
bacteria and never congregate to form ancillary bodies such as
skin, livers or bark. Bacteria even look different from other
creatures and come in the shapes of tiny rods, spirals and
spheres. Under a microscope the tubercle bacillus, for example,
looks like a maneless sea-horse. The rickettsia or typhoid fever
resembles a mouse stool and the plague bacillus has a jelly bean
shape. Syphilis takes the form of a thin slice of corrugated roof
metal. Three hundred years ago a Dutch dry goods merchant,
Anthonie van Leeuwenhoek, first spied some of these "animal-
cules" and "wretched beasties" under his home-made microscope. He found them in drinking water, on his teeth, in the
stomachs of frogs and horses, on cheese and even in his own
excrement after a bout of "looseness." Their behaviour made
Leeuwenhoek an ecologist: "Life lives on life—it is cruel, but it
is God's will."

Much to scientists' eternal discomfort, bacteria will always
outnumber the human race in spite of our best reproductive
efforts. Each gram of soil houses between 1 and 10 billion bacterial cells, twice the human population on earth. A single hand-

held laboratory test tube can grow several billion microbes from one cell in a day. No one knows how many different bacterial species there might be, but scientists agree that there are more rod-shaped and sphere-shaped creatures in the world than the 1.5 million higher species such as beetles and elephants.

Bacteria's weight of numbers is the product of elementary school math. They reproduce asexually by division, swelling up and splitting in two. With the right amount of food, bacteria can divide every twenty minutes and produce more of themselves in two days than human beings have in their entire history.

Bacteria are also enduring creatures. When strapped for nutrients some soil bacteria will join together to form a "fruiting body." The top consists of spores that can survive for hundreds of years. In fact, scientists recently awakened one 25-million year-old spore from the gut of a bee trapped in amber.

Aided by longevity and flexibility bacteria cover the world like a fine invisible crust which is very thick in places. They have been found at heights of thirty-two kilometres and at depths of eleven kilometres beneath the Pacific Ocean. Their ancient and traditional haunts include hot springs, desert soils and buffalo stomachs. More recent housing projects include air conditioners, whirlpools, toilets, hospitals and discarded coffee cups. People also make good hosts. Bacteria long ago colonized the human skin, nose, mouth, intestines and genitals where they live as peacefully as grass in a middle-class suburb. Our ancestry can be traced by counting our cells. The human body is held together by 10 quadrillion animal cells and 100 quadrillion (100,000,000,000,000,000) bacterial cells. Humans are made of bacteria, surrounded by bacteria and dependent on bacteria.

Microbes are the planet's busiest creators and destroyers. Without them the earth would be a static dung heap of dead animals, plants and humans. The Harvard biologist Lynn

Margulis says bacteria can assemble and disassemble all the molecules of modern life except for a few plant hallucinogens and snake venoms. Working in teams, bacteria recycle and transform the dead, whether animal or vegetable, into food for worms and fertile soil for farmers. From the air they fix or capture nitrogen gas and return this life-giver to trees and other creatures. No other life-form can do this. When breathing oxygen they make iron and manganese. In the stomachs of goats and cows they turn half-chewed grasses into digestible sugars. They sour milk, ripen cheese and ferment wine. With the help of algae and other micro-organisms they purify water of the natural human and animal residues. And bacteria don't rest on Sundays.

Aiding bacteria in all of this work are a number of microbial allies, including protozoa (unicellular animals), fungi and viruses. Viruses are floating bits of genetic material and members of the living dead. They don't really come to life until they invade a specific cell belonging to an animal, plant or bacterium and hijack its life-support system to reproduce themselves. As primitive genetic messengers, viruses can provoke evolutionary change in a species and even alter the colour of tulips. Humans contain a lot of genetic information deposited by viruses. Although smaller than bacteria, these tiny microbes are just as ubiquitous. Many keep bacterial communities in check by causing great epidemics and die-offs. The superorganism respects viruses and employs them as freelance evolutionary anarchists.

If a team of bacteria had written the world's history, humans would appear as a period at the end. Earth's very first living creature was a bacterial cell that breast-stroked across the planet's Archean murk. Using rocks, gases and light for energy, bacteria did what they do best: over two and a half billion years they multiplied. With their fermenting billions, bacteria changed the earth from a volcanic wasteland into a green land capable of supporting plants, fungi, animals and humans. A bacterial history might also boast that bacteria invented photo-synthesis, as well as pigments and vitamin A for protection against ultraviolet light. There is also the heroic story of how fearless armies of bacteria dined on hydrogen and farted oxygen. This gas, combined with bacteria's other explosive wastes (ammonia, carbon dioxide and methyl chloride), created the friendly atmosphere that supports all other living creatures. The planet's very stability still depends on the collective farting, belching, feasting and shitting of bacteria.

Through history bacteria have witnessed some amazing calamities. Unexpected ecological catastrophes have frozen and warmed the Earth over the millennia but bacteria have always come out smiling. Their indomitable hordes have adapted and increased while dumber creatures such as dinosaurs and woolly mammoths have died off. Ninety-nine percent of the species that have inhabited Earth have ultimately become no more than curious fossil records. Bacteria, however, have resisted extinction as stubbornly as they have resisted antibiotics.

The big secret of bacteria's survival is their ability to solve problems. Unlike humans, bacteria share an incredible genetic unity. Faced with a threat to their well-being, bacteria simply order up life-saving genetic information from other bacterial cells, with the same ease that human beings order take-out pizza. Unencumbered by a closet full of genes, bacteria have simply exchanged hereditary life-information whenever neces-sary. Scientists compare this bacterial gene-pool exchange to consumers using the central data bank of Bell Telephone, Interpol or American Express. The only difference is that bacte-ria are much better and faster at exchanging information than humans are.

Scientists didn't appreciate this genetic unity until doctors started overprescribing penicillin in the 1940s. The primary bacteria under assault were staphylococci, grape-like clusters of germs that poison the blood and lurk in hospitals where unhealthy patients provide them with ample food and warmth. Faced with extinction, the staphylococci put in a call to the great bacterial gene pool where they located an enzyme among a community of soil bacteria that could digest the antibiotic and render it harmless. The life-saving information was quickly relayed back to the staphylococci. This bacterial exchange has been repeated across the globe for almost every antibiotic ever designed. Both tuberculosis and gonorrhea have developed successful drug-resistant strains. Sorin Sonea, a Montreal physician who has a great respect for bacteria's resilience, recently observed that any other species needing a similar enzyme "might have required approximately one million years to synthesize it by means of random mutation attempts." In self-defence, bacteria have removed most of the magic from "magic bullets."

Until about ten thousand years ago, humankind and the superorganism lived together in relative peace. In this era of mutual tolerance hunters and gatherers left few footprints on the land because they kept their numbers at a level the local jungle (the original grocery store) could sustain. They didn't build great piles of garbage and they didn't jet from one hunting ground to another, exposing themselves to unfamiliar microbes. Aside from the odd intestinal parasite, their only fatal encounter with disease may have been food poisoning. To avoid diarrhea and stomach cramps, hunters gradually learned how to dry and cure meat. The spear carriers and nut gatherers of old were noble specimens: they stood tall, had good teeth and were generally so healthy that the only way they could really control overcrowding was to kill children. The routine drowning, strangling and abandoning of infants was for hunting people what measles, malaria and smallpox would later become for farming people. Infanticide kept the number of mouths roughly equal to the number of four-legged steaks available.

This brief era of bacterial tolerance disappeared as soon as

people began their famous "population avalanche" and started
to colonize the earth. René Dubos calls it an avalanche because
the human species didn't explode, it just started to accumulate
dangerously like packed snow on the side of a mountain. Ten
thousand years before Christ, 10 million humans hunted and
gathered on the planet. But after the invention of the plough,
more than 200 million had embarked on crusades to civilize the
landscape. The agricultural revolution began in earnest when
hunters ran short of woolly mammoths and other big game to
kill, and started to tame plants and animals. In the Middle East
they "conscripted" wheat, barley, peas, lentils, donkeys, sheep,
pigs and goats. In Southeast Asia they chose rice, sweet potatoes, taro, ducks and chickens. Everywhere people started to
congregate in great numbers, they all preached the new gospel
of agriculture: thou shalt enslave other species to help humans
multiply and dominate more species.

This aggressive drive didn't take into account the superorganism. By breaking up the soil and taming herds of cattle and
goats, humans collided with more microbes than they had ever
met before. Agriculture created a common market of diseases by
bringing together all manner of viruses, fungi and bacteria in
human gardens, houses and villages. When the dog became
man's best friend so too did measles. With the cow came tuberculosis and diphtheria. Rhinoviruses (the common cold) probably came riding in on a horse. Anthrax popped out of the soil.
These biological collisions were probably a shock for all species
involved.

Thrust into totally new environments, some of the microbes
panicked and died while others went on killing sprees. Over
time many gradually learned to live with farmers because dead
humans make poor food supplies. After taking an initial beating, the human immune system also changed and adapted as it
became exposed to more infections. But the Fourth Horseman
wasn't fully roused until farms allowed increasing numbers of

Early farmers uprooted microbes and annually harvested an alarming array of deadly epidemics from measles to anthrax.

idle people to build cities. Human beehives have always created enormous opportunities for the superorganism to flourish. A metropolis, by definition and design, excels at constructing garbage heaps, adding feces to water and poisoning the air.

When humans started living too close to their own garbage piles, they inadvertently became part of the superorganism's dinner and sprouted an endless variety of skin and gut diseases, including leprosy, cholera and dysentery. To avoid stomach cramps and loose bowels, the Chinese started to boil their tea while the French opted for fermented grape juice.

Unlike vigorous hunters and gatherers, relatively sedentary wheat growers and lentil planters were a stooped and hungry lot. They ate too many carbohydrates and their teeth rotted out. Because of foul water supplies, many drank too much wine and became alcoholics. Growing cereals and roots was no more a stable enterprise five thousand years ago than it is now. Periodic droughts, baby booms and greedy ruling élites introduced famine as an historical constant. Humans stressed by hunger can't help but attract germs to do their bacterial duty: to dismember and decay.

The ceaseless ploughing of land and chopping of forests, which agricultural empires celebrated as progress, also invited other parasites. The killing of wild lands forced rats, mice, ticks, fleas and mosquitoes to live closer to humans. These scavengers brought genuine surprises such as plague, tularemia, typhus and malaria. When cities of a hundred thousand people began to appear, great die-offs became as common as thunderstorms. To city builders such as the Sumerians, Egyptians and Israelites, pestilence became such a routine event that everyone concluded epidemics were divinely inspired. Horsemen, demons and Pest Maidens appeared everywhere.

The periodic depopulation of ancient cities by epidemics set in motion a variety of crude biological forces. Because the conditions of urban life exposed humans to more stress, famine and microbes than their immune systems could control, cities had to import peasants regularly or become ghost towns. To counter rapid urban die-offs, governments, clerics and the whip encouraged peasants in rural areas to marry young and have lots of children. Big families still remain a feature of peasant life because great biological lessons take a long time to unlearn.

Throughout most of "civilized" history, peasants have been biological fodder for the great microbial communities that cities grew and nurtured. Until the 1600s, most of the world's great metropolises renewed their wealth by swallowing the sons and daughters of soil tillers. Whenever the peasants multiplied too quickly, city states usually disposed of the surplus through famine or by declaring war on a neighbour. The outcome of the war generally depended on which side had accumulated the greatest disease resistance. The Arabs, for instance, defeated the Crusaders with malaria, while the Russians repelled Napoleon's armies with typhoid. One of the reasons the Army of the Union won the American Civil War was that it could afford to lose more men to diarrhea than the Confederate Army could. When battling expansionist Europeans, nomads, hunters and New World aboriginals have usually lost the war because of their lower exposure, and therefore lower resistance, to germs. In this respect, until this century, all warfare has been fought with germs and won by farm and city people with the tougher immune systems.

Our ancestors took a long time to appreciate the logic of great die-offs. One of the first to notice that war, drought, famine, humidity and even the wind played a role in these complicated dramas was Hippocrates. He referred to these environmental forces as "air, water and places." The Greek epidemiologist believed that rapid changes in any of these factors brought about epidemics. He concluded that a doctor should be "skilled in Nature and must strive to know what man is in relation to food, drink, occupation and which effect each of these has on the other." Unlike most of his contemporaries, he recognized that disease didn't come calling unless there had been either great changes to human health or great changes made to the health of the land. He didn't know about the superorganism but he could recognize its handiwork.

The Hippocratic idea that humans make epidemics as easily as bakers bake pies found its wisest convert in Rudolf Virchow. He was a nineteenth-century bacteria watcher, doctor, anthropologist and medical reformer and a robust Prussian. Virchow kept so many bones in his office that he had to meet people in a nearby hotel in order to talk. During a long career of studying microbes, Virchow invented the best and shortest definition of disease ever written: "life under altered conditions." By altered conditions he meant changes in diet, trade, travel, housing, clothes and weather—in short, the total environment. Meddle with the conditions of life, predicted Virchow, and the relationship between humans and microbes will change in unforeseen and often fatal ways.

As the father of modern epidemiology, Virchow first assembled these thoughts in 1848 when he went to Upper Silesia, now part of Czechoslovakia and Germany, to investigate a typhus epidemic among poor cotton workers. His visit later became the subject of a long and famous report that implicated heavy rains, bad housing and poverty more than typhus germs. "Epidemics," he concluded, "resemble great warnings from which a statesman in the grand style can read that a disturbance has taken place in the development of his people." Virchow's prescription for the people of Upper Silesia had nothing to do with doctors or drugs but included agricultural reform, self-government, democracy and industrial co-operatives. To Virchow, medicine was not a matter of hunting microbes but of uncovering the ecological and social forces that fed disease.

Virchow knew that humans, because they are humans, have a knack for constantly changing their living space and uprooting the homes of other species. In this historical drama people inadvertently construct one "abnormal condition" after another. The march of civilization is really the story of how changes in human economies and health have begot abnormal situations and much disease. Despite what the germ theorists might say, the superorganism merely signals these social crises with epidemics as part of its ancient mission to maintain the earth's life-support system in good working order. The earth's first-line defence mechanism will only tolerate so much crowding, pollution and deforestation before some of its members intervene. The superorganism, because it is the superorganism, can't behave any other way.

Virchow didn't know about the unity of bacteria but he did understand the meaning of epidemics. Throughout his career he lamented that the knowledge of pestilential disturbances seemed to decrease with each new generation of medical students and politicians. Not much has changed in the last hundred years except that the germ theorists, microbe hunters and pharmaceutical companies are now doing an even better job of obscuring the truth: that humans are the aggressive architects of plagues.

2

MALARIA:

THE GREAT WINNOWER

And it is as though she who visits me were filled with modesty
For she does not pay her visits save under the cover of darkness
I freely offered her my linen and my pillows,
But she refused them and spent the night in my bones.
My skin is too contracted to contain both my breath and hers
So she relaxes it with all sorts of sickness.
When she leaves me she washes me (with Perspiration),
As though we had retired apart from some forbidden action.
Ahmad Ibn-al-Husayn Al-Mutanabbi

Major Ronald Ross spent half of his life trying to solve "The
Great Problem": how malaria infected humans. Soldiers of the
British Empire were dying in heaps overseas from fever, and the
army surgeon knew that pinpointing the cause would bring him
imperial fame and fortune. In pursuit of both rewards, Ross
looked for the answer in England, in India and under micro-
scopes. He received the Nobel Prize in 1902, after he had finally
identified the life-cycle of the malaria parasite in birds. In

between dissecting mosquito stomachs, Ross wrote bad poetry in which he dubbed malaria "O million murdering death." His poetry suffered the same lack of imagination that prevented him from figuring out that only one kind of mosquito, anopheles, carried malaria. "O billion murdering death" would have been more accurate and would have given both malaria and the mosquito the credit they deserved.

Since the beginning of history malaria has killed half of the men, women and children that have died on the planet. It has outperformed all wars, all famines and all other epidemics. Until World War II it still accounted for 50 percent of the business at most cemeteries. Even today the reach of the plasmodium parasite, the smallest animal on earth, is impressive. Each year it occupies the bodies of nearly 600 million people, and each year it buries 1 million African infants. "Of all infectious diseases," says Sir Macfarlane Burnet, one of the world's great microbe story-tellers, "there is no doubt that malaria has caused the greatest harm to the greatest number."

But unlike the hungry armies of influenza or plague that strike with the suddenness of meteor showers, the malarial parasite has generally avoided abrupt die-offs. It is a winnower by nature, a slow and patient pruner of what the Roman Tertullian called "the luxuriant growth of the human race." By swimming and reproducing in human blood, plasmodium has pruned whole branches of the human tree by inducing fevers, inflaming spleens and raising pulses. Given the right conditions, the parasite can put human life into a dark coma and kill quickly. But as a committed winnower it mostly weakens the body, invites anemia, shuts down the immune system and encourages other diseases such as typhoid, influenza, dysentery and malnutrition to finish off the exhausted host. For every human directly killed by malaria, another four or five succumb to its indirect flirtations.

Like all hardy and efficient parasites, plasmodium favours the most vulnerable of the species by habitually targeting pregnant women and children. The women simply lose their immunity to the parasite while pregnant, and the children have no tolerance for animals swimming in their blood until their immune systems mature at five years of age. As a consequence, malaria leaves in its wake a wide trail of still births, miscarriages and premature infants susceptible to all manner of illness. Because its fevers can produce temperatures of 104° F—thereby cooking sperm— malaria also diminishes male fertility. These simple facts have long convinced malariologists, a very sober-minded group of scientists, that malaria has superhuman powers. The famed Italian student of plasmodium Angelo Celli concluded that malaria sabotaged national economies "by destroying blood, weakening physical resistance, and ruining mental energy and moral determination." Malaria, he said, also paralyzes and annihilates human energy and resources "by rendering the earth, our mother, inhospitable and pestilential."

Malaria's strong grip on human society is best illustrated by the impact of its absence. Sri Lanka, a tear-shaped tropical isle in the Indian Ocean, began a systematic campaign to wipe out malaria-carrying mosquitoes with DDT after World War II. The chemical assault not only reduced the incidence of fevers but also of infant diarrhea and other opportunistic infections. As the death rate dropped by half, the island became more crowded. By 1960 the seemingly benign campaign to eradicate malaria had already added 1 million more people to the island's population of 10 million. Today, as Sri Lanka struggles to support 17 million people, civil war has become the island's preferred means of ending life, controlling crowds and settling racial disputes. A society whose political and economic institutions, from open-air markets to tea plantations, had once been designed to accommodate malaria's high mortality rate, collapsed and exchanged mosquitoes for guns. When people tinker with malaria, they ultimately tinker with the structures of everyday life.

As the quiet and languorous subversive of epidemic diseases, malaria has undermined human history with the skill of an invisible guerrilla army. It has long preyed on bloated empires, participating in the decline of Greece and Rome with an effectiveness that neither decadence nor pornography could equal. It has also bled every army of any significance from Alexander the Great to General Westmoreland. (In Vietnam, U.S. troops suffered alarming attack rates as high as 53 cases per 1,000 troops per day.) When not crumbling empires or wounding armies, malaria has marked the world's demography with its own peculiar stamp. It has been "the white man's grave" in Africa for nearly four hundred years. The predominantly black population in the Caribbean reflects malaria's active participation in the slave trade. And had it not been for our obsessive desire to eradicate malaria, DDT would not now be present in the tissues of most living things on earth.

The origins of malaria, like those of all great infectious diseases, are ancient. The parasite likely arose in Africa where a hundred of its cousins still swim in the blood of apes, birds, reptiles and chimpanzees. Of the four tribes of plasmodia that crave human blood, *Plasmodium falciparum* is the most lethal. Because diversity is a hallmark of evolution's survivors, there are as many strains of *falciparum* as there are human beings. In choosing the gut of anopheline mosquitoes for transport, the parasite picked an efficient and indestructible mode of transmission. Anopheles is a distinguished race with more than four hundred tribes all over the globe. Some anopheles strike at dawn; others at dusk. Some enter homes and some stay in the bushes. Some feed on white people and some prefer blacks. Some thrive in still water; others bathe in fast rivers. With so many different strains and so many talented carriers, malaria has always comprised a vast batch of feverish diseases occupying an almost endless variety of landscapes.

African farmers probably prepared the ground for malaria's long relationship with humans when they cut down the first rain forest to grow yams and other starches. These early slash-and-burn techniques created the water-filled, sunlit ruts that anopheles need for quick breeding. After plasmodia swam long and hard in the blood of Saharan men and women, the two species negotiated a truce and achieved a mutual tolerance. For Africans this negotiation meant developing the sickle cell and a blood anomaly called G6PD deficiency. Although these genetic adaptations make it harder for the parasite to reproduce in the body, crowded cemeteries still remain the penalty for acquiring group immunity to fevers. When malaria took up long residence in Greece and Turkey, the people developed the same kind of immune defences over thirty-five generations.

Once out of Africa, malaria travelled in the blood of black slaves and seeded India where Hindus still regard the fever as the "King of Diseases." When it penetrated China several centuries before Christ, wise men assumed the new disease was three devils. They made the common mistake of confusing the tell-tale symptoms of headache, chill and fever with divine mischief. In this otherworldly trinity, one demon carried a hammer, the second a pail of cold water and the third, a stove.

Malaria's occupation of the Mediterranean attracted few metaphors but a variety of critical medical notices. Hippocrates, one of the founders of modern medicine, knew malaria intimately and described its signature in the time-tables of quotidian, tertian and quartan fevers. Drink marshy, stagnant and fenny waters, he warned, and "the physique of the people must show protruding bellies and enlarged spleen." Such a fate befell the most powerful of the Greeks, Alexander the Great. When he was thirty-three his armies had conquered Persia, Syria, Phoenicia, Arabia and Egypt, but he couldn't defeat malaria in the city of Babylon. His loyal and warlike Macedonians marched into his tent to bid farewell to a feverish near-corpse, soaked in sweat.

Unknown to the general, his malarial end foreshadowed that

of Greece. When plasmodium reached the empire via armies returning from foreign shores and in cargoes of black slaves, it had an easy time because the Greeks were great deforesters, soil-eroders and mosquito-breeders. As malaria secured a hold on the land, it sapped Greece's political energy, rendered couples childless and made farmers too sick to work. It also popularized "melancholia," a depression that appeared most commonly at the onset and peak of the malarial season. Running a country with a bunch of depressed and infertile men is a good recipe for failure. Cities fell into ruin and the anemic inherited the cradle of European democracy. Green historian W.H.S. Jones also detected a parallel collapse in Greek philosophy, which "became deeply pessimistic even in the hands of its best and noblest exponents." When "absence of feeling" and "absence of care" invaded the once conscientious halls of Greece's public affairs, malaria enjoyed its own golden age. It didn't relinquish the Greek countryside until the twentieth century.

The parasite won a similar but much greater victory over the Roman Empire. There, however, it patiently waited for the sophisticated society to complete the hydraulic engineering that would contribute to its own undoing. Like that of most empires, Rome's urban wealth depended on a network of canals, aqueducts, peasants and agricultural bureaucrats. If peasants went to war or the bureaucracy grew fat and lazy, the irrigation works plugged up, inviting mosquitoes to breed in pools of stagnant water. An outbreak of malaria usually wasn't far behind. The first terrible epidemic occurred during the first century B.C. in the Roman Campagna, a fertile and marshy market garden that fed the citizens of Rome. Its impermeable soil, *tufo terroso,* quickly filled with stagnant pools whenever peasants and bureaucrats failed to maintain drainage canals. The epidemic proved so lethal that it killed livestock and drove both farmers and the parasite into the city. Shipbuilders clear-cutting trees on mountainous slopes near the Campagna accelerated the spread of fevers by expanding the mosquito's breeding and killing grounds.

For the next five hundred years malaria chilled and wearied Romans. Whenever a citizen inherited an estate in the Campagna, relatives all gave the same advice: "You must sell it for as many pence as you can get or if you can't sell it, you must quit it." Good architects advised their clients to build on hills, "away from marshes, the poisonous exhalations of which exert a morbid influence on man"; bad architects didn't. Malaria's hold on Roman affairs even earned the fever a respected religious status. Poor and rich alike hailed the goddess Febris (fever), who was portrayed as a hairless old hag with prominent belly and swollen veins, as "the great, the mighty, the holy." The poet Lucretius noted that the goddess killed fairly, sparing no class: "Nor do hot fevers sooner quit the body if you toss about on a pictured tapestry and blushing purple, than if you must lie on a poor man's blanket."

A popular Roman remedy for malaria (and plague) required the educated to practise an early form of deconstructionist poetry. "Write several times on a piece of paper the word 'Abracadabra' and repeat the word in the lines below, but take away letters from the complete word and let the letters fall away one at a time in each succeeding line. Take these away, but keep the rest until the writing is reduced to a narrow cone. Remember to tie these papers with flax and bind them round the neck." The charm only worked, according to physicians, if it was worn nine days and then thrown over the shoulder into a stream flowing to the east.

Malaria ignored the Abracadabra talismans and emptied the Campagna of farmers. It also lowered the birth rate of Italo-Romans so fast that Barbarians, whose numbers were increasing, had to be recruited to fill the ranks of the empire's legions. By the fourth century A.D., men of Germanic descent commanded whole armies. Whenever Rome tried to repair the irrigation works in the Campagna, malaria simply waited for the hour of bureaucratic neglect and despotism to strike again. The emperors Hadrian and Titus had fever; Tiberius and Julius Caesar shook and trembled like leaves. When the Visigoths and Vandals marched on the ailing empire, "the air of Rome" met them at the gates, suffocating Alaric and all other would-be conquerors for centuries to come. Too weak to defend itself, Rome at least had one ally: malaria.

By the Middle Ages, plasmodia occupied most of temperate Europe where they picked off peasants in the continent's fertile lowlands. Each fall, families from the highlands would arrive in these malarial regions to harvest and thresh wheat for good wages. But because the seasonal migrants had no previous exposure to the parasite (it was too cold in the mountains for anopheles), malaria inevitably harvested peasants as rigorously as the highlanders harvested grain. They died "without medicine and without priests," the way most peasants died. In Bohemia, soil tillers composed a special prayer to fend off malaria. They rose at dawn, knelt in their fields, invoked the Holy Cross and uttered three Paternosters and three Aves. Without saying Amen, they then spoke directly to God: "Lord Jesus Christ, why do you tremble so? Have you perhaps a fever? I have none and will have none, and whosoever thinks of my sufferings, He also will have no fever."

While the peasants said prayers, their popes considered emigration. Malaria dispatched the holy men with such demonic regularity that papal candidates from outside Italy considered the appointment an early death sentence. Many cardinals specifically refused to serve in Rome because of its "bad airs" (mal'aria). Until foreign-born popes were allowed to rule from their country of birth in the fourteenth century, Catholics regarded their spiritual centre with more fear than respect. Malaria is also one reason why the papal court was moved to Avignon, where cardinals and popes died of plague and typhus instead.

Malaria did not begin to recede from Europe until the eighteenth century. Progress and its handmaidens had by then drained many large marshes and nearly denuded the continent of its wildest forests, a reservoir for mosquitoes. At the same time, farmers began to keep larger cattle herds, providing anopheles with a meal more to its taste than people. These changes to the land in addition to the building of better ventilated homes slowly separated Europeans from mosquitoes and fever.

In the New World, however, malaria found ample opportunities to meddle in human affairs. It arrived directly from Africa aboard the slave ships, and as soon as it had unpacked, it quickly exterminated aboriginals in the Caribbean and the coastal lowlands of Latin America. Its impact was so devastating that it left the descendants of slaves to populate Veracruz, Cartagena and Bahia. Black people's well-established resistance to malaria determined that the residents of Latin America's coast would dance to African rhythms while fever-free highlanders would play Amerindian flutes.

White European colonists did not understand the slave's tolerance to malaria and frequently attributed the characteristic to "thick skins" or "offensive odours from their persons." Fevers and fear of fevers not only monopolized the correspondence of sugar planters (and most seventeenth-century literature) but also gave rise to a scientific racism. In the eyes of the anemic slaveholder, the black's resistance to "hot fevers" biologically proved the slaves' "subhumanity." Malaria also convinced the slaveholders that their role in tropical climates was to govern and rule blacks because any outdoor labour for a white person could be fatal.

Malaria and yellow fever (a fatal virus carried by mosquitoes) entrenched a disease culture in the Caribbean that did not ensure slaves a long or happy life. It produced a class of young and brutal plantation owners who "lived fast, spent recklessly, played desperately and died young." Their cruelty and callousness knew no bounds. In what became "a race between quick wealth and a quick death," slaveholders over-worked and underfed their human property. Slaves that rebelled faced a summary disembowelment or a beating with bulls' penises. But in the American South, where malaria and yellow fever didn't pose as grave a threat to rural landowners, U.S. planters aged naturally and let a strong paternalism rule the welfare of their slaves.

The insalubriousness of plantation life in the Caribbean prompted a priest to write that "of ten men that go into the Islands, four English die, three French, three Dutch, three Danes and one Spaniard." In fact 30 to 40 percent of the Europeans that sailed into the Caribbean in the seventeenth and eighteenth centuries succumbed to one fever or another. But in addition to discouraging white immigration, disease also drove landed whites out. In 1643 Barbados counted 37,000 whites. In 1665 it had 23,000 whites and 20,000 slaves. And by 1712 blacks outnumbered whites nearly four to one. This pat-tern repeated itself in the Leewards, Jamaica, Guadeloupe and the Virgin Islands. Dread of early fever death ("Fear kills Bawkra," said the slaves of their bosses) eventually created an epidemic of absentee landlords. A headless political culture, in turn, left a legacy of economic mismanagement, treeless and eroded islands, and the feverish belief that "the best people" make quick fortunes and even faster exits.

Although vacationing whites now, ironically, regard the Caribbean as a place to rest and restore health, the region still labours under economic and political institutions defined by a pathological fear of disease. The underdevelopment that many tourists regard as a symbol of black backwardness is actually the outcome of a paranoid European imperialism that sought to rape and pillage the region before its "fevers" undid the world of the slaveholders and their economic ambitions.

Death halted construction on the Panama Canal until American engineers
imported a malaria-resistant workforce: the descendants of black slaves.

In the twentieth century, public health officials have uncon-
sciously inherited the slaveholders' terror of malaria. Their well-
intentioned campaign to eradicate the disease has been just as
disastrous for Third World environments as was the disease culture that drove the Caribbean into a Roman decline. Single-
minded goals, of course, rarely achieve single results. The slavish efforts of educated scientists to rid the world of both plasmodia and mosquitoes—a fantasy akin to removing the stars

from the sky—are a classic case of the species destroying more life than it has saved.

In 1957 the World Health Organization deemed malaria's destruction an attainable goal, an assertion based largely on the availability and effectiveness of a new pesticide called DDT. First tested as a killer of Colorado potato beetles in 1939, DDT soon became a slayer of lice on European refugees, and a "killer of killers" in the mosquito-infested islands of the South Pacific. In seizing the Dutch Indies (then the source of quinine, malaria's only known reliable treatment), the Japanese calculated that they could count on mosquitoes to reduce Allied armies to an indolent mass of invalids in Pacific jungles. (Malaria did indeed hospitalize nearly half a million U.S. troops between 1942 and 1945). However, the development of atabrine (a synthetic drug) and the Marine Corps' liberal use of DDT defeated Japan's insect allies and its first line of defence.

But once DDT had established a reputation as "the atomic bomb of the insect world," public health officials adopted the weapon with unquestioning fervour. By the 1960s when the World Health Organization's anti-malarial campaign peaked, 76,000 tons of DDT had been dropped on 76 countries. Although the chemical initially killed anopheles with clinical efficiency, it soon bred a stronger and more resistant adversary. At least 57 mosquitoes can now swim in DDT and other insecticides without suffering any ill effects. Gallons of DDT sprayed randomly also produced a myriad unforeseen health problems.

A typical case of good intentions gone awry occurred in Sarawak, part of Borneo. Here the spraying of homes with DDT killed not only mosquitoes but also cockroaches. Free of predators, the Malaysian field rat, a carrier of plague and typhus, overran the mosquito-free villages. Fearing an outbreak of plague, the WHO eventually asked the Royal Air Force to drop cats by parachute over the isolated villages. Fortunately for Sarawak's peasants, "Operation Cat Drop" helped avert an epidemic of plague that DDT and malarial control had invited into their villages.

Aside from poisoning birds, fish and mother's milk, DDT also left another powerful legacy. Public health officials became so infatuated with the insecticide that the study of bugs and bug habitats fell into disrepute. In the 1970s the number of American Ph.D. students studying insects numbered 170; today that figure is 100 or less. "DDT didn't eliminate malaria," says American entomologist Robert Gwadz of the National Institute of Allergy and Infectious Disease, "but it did eliminate malariologists."

This decline is one of the more unfortunate consequences of the WHO's campaign against malaria because the disease is once again on the resurgence. Although the WHO temporarily succeeded in removing malaria from 80 percent of its original range, the parasite still remains strongest where human populations are greatest. It has also reappeared in old haunts such as Sri Lanka and Guyana (formerly British Guiana). India spends nearly half of its health budget battling fevers, and in Brazil malaria cases have jumped from 50,000 to 600,000 a year in the past two decades.

Malaria owes its renewed vigour almost exclusively to human tinkering with the environment. The systematic logging and mining of the Amazon basin has left the kinds of holes, ruts and sunlit areas that DDT-resistant anopheles need to produce 20 million offspring in two months. In the forests of Thailand and Sri Lanka, gem mining has produced similar malarial outcomes: holes dug for precious stones in the forest serve as nurseries for anopheles. Even the planting of a forest has created new malarial epidemics. In Trinidad, the introduction of immortelle trees as shade for cacao plants merely gives anopheles an opportunity to breed in the water collecting on little parasite growths (bromeliads) that thrive on immortelles.

Across Africa, both mosquito and plasmodium faithfully dog the progress of humans by breeding in the stagnant pools created by new building, roads and irrigation works. In fact, wherever people have introduced rice farming in the tropics (more open pools of water), epidemics of malaria have followed as predictably as rain—in Kenya, Venezuela, Tanzania, India and Syria. Just as irrigation created problems for the Romans, it is now unleashing a familiar chain of events in India and Africa. The Kalimave Dam in Tanzania, for example, allowed farmers to cultivate more land, which meant that their cattle—the local mosquito's favourite meal—had to graze farther from the villages. With no easily accessible meal in sight, the mosquito simply changed hosts and dined on the human inhabitants with malarial consequences. Such fables of plasmodium's ingenuity appear daily in Third World newspapers.

Thanks to the WHO, malaria is a much leaner and meaner regiment of diseases today. Not only are its carriers resistant to chemicals, but the plasmodium parasite itself has developed a similar resistance to the battery of drugs that are overprescribed to eradicate it. Chloroquine, the cheapest and most effective of these weapons, is now quite useless in Asia and increasingly ineffective in Africa. The parasite has also developed a tolerance for mefloquine. For tropical doctors and visitors very few alternatives remain, other than praying to the goddess Febris.

Like a faithful dog, malaria follows in the energetic footsteps of civilization and reduces to a crawl empires that threaten to overtax the land. In the 1950s, Sir Macfarlane Burnet suggested that humans have never appreciated malaria's complicated role in the scheme of things. His sobering observations ring as true today as they did forty years ago: "If malaria could be suddenly eliminated from the globe, the racial, economic and political consequences within a very few years would probably be appalling." He knew the sudden population growth that follows the temporary removal of malaria would produce famine, mass immigration and bloody social upheaval. Life with malaria, then, is ultimately a reminder of what life would be without it.

3

Leprosy:

Immortal Blemish

I forbid you ever to enter churches, or to go into a market,
or a mill, or a bakehouse, or into any assemblies of people.
I forbid you ever to wash your hands or even any of your
belongings in spring or stream of water of any kind....
I forbid you ever henceforth to go out without your leper's
dress, that you may be recognized by others....
I forbid you to have intercourse with any woman except your
wife....
I forbid you to touch infants or young folks, whosoever they
  may be, or to give to them or to others any of your
  possessions.
I forbid you henceforth to eat or drink in any company except
that of lepers....
Manuale ad Usum Insignis Ecclesiae Sarum

In the French town of Arras at the turn of the twelfth century,
Jean Bodel, municipal worker and poet, introduced himself to
the leprosy germ. Medieval men were more likely to catch the

disease than were medieval women because men ran most of
the errands. Travelling was a hazardous business on medieval
streets and a city worker such as Bodel had to dodge dead animals, piles of garbage and cascades of watery stools from the
arbitrary emptying of chamber-pots. Splashing and wading
through this muck didn't improve a man's health but did expose
him to a wealth of bacteria. The record doesn't say, but Bodel
may also have had a leprous lover. In any case, by the year 1202
Bodel had begun to discover large hard swellings and spots on
his body. Like a lot of lepers he illegally tried to hide the spots
with extra clothes, but the blemish betrayed him to his watchful
neighbours. In desperation he visited a doctor and marvelled
how the man dared to undertake to shave and fissure such a
head, which was entirely diseased. The physician greased Bodel
with a few mercury ointments but everybody knew that leprosy
had no real cure. After a few weeks of denial Bodel realized that
he was bound for the clapper, the alms bowl and leperdom.

Once identified as a leper by the good citizens of Arras,
Bodel wrote a long letter announcing his departure from the
world of the living. A cast-out leper hardly ever saw his parents
or friends again, and writing a good *congé* was an ideal way to
say goodbye. Words for Bodel, the poet laureate of lepers,
flowed like tears. "I am so sorrowful that my heart breaks...."
His letter cries that he can no longer eat with the living, no
longer visit friends and no longer walk the streets of his home
town. "My sadness surpasses all others." A leper, thought Bodel,
can hide nothing, not even his despair. "God, you who give all
good, you who have beaten me with your ferule...."

Bodel had good reasons to grieve. The ceremony for separating a leper from the community (*separatio leprosarum*) was a
funeral mass. It took place in a church draped with black cloth
and the condemned sometimes arrived on a bier covered in a
black shroud. After a goodbye mass, the leper stood in a freshly
dug grave holding a candle while the priest dropped three

spadefuls of earth on him or her, saying, "Be dead to the world, be reborn to God." Bodel probably replied: "O Jesus, my redeemer, you formed me out of earth, you dress me in the body; let me be reborn in the final day." Everyone then sang a rousing rendition of *Libera me, Domine*. At the end of the mass the priest read the rules of the dead: no church-going, no touching of children, no drinking from public wells, no love-making (spouses could live with the smitten or get divorced) and no travelling without a leper's tools. Friends and relatives were allowed to stay with "the living dead" for the first night in case the leper got very depressed and had a "spiritual crisis." The priest set an example by putting the first donation in the leper's alms bowl.

Bodel was too poor to buy a room in a decent leper house, so he camped in a "wretched spot" downwind of Arras. He asked his former employers for assistance by arguing that he had caught the disease while on town business: "Messeigneurs, before I leave you, I ask you at this crisis, in the name of God and our birthplace, that you get up a subscription among you to put an end to this difficulty, for which each one ought to have pity." He learned that the leper only sees the backs of men: "The world excluded and persecuted me." In 1210 Bodel died a leper among lepers, believing, as only a leper could believe, that the last years of his life would cleanse his soul, give him eternal life and free him from leperdom.

The fate that cast Bodel out of society was not strictly medieval. As one of our oldest diseases, leprosy has thoroughly shaped the way we think about sickness and the treatment of the sick. The Egyptians called it "death before death," and sent their lepers out to a place called the City of Mud. In ancient China and India, lepers were killed or burned outright. Abandoning lepers was not a European invention, simply part of an old custom. But no matter how old the tradition, epidemic waves of leprosy so rattled Europeans during the Middle Ages

that the memory of leprosy still hangs over the continent like a
dark cloud. When writers and politicians need a gutsy metaphor
for defilement and abandonment, they still pick leprosy.
Graham Greene once defined innocence as a "dumb leper who
has lost his bell, wandering the world, meaning no harm." Even
today the righteous still speak of "moral lepers," beggars cry, "I
am no leper," and we all understand the meaning. This is a
remarkable achievement for a disease that disappeared from
most of Europe in the fifteenth century.

The most impressive memorial that leprosy left Europe was
the hospital. All of the oldest and most famous infirmaries in
France, Italy and England began as leper houses. Leper charity
made these early hospitals wealthy enough to expand and nurse
the sick on a regular basis. The survival of these institutions
stands as a powerful reminder of leprosy's influence on human
behaviour because the invention of the hospital, as a place to
segregate and house the sick, merely formalized a very primitive
custom. Casting out and forsaking the incurable and the
deformed began with hunting and gathering people, and even
today every chronic, long-term disease looks a bit like leprosy to
us. Had Bodel lived in this century and been struck with multiple sclerosis, chronic fatigue syndrome or even AIDS, people
would have given him leper looks. Shunned by relatives, forgotten by employers, ignored by physicians and forced to plead for
lodgings and care, Bodel would have found life today a misery—
and all without the medieval comfort of knowing that, like the
spotted Lazarus, his place in heaven was reserved.

Although we don't sweat in the presence of lepers as much
as our ancestors did, we remain just as baffled by the illness.
Leprosy is such an ancient disease that nobody really knows its
origins. It may come from the water buffalo, the armadillo or be
a purely human infection. Although the Norwegian physician
Armauer Hansen first associated the bacillus *Mycobacterium leprae* with leprosy in 1874, doctors still don't know how it is

spread. Most scientists agree that the health of the infected host has a greater say over the course of the disease than the bacterium itself. Like AIDS, leprosy seems to prey on faltering immune systems. Because the unwashed, the undernourished and the ill-clothed generally have immune defences with more holes than the ozone layer, leprosy has mostly been a disease of the poor. Africa and India are home to 15 million lepers today.

Leprosy can dress the infected in as many different looks as an Italian fashion designer. Textbooks list an endless variety of physical symptoms, including ulcers, spots, bumps and disfigurements. Their shape, number and form tell how well the immune system is fighting the bacteria. The symptoms of success are mild joint pains and pale skin (tuberculoid leprosy or white leprosy). Defeat comes in the grotesque and infectious costume of lepromatous leprosy, which erodes noses, swells lips and tongues, erases eyebrows, uproots hair, sculpts facial skin into leonine folds and contorts hands and feet into claws. Lepromatous leprosy also reduces the voice to a hoarse whisper, fixes the eyes into an unwinking stare and changes the gait to "someone about to mount a step." Over time lepers lose all sensation in their skin and muscles, and start to knock off knuckles and toes by accident. A leper can survive in such a deteriorating condition for more than a decade.

The bacterium responsible for leprosy's flesh-eating penchant is among the world's slowest growing germs and may incubate for ten, fifteen or even twenty years. Its degree of contagiousness is still being debated. Fewer than 10 percent of the people exposed to *Mycobacterium leprae* ever develop leprosy, and only half of these people ever sprout disfiguring bumps and blotches. Doctors suspect that the fastest way to catch the leprosy germ is to sleep with a leper or inhale his or her breath. But close contact doesn't always seem necessary; many people have developed leprosy without ever meeting a leper. Physicians hide their confusion by labelling leprosy "slightly contagious" or "feebly contagious." The thousands of lepers that suddenly clogged medieval highways in the fourteenth century indicate that the germ either had a more forceful personality during the Middle Ages or a better diet. Medieval people believed that leprosy was extremely contagious and feared it as the worst scourge that could befall them. Anglo-Saxons even called it *seo mycle adl*, "the great disease."

Although scientists still have big questions about leprosy, medieval thinkers supplied as many answers as they could reasonably invent. Physicians of the Middle Ages generally defined leprosy as a venereal disease and considered lustful behaviour ("many burn with a desire for coitus") an important symptom; Rufus of Ephesus said lepers were particularly seized by "ardour for coitus" when their eyebrows swelled and their cheekbones went red. Men also had to be careful during the time of women's "flowers" because menstruating women poisoned animals and stained mirrors; "on some occasion those men who lie with them in carnal intercourse are made leprous." Men could also catch leprosy from the bite of a poisonous snake, the consumption of rotten fish and "lykynge by a womman soone after that a leprous man hath laye by her." Linking leprosy with wanton sex probably started when people noticed either that skin contact spread the disease or that individuals anticipating a leprous verdict (and years of isolation) simply went on wild coupling sprees. The belief that full-blown lepers performed like sexual acrobats (similar to the myth of the virile drug user) made a good story but just wasn't true. It helped justify casting lepers out, but men and women with rotting limbs didn't usually have the energy for "arduous coitus" of any kind.

Not surprisingly, most people thought lepers were a bad-tempered and foul-mouthed lot. Theodoric, a surgeon, wrote that lepers "grow angry very easily" and that "patients suspect everyone of wanting to hurt them." Guy de Chauliac, surgeon to the Papal Court of Avignon and medieval Europe's greatest physician, called lepers "schemers and deceivers" who "wish to impose themselves upon the people....They have heavy and grievous dreams." At the time nobody really linked surly leper behaviour with being cast out of society like the foul contents of a chamber-pot.

According to the Catholic Church, all lepers were sinners, and avoiding one was simply a matter of escaping an obvious symbol of God's wrath. The Church mistakenly based its judgment on ancient Levitical laws for dealing with cleanliness (what pleased God) and defilement (what displeased Him); the leper unhappily fell into the filthy camp. The Church faithfully applied the ritual teachings of Leviticus to lepers. In Leviticus, the writer describes an ugly and disfiguring skin disease that the Hebrews called *tsara'ath*, a word that could also represent a blemish on a cloth or a wall. Those afflicted had to be separated from "the clean" until the short-term blemish went away. But sloppy translations of the Old Testament from Greek to Arabic and finally Latin mistakenly rendered the word as *lepra*. This error dramatically changed the tone of the Book of Leviticus. It commanded that "whosoever shall be defiled with the leprosy, and is separated by the judgment of the priest, shall...cry that he is defiled and unclean. All the time that he is a leper and unclean, he shall dwell alone without the camp." The Church read Leviticus correctly but applied it to the wrong disease, making the poor leper a symbol of God's displeasure.

Although the Church regarded all lepers as diseased souls, it also conferred upon them a special grace. This remarkable contradiction owes its existence to the parable of Lazarus. Lazarus was a hapless beggar, so "full of sores" that the dogs licked them. He fed on the crumbs that fell from the table of a nameless rich man clothed in purple and fine linen. When Lazarus died he went to heaven, but the rich man descended to hell where he demanded an explanation. God replied, "Thou didst receive good things in thy lifetime and likewise Lazarus evil things, but

In this startling medieval fresco, hapless lepers with claw-like limbs and saddle noses dare to express their anger and despair.

now he is comforted and thou tormented." Both priests and doctors offered the parable as a psychological anodyne when breaking the news to neighbours that they had leprosy. Guy de Chauliac instructed fellow doctors to tell patients that leprosy is the salvation of the soul, "and that they ought not at all to fear to say the truth: for if they are found lepers, that will be the purgatory of their soul, and if the world loathes them, God—who loved the leprous Lazarus more than others—does not." This was Bodel's and every other leper's consolation: salvation after death.

Medieval leper detectors often had a tough time separating leprosy from an army of medieval skin problems. In an era of intense population growth, hygiene just wasn't a priority. Nor was it a virtue. Many theologians preached filthiness as a form of sanctity while most of the saints never touched water. A lousy St Jerome said, "Who is once washed in the blood of

Christ need not wash again"—and didn't. St Simon Stylites had so many worms crawling out of his skin that most visitors couldn't stand to watch. The saints weren't alone in their filth or smells. Soap, a taxed luxury for the rich, remained about as common as comets for the poor until the nineteenth century. Cotton underwear had not yet been invented, and when it appeared in the 1800s people wore it to protect fancy outer linens from body grime. In the thirteenth century most people donned coarse wool, bathed infrequently and slept in the nude with a variety of animals and relatives for warmth. It's not surprising that their skin broke, scaled and cracked. Psoriasis, eczema, fungi, leucoderma and ergot (dermatologists missed their century) sprouted on the medieval family like a garden. Every now and then people with poor complexions were condemned to leperdom, a mistake still made by modern doctors.

The fine art of spotting a leper was serious business. Usually a tribunal of lepers, village elders or priests did the job. If necessary they made as many as twenty-two successive investigations, checking everything from the hair to urine samples. If suspects didn't look "loathsome" or "satyr-like", leper tribunals kept them under observation for a year. In some villages the entire parish would examine an individual: if they "shuddered" at their neighbour's leonine face or saddle nose, no more had to be said. The Danish bone expert Vilhelm Møller-Christensen recently proved the accuracy of these diagnostic techniques when he exhumed a leper cemetery dating from 1250 to 1550, located behind an old Danish hospital in Naestved. Seventy percent of five hundred skeletons had the warped facial bones of a leper.

The first hospital ever built in Europe was constructed by a rich leper named Zodicus in Constantinople during the fourth century. When a famine emptied the city's markets of food, the hospital caused an uproar because hungry peasants wanted to know why Zodicus was feeding so many useless mouths. Quoting the Bible, the masses argued that sheltering sinners had made God angry and brought on the famine. Emperor Constantius arrested Zodicus, and when he learned that the wealthy leper had a great collection of jewels, he demanded that Zodicus give them up. Zodicus agreed. He took the emperor to his leper house where all the lepers, including the emperor's own daughter, greeted the two men. Each leper held a lighted candle. "Here are my jewels," said Zodicus. Enraged, the emperor ordered that Zodicus be torn apart by wild mules and that his own daughter be drowned in the Bosporus. The emperor later had a change of heart and actually donated money to the house. Over the years it survived riots, fires and earthquakes, expanding to ten thousand beds.

Leprosy travelled across Europe in waves and first appeared in edicts and prohibitions around the 600s when lepers started to pop up on street corners like homeless New Yorkers. The number of deformed beggars in Europe's growing towns alarmed the powers-that-be and for different reasons they arrived at the Zodicus solution, concluding that the best way to remove the ugly loiterers was to put them into leper houses. The Catholic Church made the leper house an attractive investment for nobles by promising that the occupants would fervently pray for the souls of the benefactors. Funding a leper charity was like sponsoring a personal prayer service and buying a ticket to heaven at the same time. The English nobleman Robert de Roos admitted founding a leper house "partly for the general welfare and partly to promote his own eternal happiness." Alexander II of Scotland also set one up for the "health of [his] soul and for all [his] predecessors and successors." By the thirteenth century nearly a third of England's 1,103 hospitals were devoted to lepers while France maintained 2,000 lazarettes. At the peak of the epidemic in the thirteenth century, 19,000 leper houses lurked downwind from Europe's towns. Nearly every village and burg had one—rather like a Holiday Inn or a Sleep Cheap Motel.

Fortunately for lepers, early hospitals didn't look anything like the monstrous square boxes that the sick go to now. The first hospitals actually dispensed hospitality and served more as inns or roadhouses. In fact, England's very first hospital, Carman's Spittle, was set up to protect travellers from hungry wolves and other beasts. The innkeepers of these primitive hotels were usually clerics, who entertained the poor, the sick and the weary when not saying prayers to their benefactor. Nursing was never much of a priority. The leper house combined these varied functions with its own specific needs and was part prison, part monastery and part almshouse; many lazarettes actually housed more clerics than they did lepers. Leper historian Charles Mercier says the main duty of the leper house was to be "a compulsory isolation hospital," and in Scotland lepers caught leaving a leper house were hanged; in Denmark they were expelled and directed to the nearest road. Other communities ran their houses like hotels, letting lepers come and go as they pleased.

Conditions in the lazarettes varied like those in hotels on a city strip. Some had clean beds; others didn't. Some had good kitchens with cooks and others left the lepers to fend for themselves. Rich or ordained lepers didn't have to put up with bad care or abusive clerics, however. Nobles and ladies of the court in Dauphigne had their own separate leper colonies as did leprous nuns and priests. Whenever noble lepers were forced to mix with poor lepers in a colony, they usually built separate little cottages. Poor lepers packed themselves into one small dormitory and said Paternosters and Aves morning, noon and night. The Norwegian Peder Feidie survived seventeen years in such a place and passed the time writing bitter leper poetry:

> We lepers here can no doctors get:
> Here must we stay and wait and fret
> Until our time is up.

Peter from prison did escape
Because on God's grace he did wait:
O God, break now the chains
Which bind our limbs with pains.

A typical leper asylum usually consisted of a couple of huts
and a garden enclosed by a fence. Many had their own cemetery
and chapel. The lazarette on the Åland Islands, off the coast of
Sweden, had a leaky roof, unstable ceiling and dirt floor.
Conveniently, the inmates often didn't need to go outside to
check the weather. One winter the lepers broke up their water
barrels to cover the floor "because snakes crept in during the
night and they didn't dare all to sleep at the same time." But
bad housing didn't preclude the strictest of clerical rules. Lepers
couldn't play dice, gamble, dance or touch ecclesiastical orna-
ments. According to the rule book at St Albans, a leper had to
live like a leper. "Amongst all infirmities, the disease of leprosy
may be considered the most loathsome, and those who are smitten with it ought at all times and in all places, as well in their
conduct as in their dress, to bear themselves as more to be
despised and as more humble than all other men."

Charity and endowments made some leper houses as wealthy
as banks and good targets for robbery. When Philip the Tall of
France needed money in 1318, he made up a story about lepers
poisoning wells and spreading disease. Then, after burning several hundred lepers at the stake, he confiscated the revenues
and property of the empty leper houses. Looting leper houses or
bashing lepers gave many local communities a chance to work
out their frustrations during famines and other misfortunes.
Accusing lepers of stealing children and polluting wells was
quite routine. Edward I of England enjoyed burying lepers alive.

Medieval communities didn't segregate lepers for biblical
reasons alone. A person with a leonine face and rotting limbs
genuinely scared the hell out of most Christians. Leprosy's

contagious consequences, abandonment by family and friends, also terrified people. Most families, whatever their desire, couldn't afford to look after a leper for ten or fifteen years of slow rotting before death. Even the Vikings, the Old World's earliest and toughest gangsters, made a point of avoiding "the houses of prayer where the men of God and lepers stayed." The fear of leprosy paralyzed artists as well. Most medieval painters and lithographers relied on inaccurate biblical descriptions of leprosy as pepper-like red spots in order to avoid examining the real thing. The first painter to capture the physical and moral despair of the leper was the Italian artist Francesco Traini in 1355. His dark fresco "The Triumph of Death" shows eight angry lepers and beggars with bandaged limbs and melted noses. One holds a scroll that reads, "Since prosperity has abandoned us, Death, medicine for every pain, Come and give us now the Last Supper."

To protect themselves from wandering lepers, medieval authorities spent a lot of time monitoring and regulating leper movement. In 1278, police in the French town of Metz had orders to fine people caught giving lepers alms because charity encouraged lepers to hang around. Police officers who didn't take the bylaw seriously were hung upside down over a cesspool and dunked until they swore to uphold the law. In 1346, Edward II of England declared that anyone sheltering a leper would lose his house. He also excluded lepers from the city of London for "endeavouring to contaminate others with that abominable blemish, (that so, to their own wretched solace, they may have the more fellows in suffering), as well in the way of mutual communications, and by the contagion of their polluted breath, as by carnal intercourse with women in stews [houses of prostitution] and other secret places, detestably frequenting the same, do so taint persons who are sound, both male and female, to the great injury of the people dwelling in the city...."

It was easy to spot a leper on the road because they all wore the same uniform, consisting of gloves and a white or grey wool robe (the earliest version of the skimpy white hospital gown). Some lepers also wore masks over their mouths. In parts of France, clerics sewed a large letter L onto leper costumes. What further distinguished lepers from priests and other poor people were all the tools that they carried. Lepers usually had a rattle, clapper or horn to warn the healthy of their whereabouts, a stick to point and indicate wants, a stoup for water and a bowl for alms. In Arles, lepers sang a hoarse version of *De Profundis* instead of shaking clappers.

Despite the building of thousands of leper houses, authorities still had trouble keeping lepers off the streets. The Scots finally admitted that lepers were limping about everywhere and allowed them to visit on Sundays, Wednesdays and Fridays, provided there was no market on those days. The French set aside feast days and Christmas for leper visits. But officials still complained that charity hadn't kept them out of sight. Medieval edicts complained again and again of "multitudes of lepers" invading cities, eating and drinking in the streets, squares, and other public places and frequently getting in people's way.

In the fourteenth century lepers and leprosy began to disappear mysteriously from Europe. Beginning in the 1340s, leper houses that had been overflowing reported that they were now taking care of no more than two or three lepers. Some lazarettes, such as the Hospitals of St John and St Leonard at Aylesbury, went to ruin for lack of boarders. By the 1550s France had closed two thousand leper houses or reassigned them as general hospitals. The English simply refilled their lazarettes with students, monks or beggars. Italy turned its asylums into quarantine stations for plague victims. Leprosy lingered only in Scandinavia where the poor slept on earthen floors well into the nineteenth century. In these leper frontier territories, citizens muttered, "He is a leper; may God be near us and watch over us" until the 1880s.

Leprosy's sudden demise coincided with the emergence of its half-brother, tuberculosis. Like leprosy, TB is a disease of poverty and urban crowding, and an ancient member of the mycobacteria tribe. Because of their genetic closeness, the diseases provoke similar immune responses. Although leprosy confers no immunity to tuberculosis (the bane of most lepers), TB does fortify the immune system to help repel the leprosy bacillus. Forced to compete with the rapidly moving TB germ, the slower moving *Mycobacterium leprae*, confined to leper houses, surrendered its 700-year-old reign in Europe and died out.

At the same time that tuberculosis replaced leprosy, the Black Death rode through Europe subtracting people and adding sheep to the landscape. As the wool supply increased, peasants seized upon this rare abundance to clothe themselves with more and better garments. By dressing better, historian William McNeill speculates, "Europeans may very well have interrupted old patterns of skin-to-skin dissemination by Hansen's Disease [leprosy]." This theory also explains why leprosy loitered the longest in Iceland, Norway and Poland where poverty, cold and a shortage of wool provided a terrain of dirty and immune-depressed people well into the 1800s. Norway didn't actually banish leprosy from its borders until it forbade lepers to wander from farm to farm for food in 1877, and started installing wood or stone floors in its houses.

Perhaps the most startling feature of leprosy in medieval society is how different cultures responded to the disease in remarkably similar ways. The connection between leprosy and immorality has popped up everywhere. The Chinese said it was "as an open indication of spirit displeasure." Confucius, normally a humanitarian, refused to look at a leprous follower, and said that "Fate kills him, For such a man to have such a disease!" The Mesopotamians chased lepers out into the wilderness to live "like wild-asses." The Koreans thought of the leper as a "dead dog" and a curse from heaven. In India many Hindus still believe that it is fatally dangerous to aid a leper for fear of associating with "an enemy of God." Lepers have always been on everyone's blacklist.

What this pattern says about human beings, both ancient and modern, is that they don't like blemishes, whether on people or fruit. Nor do they know how to contend with incurable and lengthy illnesses. There is still a bit of the hunter-gatherer's fear in everyone when it comes to caring for the sick, and in the face of the chronically ill, we still see some of the leonine folds of the leper. We unthinkingly abandon our "abominable blemishes" in institutions because old leper traditions are hard to break. Although we may give the elderly or Alzheimer's patients clean sheets and plenty of pills, we keep them strictly hidden from public view. This policy wouldn't have surprised Bodel or his family, and probably shouldn't surprise us.

4

THE BLACK DEATH:

AN ECOLOGICAL DISASTER

Ring around the rosies,
A pocket full of posies,
Achoo! Achoo!
All fall down.
Children's plague rhyme

In 1966 the U.S. Atomic Energy Commission recognized that it
actually didn't know how an atomic war might poison a continent. It had the work of two bombs and the radiated record of
Hiroshima to draw upon but the question remained unan-
swered. So, in order to paint a much broader Breugelian picture
of a nuclear holocaust, it hired the Rand Corporation, a sunny
California think tank, which in turn sent one of its crew-cut
academics to the library. After much reading, the think tank's
analyst wrote a thirty-one-page memorandum on the Black
Death of 1348. The memorandum eventually formed part of a
larger study on the "biological and environmental consequences
of nuclear war." Rand's thinker chose this epidemic ("one of the

very greatest disaster-recovery experiences ever recorded")
because it killed a third of Europe's population, or 30 million
peasants, in two years. He concluded that the plague compared
favourably to a hypothetical thermonuclear war "in suddenness,
geographical scope and scale of casualties." Only one aspect of
the epidemic disappointed the analyst: unlike a war, the Black
Death did not destroy property.

The obscure Rand memorandum was a document of considerable understatement. Although the Great Mortality (as it was
then called) spared homes and monasteries, it emptied them of
their residents so rapidly that the plague hit Europe with the
force of several nuclear wars. It achieved a fearful symmetry by
recurring in two- and twenty-year cycles (albeit with decreasing
intensity) over a period of three hundred years until 1720. The
great die-offs that accompanied these epidemics produced great
change. Depopulation inexorably raised the scale of wages, subverted feudalism and conserved forests. It also enlarged graveyards, ignited Jew-killings, multiplied sheep, inspired flagellants
and even introduced English as the common language of intellectual discourse. "This disease," wrote one exasperated
medieval physician (and there were many of them in the fifteenth century), "changed all the times of the year into one
time and all diseases into one disease."

To the shell-shocked survivors of the plague's visitations, it
appeared as though God and His able assistant Nature had con-
spired to destroy human beings. Just as the modern world can
imagine no greater horror than nuclear war, so the medieval
world had no measuring stick long enough for the plague.
Petrarch, the popular Florentine writer, watched with disbelief
as the pestilence cleared out his city the way a fire might empty
a theatre. He feared that the disease's grand entry into European
affairs in 1348 would become unfathomable to his descendants:
"O happy posterity, who will not experience such abysmal woe
and will look upon our testimony as a fable." It took scholars

nearly six hundred years to gauge the plague's fabulous impact, but they now agree that the writings of Petrarch and his friend Boccaccio are not early science fiction. The writers' descriptions are genuine eye-popping accounts of the greatest ecological disaster to strike the Old World.

Long before the plague, bacillus, fleas, rats and Genoese merchants all collided in Italy for their epic encounter, medieval society prepared for the disaster by inviting misery and famine into Europe's crowded household. Climate played a subtle role in this drama. Throughout the Middle Ages a run of long hot summers and short cool winters encouraged peasants to grow more crops and produce more peasants. This baby boom turned Europe into a fermenting test tube of bacteria as its population grew from 25 million well-fed souls in the year 700 to 75 million hungry ones in 1250. Humans rarely recognize their good fortune until they give it away.

The first signs of calamity appeared in Europe's overworked and degraded land. To feed their expanding numbers, peasants chopped down forests, drained marshes and planted crops on steep mountain slopes. Much of this newly broken land was so rocky and infertile that it hasn't been cultivated since. To make room for more grain, peasants invaded pasture land, displaced cows and sheep and effectively curtailed the production of manure and soil fertilizer. This thoughtless agrarian rape of Europe's soils didn't improve harvests. Wheat and rye yields became lighter as the soil became anemic and eroded. At the peasant's table loaves of dark bread became shorter than fingers.

While peasants toiled harder for less food, Europe's weather changed as insidiously as it did in the 1980s. This cooling, or greenhouse effect in reverse, later became known as the "Little Ice Age." It expanded glaciers over pasture land in the Alps and froze the Thames River and the Baltic Sea more than once. It also isolated the Viking settlements in Greenland where ice-locked colonists died of starvation. Cloud-filled skies and early frosts produced one crop failure after another across Europe in the early 1300s. With so much rain and so little sun, peasants couldn't even preserve meat with salt.

The resulting famines that thinned out Europeans from 1308 to 1332 forced people to eat nettles, dove shit and even children. While the cat and dog populations of many towns disappeared into cooking pots, hungry crowds rushed the gallows to hack at the flesh of murderers and thieves. In England only the rich could afford horse meat. Medieval painters had no shortage of wan and rickety subjects. By the time the plague arrived in 1348, the continent had placed itself in the stranglehold of a classic Malthusian subsistence crisis. "Viewed in this light," says the erudite plague historian Philip Ziegler, "the Black Death is the nemesis that met a population which bred too fast for too long without first providing itself with the resources needed for such extravagance."

Yersinia pestis, the bacterium that exploited this troubled terrain, originated in the Mongolian steppes and still flourishes there as a flu-like nuisance among voles (a rodent) or in mortal form among burrowing marmots and squirrels. In the 1330s the world's changing climate uprooted rodent life on the steppes. Warm dry winds drove bacteria, fleas and animals out of the desert and into unsuspecting camps of Mongolian caravans. Fleas with stomachs full of yersinia then rode on the Mongols as they travelled across Asia to Europe with fresh supplies of spices, silk and disease. Encountering no natural immunity in China, India and Armenia, the plague left piles of dead so high that highwaymen recycled them for ambushes.

The first Europeans to catch the plague were early victims of biological warfare. Besieged by Tartars in the Crimean trading city of Caffa, Genoese merchants watched with alarm as the plague-stricken attackers, who were clearly "fatigued, stupefied and amazed" by the pestilence, lobbed their plague dead over the city walls as a parting gesture. Merchants that survived the bacterial bombardment soon fled to their home ports carrying the plague with them. The residents of Genoa and Messina initially welcomed their ships, only to discover cargos of sick and dead. In city after city, terrified residents repelled the galleys and their ailing sailors with flaming arrows. Now allied with fear, the plague saturated Europe and took up residence among the black rats and fleas that abounded in every medieval home. Within two years the wooden, earth-floored, straw-filled shanties of Europe resembled the rodent burrows of Central Asia.

At least two different kinds of plague, bubonic and pneumonic, dined on Europeans. Bubonic plague began with the bite of an infected flea, which produced a blackish rash (a rosie) followed by egg-like buboes in the armpit, groin or neck. Accompanied by fever and delirium (the dying often performed a dance of death), bubonic plague killed more than half its victims within a week. Before the sick expired, their sweat, excrement and spittle became so fetid "as to be overpowering." Pneumonic plague worked without fleas, appearing in cold weather when the germ lodged itself in lungs and sprayed blood out the nose. Spread by the coughs and spit of the infected, this highly mortal brand of plague dropped people dead within twenty-four hours and ran through a crowd like a wild sex rumour. Pneumonic plague eventually forced Europeans to dig great open pits, where busy grave-diggers sprinkled dirt over the dead "like cheese between layers of lasagna."

Travelling across Europe during the Great Mortality was an alarming experience. Abandoned ships bobbed across the Mediterranean, drifting from one shore to another. Harvests went uncut while farm animals roamed unattended. Unruly and noisy flocks of ravens and vultures blackened the skies, making people's skin crawl. Hungry wolves ventured into Paris where they fought with dogs, pigs and cats over the unburied dead. On Sundays clerics read and reread the Book of Revelation, especially the part about the Fourth Horseman. As a public service, church steeples flew a black flag to warn parishioners of the plague's comings and goings.

In the cities, beggars and other folks gathered around bonfires of orange leaves, camphor and sage that cleansed the air, if nothing else. The plague-weary also watched the latest dance craze, a sort of medieval rap in which peasants dressed up as skeletons. The dancing cadavers coarsely reminded spectators that they would soon be "dead, naked, rotten and stinking" and that "power, honour and riches" meant nothing. For a little levity people also sought out performing Companies of Fools, who tried to dispel plague fright with jokes and pranks about dead relatives.

During the pestilence of 1348, people needed all the relief they could get. In Siena, the Italian banking centre, Agnolo di Tura (the Fat) couldn't find anyone to bury the dead for money or friendship. Fathers abandoned children and wives abandoned husbands. Di Tura buried his five children with his own hands. "It seemed that almost everyone became stupefied by seeing the pain." Two thousand miles away in Ireland the scene was just as black. After making extensive notes about empty towns and confessors dying with abscesses under their armpits, the friar John Clyn saw Death approaching, and left some blank parchment in his diary to continue the story, "If haply any man survive, and any of the race of Adam escape this pestilence." Clyn was a man of foresight. In the next sentence someone with a stronger constitution write, "Here it seems the author died." Clearly these were not the best of times.

As the plague danced its way across Europe, many fearful citizens vented their frustrations by burning Jews. Excluded from most other jobs, Hebrews worked as pawnbrokers, gravediggers or money-lenders during the Middle Ages (Christians wouldn't let non-Christians pollute any other trades). Although Catholic kings and queens took most of the profit from 20 percent interest charges, they let the Jewish money-lenders take all the resentment. When hysterical plague victims accused Jews of poisoning well water and "corrupting the air," debtors and the poor began to kill Jews in mass immolations. In Basle, Christians constructed a special wooden house to barbecue several hundred "well poisoners." In some cities, Catholic mobs nailed Jews to stakes before they fried them, while others sealed Jews in wine casks and floated them down the Rhine. Jews often denied their pyromaniacal persecutors satisfaction by burning themselves in their own houses. By 1351, just two years after the Great Mortality, hardly a Jew was left alive in Central Europe. After the plague pogroms, most European Jews fled to Russia or Poland where their skills and education were then welcomed. Jews remained in these precarious havens for six hundred years until Hitler sealed off the Warsaw ghetto and started the burning all over again.

Some of the most avid Jew burners were flagellants. These bands of back whippers usually consisted of fifty to three hundred men who wandered from town to town flogging themselves or each other with knotted leather and iron spikes. To expiate the sins of humanity, the men stripped to the waist, scourged each other on crosses and sang mournful songs about the Virgin Mary. Their bloody performances moved crowds to tears and shouts of ecstasy, especially if one or more of the flagellants died during the frenzy. The flagellants, who believed that they had a sacred mission to stop the plague and halt the destruction of the world, fingered Jews as popular scapegoats. Before or after the whipping ceremony they often led crowds on Jew burnings. Throughout most of Europe the poor received the members of this sect as genuine heroes and martyrs, hoarding their hair, blood and nail clippings the way children now collect baseball cards.

But as the so-called Brotherhood of the Cross became bigger and bloodier, the movement also became bolder. Flagellants started to make a lot of false claims about raising the dead, took part in sadomasochistic sex orgies and preached that the rich would be forced to marry the poor as soon as the world ended. In 1349 Pope Clement VI finally outlawed the revolutionary whipping sect and ordered the execution of its "masters." By 1350 flagellants had become as scarce as Jews. The spontaneous movement died as quickly as a plague victim.

Death became such an everyday event during the Great Mortality that artists gave it a brand new personality. Using skeletons for models, painters and woodcutters imagined Death as a lively and boney fellow who danced, sang and even fornicated. They often gave Death a mocking grin and portrayed him accosting peasants, bankers and kings. German artists developed the greatest fondness for the bold Leveller and frequently put a scythe or an hour-glass in his hand. During the plague years no portrait was complete without some reminder of Death. The famous painter Hans Burgkmair even drew his comely wife sitting in front of a mirror that reflected, not her beauty, but skull and bones.

Although nobody knew the real cause of the plague, most Europeans agreed on its divine origins. Magnus II of Sweden, like most aristocrats, followed the standard clerical line: "God for the sins of men has struck the world with this great punishment of sudden death." Medieval physicians, who were better astrologers than doctors, read the stars and concluded that God's vague instrument consisted of "corrupted airs" and "pestilential vapours" induced by the misalignment of Mars and Jupiter. To different peoples these hostile airs took different forms. In Vienna citizens recognized the plague as a *Pest Jungfrau* (plague virgin) who emerged as blue flame from the lips of the dead. In Lithuania the same maiden raised a red flag to infect the living. In other countries "God's disease" took the shape of blind women, cripples, wandering Jews and men on black horses. Only one medieval commentator dared to dismiss the theory of divine punishment by logically arguing that "nothing so promiscuous in its results could possibly have been intended by God." But his heretical work was ignored.

A London pamphlet of 1625 describes a routine plague visitation: God's wrath descends as a thunderbolt, corpses litter the fields and Death pursues the infected.

In Florence, Boccaccio watched his neighbours accommodate the plague by joining one of four plague camps. The cautious Florentines lived entirely apart from everyone else (forming a kind of plague society) and ate the most delicate of foods and drank the finest of wines in moderation. They also forbade their members to speak of or listen to anything said about the sick and the dead outside. The reckless drank too much, sang loudly and believed that "making light of everything that happened" was the best medicine. The middle of the road gang went about their business with no more protection than garlands of flowers and spices, trusting that herbs purified "the brain," banishing the stench of dead neighbours.

The last group, the survivalists, merely fled, "not caring about anything else but themselves." All in all, plague psychology did not impress Boccaccio. The dead were honoured with neither candles nor tears, and "were cared for as we care for goats today."

Body counters for Pope Clement VI estimated that between 1348 and 1351, the Great Mortality killed 23,840,000 people— 31 percent of Europe's population. In densely packed countries such as France, *Yersinia pestis* likely emptied the land of half of its inhabitants. England recorded about a million plague dead or one-third of its people. In Eastern Europe where the plague found fewer inhabitants and probably arrived in a less aggressive mood, the first epidemic claimed no more than 15 percent. After the grand pandemic of 1348, the plague returned in 1362 (*pestis secunda*), killing great numbers of children, and again in 1369 (*pestis tertia*). After eight major plague epidemics the city of Florence, which had boasted a population of 120,000 in 1330, counted no more than 37,000 inhabitants in 1427. For the next hundred years this fantastic winnowing became the norm as the plague harvested between 10 and 15 percent of each new generation. In so doing it effectively ended the continent's crisis of too many mouths and too little bread. Europe did not attain its thirteenth-century population levels again until the sixteenth century.

Accommodating so many dead, particularly in city cemeteries, was no easy task. The stench from piled-up corpses forced municipal authorities to dig new common graveyards outside of town. In Siena and other cities, workers couldn't dig pits fast enough. Some contained as many as 1,500 bodies. The need to dump dead paupers into anonymous thirty-foot ditches survived well into the eighteenth century. Holes for commoners mostly went unmarked but those with gravestones told minimalist plague histories:

Is that not a painful sight
Seventy-seven in the same night.
Dead of the plague in the year 1637.

Or:

Was that not said and painful to relate,
I died with thirteen of my house on the same date?

It didn't take long for the miraculous rotting powers of common graves to gain wide fame. The soil of one Paris cemetery, Les Innocents, was so putrefying that it consumed a human body in nine days. After worms and bacteria picked off the flesh, grave-diggers nonchalantly removed tibiae and vertabrae to make room for more plague victims. Bishops considered the "flesh eating" qualities of common graves so beneficial they even demanded that a couple of spadefuls be placed in their own coffins. The appeal of rapid rotting was just another short-lived plague fad.

The Great Mortality changed every aspect of life in medieval society. Chroniclers weren't exaggerating when they wrote that the plague "turned Europe upside down." The first institution to be overturned was feudalism. Waves of peasant die-offs translated into acute labour shortages and ended the chronic underemployment that characterized life in the thirteenth century. To retain some semblance of order, panicky landowners doubled wages, broke up their estates and rented land to individuals whose sweat they had previously assumed they owned for life. Accustomed to being expendable, peasants took advantage of their new economic freedom and began to walk for better working conditions, beginning an era of mobility that mirrored the twentieth century's love of transiency. The post-plague labour market also broke the traditional bonds of respect between peasant and landlord as each class struggled to set the new rules of exploitation. The bloody peasant revolts that arose after the first plague epidemic reflected this contest.

During the plague, merchants also rediscovered the merits of travelling. Faced with a shortage of customers in their home towns, English, Iberian and Dutch traders sailed far and wide to sell their wool, wine and cheese. Their efforts were rewarded by Europe's new-found interest in material goods, particularly in more colourful clothes, and by rich lawyers, clerics and doctors with more money to spend. Depopulation also inspired Europe's merchants, who properly called themselves Adventurers, to seek more customers in Africa, Asia and the New World. The continent's shrunken populace and fragmented markets imbued these entrepreneurs with a new brazenness. The unwilling hosts of Europe's new economic quest for markets and consumers would later call it imperialism.

The Black Death also introduced "merchant's time" or the frenzied commodification of minutes and hours. Prior to the plague, life in Europe was unhurried. The passing of time was languidly marked by harvests and church events. But after the Great Mortality a scarcity of workers in some trades, combined with an increased demand for manufactured goods, gave clocks and schedules a revolutionary new importance. When the plague rewarded Brandenburg's surviving workers with such a surge in wages that they could afford to work just two days a week, the need to enslave working hands to bells and chimes struck employers as the only solution to fiscal anarchy. In several Flemish towns, for instance, textile workers were so few that they could even set their own hours. In such an environment the clock triumphed and began to determine the pace of life.

In the countryside, the disappearance of soil tillers brought equally dramatic changes. Fewer peasants meant more room for grass and grass-eaters. Nature abhors empty spaces and usually fills them with creatures or microbes, so after the first plague waves, untended cattle and sheep quickly multiplied. Peasants were delighted. Unlike crops, the animals required little care, offered reliable income (wool and leather) and even made a good meal. In England, where the sheer abundance of sheep created a powerful wool industry that eventually monopolized the land, a new proverb was born: "Sheep's hooves turn sand into gold." When the English peasant population began to rebound in the fifteenth century, it discovered that sheep had more rights than people. As a famous and often misquoted nursery rhyme protested, wool barons clearly preferred four-legged animals to those with two:

> Baa, baa, black sheep, have you any wool?
> Yes sir, no sir, three bags full.
> Two for my master and one for his dame
> But none for the little boy who cries down the lane.

But the plague shifted more than just animals and humans on Nature's scales. It also gave Europe's much abused forests a chance to recover some of their former greenery. By 1200 Europeans had cut and ploughed their way across the continent with such thoroughness that they threatened to create a treeless desert. Restless feudal lords constantly moved from castle to castle, not only to get away from their own garbage but to find new firewood. Wood shortages had become so acute by the 1300s that penalties for tree-cutting included death. Only the intervention of the superorganism in the guise of plague bacteria allowed trees to recolonize fields and pastures, soils to rest and heal, and bears and wolves to prosper long enough to populate Europe's fairy-tales. Without the Black Death, argues plague historian Robert Gottfried, Europe might have become a dusty and treeless Ethiopia. With a few exceptions, Europe's great forests date from the late Middle Ages.

After a few years with *Yersinia pestis*, most Europeans realized that the pestilence had a much greater appetite for the poor than the rich. The continent's malnourished masses, for whom life was already a kind of diarrhetic death, offered no resistance to the germ. Lodged in rat-filled mudflats, they also couldn't afford to flee the plague's periodic cullings. As epidemics came and went, observant Europeans began calling the Black Death "the beggar's disease" or "the poor's plague." French merchants approved of the plague's attraction to the poor as a welcome trend: "Let God in his mercy be satisfied with [the poor]....The rich protect themselves against it."

For the affluent, dependable plague protection consisted of a fast horse and a country retreat. In fact, the plague years cemented the rich's long association of good health with country homes. During an epidemic in 1456, so many nobles and "good citizens" fled Venice that the city hired sixteen boats manned by armed guards to protect "homes left without any custodian from thieves and evil men." After a couple of plague die-offs, the wealthy bought villas, not to escape summer heatwaves but to avoid early death. As sanctuaries from epidemics, these rural retreats often succeeded in preserving the life of their owners. Before they returned to their plague-emptied towns ("like those who have escaped a heavy shower"), the rich hired fumigators to disinfect their urban dwellings. After smoking the building thoroughly with sulphur (enough to kill any caged canary or sparrow), a poor woman was left inside the residence for several weeks as an early warning system. If she died, the owner enjoyed a couple more months in the country.

Though the plague spared many merchants and nobles, it did strike a disproportionate number of clerics. Good shepherds who honoured their calling (and many didn't) daily comforted their infected flocks only to find themselves afflicted with buboes. Once established among the rats and fleas that inhabited isolated clerical institutions, the plague germ also consumed monks and nuns in great numbers. In Montpellier, France, only 7 of 140 Dominican friars survived the plague, and in Marseilles a monastery of 150 Franciscans was silenced. In Germany a third of the clergy perished. In England half of the 17,500 residents of religious houses succumbed to the epidemic. And so on.

The expiration of so many clerics effectively loosened Latin's stranglehold on education and ended its reign as Europe's universal language. With fewer Latin-speaking monks, the Church reluctantly refilled its ranks with members who spoke and wrote in the common tongue. In universities, scholars had also found that the ability to conjugate Latin verbs afforded no protection against the disease. The loss of so many Latin-speaking intellectuals prompted one writer to conclude that "learning did degenerate in these times from their genuine purity, together with the elegance of the Latin tongue, and that the empty babbling of Sophisters did everywhere make a noise in the schools." Thanks to the plague, English grammar schools had to abandon French as the language of instruction because replacement teachers couldn't speak French, let alone Latin. Ignorance of Latin also prompted the translation of Aristotle's works and scientific treatises into English and other national languages. Wherever Latin tongues grew quiet, common ones invaded courts, churches and universities. Learning, once the preserve of a small class of older men who spoke an alien language, now marched into the commons.

The plague not only eroded Church Latin but seriously undermined Church authority. As each succeeding wave of the epidemic rolled over Europe, it became plain to the faithful that God had run amok and that His priestly servants couldn't provide solace to a flea. In some parts of England, a fifth of the clergy simply fled the plague and abandoned their parishes in search of ale, mistresses or riches. Italian friars regularly refused to bury the dead or hear confession, while clerics who dared to honour their vows gingerly offered the sacrament at the end of a pole. A Dominican priest from Westphalia watched his brethren "feed themselves instead of their flocks, these they shear or rather fleece," and concluded, as most Christians did, that the Church had grown contemptible.

Many of the men who replaced dead or truant clerics were neither trustworthy nor holy. Thousands of incompetent clerics suddenly found themselves delivering a sermon or administering a diocese solely because of luck or a strong immune system. One English friar spent so much time robbing his parishioners that he earned the nickname "William the One-day Priest" before they hanged him. Such corruption among the religious elect thoroughly sullied the Church's reputation in Europe. People's disillusionment found expression either in mysticism or in the growing disquietude that eventually led to the Reformation.

The plague's sheer killing efficiency clearly advanced the revolutionary notion that people were better off talking to God directly than going through a useless and impotent ecclesiastical bureaucracy. Martin Luther not only championed this idea but also challenged his fellow clerics on epidemiological lines. Unlike many of his Catholic persecutors and adversaries, he eloquently addressed the all-consuming subject of the plague (he survived three epidemics) in the pamphlet, "Is it Right to Flee from the Epidemic?" His answer was no: "If anyone is infected he should immediately isolate himself or let himself be isolated from all others." People who knowingly spread the plague, he added, deserve death. In one of several disinformation campaigns against Lutherism, the Catholic Church later condemned Germany, Luther's home, as a source of the plague. The use of biological untruths in propaganda wars is not a twentieth-century invention.

Priests weren't the only profession defrocked by *Yersinia pestis*. Physicians also lost credibility as quickly as they lost plague patients. The only effective prescription an honest doctor could offer was *fugo cito, vade longe, rede tarde* (flee quickly, go far, come back slowly). Guy de Chauliac advised Pope Clement VI accordingly and only fear of disgrace kept the doctor from following his own advice. Fearing infection, doctors donned outrageous apparel with beaked masks, or refused to visit patients. Collecting fees from the dead was also a problem. The whole experience, confessed de Chauliac, "was most humiliating for physicians."

Their inability to fight the plague, however, didn't stop them from trying. Earnest doctors dispensed plague remedies like candies. Those with means paid handsomely for a litany of prayers, charms, spices and bleedings. Plague antidotes varied from the sane to the inane: Eat figs with two filberts. Shun lettuce. Chew slowly and rise from the table hungry. Guard against weeping and fear "for imagination works havoc with disease." Light wine mixed with spring water [the original spritzer] keeps the body cool and free of disease. A German proverb summed up these whimsical prescriptions: "Neither drunk nor yet too sober, in times of plague is the way to get over."

While the epidemics demonstrated the youthfulness of medicine as a science, they also laid the cornerstones of public health. In the wealthy and independent city states of Germany and Italy, merchants and nobles tried to keep buboes out of their armpits by establishing health boards, quarantines, pest-houses and accurate Books of the Dead for keeping track of the progress of plague from town to town. In 1348 Venice set the tone by appointing a Committee of Three to isolate infected ships, people and goods on an island. At the quarantine station, porters exposed woollens to sun and air and sprinkled feathered animals with vinegar. After losing nearly six hundred people a day to the epidemic, the Committee punished quarantine violators with death. Detaining ships for *quaranti giorni* (forty days) quickly became a standard practice throughout maritime Europe.

In Milan, then one of Europe's grandest cities, officials also didn't dawdle. They entombed the sick in their homes and left them there to starve or die of plague. They also expelled the ill outside the city walls like lepers. Strict prohibitions on festivals, fairs and even church services were not popular, but kept the plague in check. Of all of Italy's great cities, Milan suffered the lowest death rate during the plague, losing only 15 percent of its people to the Fourth Horseman.

Many European towns and cities took the lessons of Milan and Venice to heart, and created a new class of plague bureaucrats to preserve the people "from contagious maladies." These epidemic fighters included municipal physicians, body removers, grave-diggers, house guards and fumigators (perfumers). These first fathers of public health had the power to ban commerce, sequester the sick, bury the dead, smoke houses, burn private property, close fairs, block streets, and arrest and torture the unco-operative. But rarely did they perform any of these duties at the right time, in the right place or with the right people. With working budgets as thin as peasants, cities paid their health officials so irregularly that one Italian surgeon spent a year lancing buboes and bleeding the sick in the same bloody and stinking suit of clothes. Furthermore, the rich and the clergy routinely flaunted quarantines and other regulations. Although they were often armed with good health goals, says plague historian Alfonso Corradi, the new health bureaucrats never overcame the overwhelming hostility to the poor or the conniving of the rich: "Cunning, privilege and private power stood above the laws, mocking the regulations that carried extremely severe, even cruel punishments for people who were less powerful or less cunning."

The most fearless of the plague busters were the grave-diggers. Recruited from slave galleys, they roamed the streets, removing and burying dead with the finesse of twentieth-century garbage collectors. These proletarians spoke to no one, lived in a separate quarter of the city and died like flies because of the hazardous nature of their work. Known as the "priests of public health" they chose "to remain dauntless among the stricken by day" and then to go out drinking and gambling by night. Without a small bribe they treated the dead like broken

At open-air plague hospitals, surgeons dissected live patients while doctors shouted their prescriptions from the street.

furniture. They frequently robbed the rich and sometimes cut
the throats of the sick to speed up their work. Their habit of
removing and donning the plague-infected clothes of corpses
often upset other health officials.

The poor also had to contend with body removers, who wore
bells on their ankles and carted both the dead and the sick to
pest-houses. Fumigators or perfumers followed, dressed in white
with red crosses. They disinfected houses of the dead with sulphur and were charged with burning mattresses or anything
upon which the plague might "stick," such as furs, clothes and
carpets. One Florentine fumigator, Bartolomeo Fagni, regularly
stood accused of stealing objects from plague survivors who had
been isolated in pest-houses. When confronted in the streets by
one of his accusers, the brazen official asked: "What is stealing
and not stealing? Fuck me in the ass!"

The most hellish public health institution was the pest-
house. While the rich escaped to their villas, the sick and the

infected from the lower classes were sequestered in large and crowded hospitals for twenty to eighty days. Some pest-houses differentiated between the diseased and the exposed by placing them in separate rooms; others did not. Physicians studiously avoided these institutions for fear of contracting plague, and shouted their cures from the street up to resident surgeons (a lower and expendable class). Most pest-houses or lazarettes had few blankets and little food. Relatives constantly complained of the sick being robbed, poisoned and dissected without their permission. In Florence, guards, cooks and nurses turned one pest-house into a small factory that magically transformed bed sheets and blankets into aprons and socks for the market-place. In Milan, public officials fainted from the odours seeping out of the rooms. And in Bologna, a cardinal visited a pest-house in 1630 and covered his eyes: "Here you see people lament, others cry, others strip themselves to the skin, others die, others become black and deformed, others lose their minds. Here you are overwhelmed by intolerable smells. Here you cannot walk but among the corpses. Here you feel naught but the constant horror of death. This is the faithful replica of hell since here there is no order and only horror prevails." To avoid being placed in these institutions, the poor buried their dead secretly, while many women, fearing rape and other forms of violence, chose suicide before internment.

Despite the injustice of these disease barriers (their greatest effect was to protect the rich from the poor), public health programs did cripple the plague's progress in isolated towns and cities. The early plague fighters also initiated the first garbage collections and the first meat market inspections. However, in busy merchant centres such as Venice where travellers and their microbes made brisk trade, the plague persisted, culling between a quarter and a third of the population in 1575 and again in 1630. Improved sanitation and public health made a mark on the disease but did not drive it out of Europe.

This humble victory belongs to the redesigning of European homes. At the time of the plague the poor built their window-less shanties with unseasoned wood and thatched roofs. The floor was made of dirt or clay mixed with ten-year-old piles of rushes. The only real difference between a rich home and a poor one was the hardiness and abundance of timber. Medieval straw ceilings provided black rats, *Rattus rattus*, with good nest-ing places and a platform from which fleas could drop like dust on unsuspecting humans. Rats also bred well in piles of rushes, in walls filled with wattle and in sacks of grain. According to Philip Ziegler, a rodent urban planning committee couldn't have designed better rat accommodation.

Fear of fire rather than black rats or big buboes finally con-vinced city dwellers that wood homes with thatched roofs invariably invited smoky disasters. Plague visited London for the last time in 1665 because the Great Fire of 1666 destroyed 13,200 wood homes. In their place Londoners constructed 9,000 brick houses with floor carpets and tile roofs. Similar fiery events transformed house architecture in Berlin, Brandenburg and other cities. While humans were making their dwellings less appealing to the black rat, the larger grey rat, *Rattus norvegi-cus*, began swimming in swarms across the Volga and displacing the black rat from all its traditional lodgings. *Rattus norvegicus*, a much wilder rodent, carried a different type of flea, eschewed humans and preferred sewers to houses. It didn't make plague-carrying a priority.

Without proper housing the plague retreated from Europe, leaving 80,000 dead in the region of Marseilles in 1720 as a final reminder of its killing power. But Europeans didn't have much of a chance to celebrate the withdrawal of *Yersinia pestis*. As the nineteenth-century epidemiologist William Farr first noted, one epidemic replaced another "whenever the condi-tions of life [were] wanting." The first microbe to fill the plague vacuum was the typhus germ, which is carried by lice. As the continent's supply of sheep grew, plague survivors wore more wool, supported greater lice colonies and became more lousy. Typhus took advantage of the wool craze and spread across Europe in the fifteenth century. Because it thrived in the dirtiest places, it was first called "jail fever" or "hospital fever." In 1477 the people of Milan suffered from such intense fevers and delirium that they hurled themselves out of windows. This particular epidemic alone killed 22,000 people and filled the city with crosses and priests as expediently as the plague had. And so the dying continued.

After the Black Death, Europe hummed a sort of plague tune in the 1700s. Now aware that too many mouths meant hunger, want and disease, the grave-filled continent declared "its independence from the world's instinctive patterns of behaviour." Peasants begot fewer peasants by delaying marriage and childbearing until one or both sets of parents (four extra mouths to feed) had died and made room at the dinner table for future generations. In French towns such as Sennely, tillers who were bent and toothless by the age of twenty-three still subsisted on the miserly fruits of sandy soil, but now distrusted priests and married late. They raised an average of five children, knowing that three would likely be borne off by smallpox or other microbial gypsies. Europe's new plague culture was absolutely unique. Ninety percent of the nubile girls around the world bore children by the age of fourteen, but only two-thirds of European women of child-bearing age engaged in such a risky business. Famine and plague simply weren't forces to tamper with.

The plague years altered human thinking not only about reproduction but also about Nature. Once revered or at least respected, Nature was now an enemy to be feared and tamed. Human beings emerged from the Middle Ages as the mean-spirited survivors of a biological holocaust. The plague's incredible die-offs conditioned people to seek mechanistic explanations for Nature's unpleasant visitations, with the hope that humankind could somehow fix or rework the environment or hammer it into submission. Retribution, the favourite theme of artists after the plague, also became the goal of Europe's new scientists. Descartes' philosophical view of the universe as a clock that could be set or reset to suit human ends had all the marks of post-plague thinking: if you don't like the time, just move the hands.

After the plague, it's not really surprising that humans decided to trust machines more than Nature. Firmly entrenched in the collective unconscious is the memory of pestilential and divinely directed vapours that nearly halved the human race in Europe. For three hundred years now scientists, doctors, economists and explorers have committed themselves to killing or subduing natural forces that might impede human progress. With railways, dams, combustion engines, antibiotics and atomic bombs, the species has set itself on one collision course after another with Nature and the superorganism. Now cursed with a belligerent and intolerant view of the world, humans must face the daily threat of nuclear winter, global warming and polluted homes. But the modern thinking that drove us this far and this darkly began with rats and fleas in the hungry year of 1348.

THE SMALLPOX CONQUEST:

BIOLOGICAL IMPERIALISM

There was then no sickness;
they had then no aching bones;
they had then no high fever;
they had then no smallpox;
they had then no burning chest;
they had then no abdominal pains;
they had then no consumption;
they had then no headache.
At that time the course of humanity was orderly.
The foreigners made it otherwise when they arrived here.
The Book of Chilam Balam of Chumayel

During the late 1800s, smallpox visited the Kiowa in the south-west corner of the Great Plains three times. The disease's depre-dations resulted in a Kiowa tale called "The White Man's Gift." The story is the shortest and saddest summary of American his-tory ever recorded. Saynday, a Kiowa joker with a good heart, was coming along when he saw a spot in the East, the place of birth and good life. The spot grew larger but didn't dance or bounce like good messengers. Soon a horse powdered with red dust appeared. A man spotted with red dust rode it. The man looked like a missionary in a black suit and high hat and his face was pitted with terrible holes. Both man and horse moved as slowly as the Kiowas imagined that death moved.

"Who are you?" the stranger asked.

"I'm Saynday. I'm the Kiowas' Old Uncle Saynday. I'm the one who's always coming along."

"I never heard of you," the stranger said, "and I never heard of the Kiowas. Who are they?"

Saynday explained that the Kiowas were his people and asked who the stranger was.

"I'm Smallpox," the man answered.

"And I never heard of you," said Saynday. "Where do you come from and what do you do and why are you here?"

"I come from far away, across the Eastern Ocean," Smallpox answered. "I am one with the white men—they are my people as the Kiowas are yours. Sometimes I travel ahead of them, and sometimes I lurk behind. But I am always their companion and you will find me in their camps and in their houses."

"What do you do?"

"I bring death," Smallpox replied. "My breath causes children to wither like young plants in spring snow. I bring destruction. No matter how beautiful a woman is, once she has looked at me she becomes as ugly as death. And to men I bring not death alone, but the destruction of their children and the blighting of their wives. The strongest warriors go down before me. No people who have looked on me will ever be the same."

The Kiowa didn't exaggerate for after smallpox the New World never looked quite the same. In the end the Great Dying probably claimed a hundred million Amerindians in less than a hundred years. If the Black Death was an ecological disaster, then the invasion of the New World was a biological

Armageddon. Historians (who can add and subtract) rate it as the greatest demographic disaster in the history of the world. With a biological arsenal that also included potent killers such as plague and tuberculosis, the Old World's invasion of the New was never much of a contest. The English pilgrims didn't need their blunderbusses nor the Spanish conquistadors their mastiffs, horses and blood lust. Missionaries and soldiers could have just walked behind each ruinous epidemic and swept away the shocked survivors with a broom. The shooting and butchering that accompanied the invasion of the New World was mostly dramatic overkill and just made a sad story sadder. "Had my pen the gift of tears," wrote the great Ecuadorian writer Juan Montalvo, "I would write a composition entitled *El Indio*, and the world would weep."

The smallpox conquest emptied the New World with a thoroughness that shattered cultures and humbled whole civilizations. Epidemics not only unhinged the Aztecs and the Incas but created a kind of wild diaspora throughout the Americas, dispersing survivors left and right. Smallpox also forced the invaders to replace millions of dying Indians with millions of black slaves to keep the hemisphere's economy working. Empty aboriginal cornfields and cities created the vacant real estate that the Europeans needed to invent a Neo-Europe, complete with Iberian cattle, Hessian flies, English starlings, Russian knapweed, Norwegian rats and Turkish Red wheat. After the Great Dying, nineteenth-century Americans grew up thinking that they lived on the edge of a "wilderness" in a land without history. Octavio Paz, the great Mexican thinker, understood this disease-sponsored fantasy when he wrote that, "the word American designates a man defined not by what he has done but what he wanted to do." Immigrants, of course, can only invent their own destinies in lands where disease has smothered the original inhabitants, and in this respect the Americas are really the first cultures ever designed by a virus. Smallpox's wanton behaviour has even bequeathed the Americas a lot of front-page legacies. Canadians and Americans read about aboriginal land claims and uprisings in their newspapers today because their Indian policies were based on the belief that smallpox would finish off the New World's original landlords. Neo-Europeans never banked on Amerindians developing a healthy immunity to Old World germs after four hundred years or outgrowing their reservations.

Smallpox, the largest of all viruses, introduced itself to the Old World long before Columbus's time. Related to monkey pox and cow pox, the virus became a human parasite thousands of years ago when people in the Middle East began to domesticate animals. The virus first appeared in Europe before the tenth century, where it probably established itself as a minor flu-like nuisance. However, in the sixteenth and seventeenth centuries (when smallpox ran wild through the New World), it also dominated Europe's mortality tables by developing an uncanny virulence. This new strain (about nine strains preyed on the New World in all) caused fevers and chills, produced fleshy circles of pus, and swelled hands and faces. The sick smelled horribly of rotting flesh, and in bad cases the pustules melted faces and backs in a sea of blood. While the virus stripped skin in red and yellow patches, it also battered internal organs like an invisible prize-fighter. Survivors of the month-long ailment often went blind in one eye, bore ugly pock-marks and carried an immunity to smallpox for life.

By the end of the seventeenth century, mild or severe eruptions of "the cruel disease" accounted for nearly a third of children's deaths in Europe and had infected nearly four out of five adults. One European poet predictably described smallpox as such a "loathsome" thing that "the Soul would hardly own the body at the resurrection." The disease's frightful disfigurement also didn't do much for romance. The onset of smallpox was enough to dissolve the vows of newlyweds and propel the uninfected partner into flight. For these and other reasons, the prolific British historian Thomas Macaulay dubbed it the "most terrible of all ministers of death"—an honour the virus gradually lost to other microbes as it evolved into an annoying but treatable childhood disease in the late nineteenth century.

Before Columbus and smallpox fumbled their way to the Americas, the New World pulsed with an incredible richness and diversity of people. Bartolomé de Las Casas, a Spanish friar with a conscience, compared the activity of New World peoples to "a hive of bees.... It seems as though God had placed all or the greater part of the entire human race in these countries." Las Casas was not a liar, and the historical record largely supports his eyesight. In New Mexico's Chaco Canyon the world's largest apartment house, *Pueblo Bonito*, rose five terraces, sheltered eight hundred rooms and took 150 years to build. The Neo-European city of New York did not erect a building of similar size until the 1800s. In Cahokia, Illinois, the celebrated Mound Builders, a group of prolific farmers near the Mississippi River, built an earthen ceremonial centre that covered six and a half acres. Forty thousand aboriginal clerics, tradesmen and bureaucrats worked within its walls. No Neo-European settlement could boast such a population until 1790. The New World also had the world's largest market-place in Tenochtitlan, the Aztec capital. Every morning sixty thousand traders and consumers packed its thoroughfares to buy maize, polished stones, cotton garments, wild turkeys, garlic, raw fish and gold. Neither Rome nor Constantinople had anything to rival it. Soldiers in Cortez's army, who wondered if the whole city wasn't a dream, said it took two days to walk through the market. The Portuguese also couldn't believe the crowds of people they encountered along the coast of Brazil. To the missionary Alfonso Braz, Amazonians grew almost as wild as rabbits: "There are so many of them and land is so great and they are increasing so much that if they were not continuously at war and eating one another it could not contain them."

In spite of this evidence, historians have long argued (with a viciousness that only academics can muster) about the actual population of the hemisphere before the Great Dying. Although the shouting continues, most scholars now agree that estimates of 1 million for North America and 15 million for Latin America are absurdly low. Henry Dobyns, a cantankerous historian, first debunked these numbers nearly thirty years ago by studying available food resources, waves of epidemics and ledgers of dead Indians. He concluded that, in order for 1.5 million North American Indians to be alive today, epidemics of Old World germs needed a base of 18 million hunters, gatherers and farmers in 1492. When he added in the Aztecs, Mayas and Incas, not to mention the 5 million or so Indians that lived in the Amazon basin, New World people probably totalled between 90 and 112 million before they were devastated. Although some historians and archeologists still consider Dobyns' calculations "exaggerations," his demographic research is well-founded and supported by other scholars. His numbers also imply that the Americas were twice as populated as Europe was before the smallpox conquest, and in many cases much healthier.

If there was ever a people that promoted and valued healthy living more than the Greeks, it was the Amerindians. They suffered none of the ailments that wobbled the legs, loosened the teeth and rattled the lungs of Europeans. There was no smallpox. No measles. No plague. No leprosy and no influenza. Malaria and yellow fever were as foreign as black people and dandelions. They also appreciated this absence of disease. For most aboriginals, the idea of living well and staying healthy formed an essential core of their religion. The Ojibway of Canada even had a name for the good living, *pimadaziwin*, which means to honour life "in the sense of longevity, health and freedom from misfortune." Cleanliness was also next to godliness in the New World. Unlike the smelly and lousy invaders, most natives washed regularly and took sweat-baths. The Inca, for instance, considered good hygiene as high a virtue as honesty, something perfumed Europeans did not believe until the nineteenth century.

The unclean invaders couldn't help but notice the "good smells" coming from so many robust people. They particularly admired the aboriginals' "white even teeth" and envied their "admirable complexion"—something most pock-marked Spaniards, Portuguese and French had lost at an early age. A New England colonialist, William Wood, noted that Amerindians possessed "lusty and healthful bodies, not experimentally knowing the catalogue of those health-wasting diseases which are incident to other countries." He also reasoned that Indians reached the astonishing age of fifty (Europeans were lucky if they saw thirty) because "they are not brought down with suppressing labour, vexed with annoying cares, or drowned in the excessive abuse of overflowing plenty." In Canada Baron de Lahontan also pronounced "the Savages" a "vigorous sort of People." The Jesuit missionary Manoel da Nóbrega made similar flattering observations about Amazonians: "I never heard it said that anyone here died of fever but only of old age and many of the Gallic malady [syphilis]."

All of this vigour dates back to the crossing of the frozen Bering Strait and the eventual peopling of the New World thirty thousand years ago. Because the entry point was cold and harsh, diseased immigrants and their microbes died out rather quickly. Prehistoric Alaska with its mountains, snow and glaciers acted as a sort of germ filter that accepted the fit and froze the unfit. Thereafter the Old World and the New World developed radically different parasites. With the exception of polio, hepatitis and syphilis, Amerindians lived a remarkably disease-free existence. But without the constant hounding of uprooted microbes, the immune system of the New World peoples grew as inexperienced as a peace-time army. Consequently smallpox found "virgin soil" in the New World and an almost unlimited terrain for growth and expansion.

The divergence in disease pools between the two worlds also reflected different farming practices. By the 1400s the Old World had domesticated goats, sheep, cattle, pigs, donkeys and horses. Europeans paid a price for all of this four-legged help and protein by sharing a lot of their microbes. Tuberculosis probably sprang from cows, chicken-pox from chickens, measles from dogs, influenza from hogs and ducks. Domesticated animals and humans probably share more than two hundred diseases in total. Although initial encounters were often fatal, long association usually resulted in some kind of mutual tolerance and immunity. Old World agriculture, then, insured that Europeans disrupted the superorganism more often and developed a greater immunity to germs than other peoples did.

Such microbial encounters didn't happen very often in the New World. Although the peoples of Central America quickly cultivated maize, beans and amaranth, they never tamed animals. The last Ice Age had not left a lot to tame besides dogs and turkeys, and what remained had either been eaten or displaced by crops. This dramatic shortage of domesticated animals prompted the Aztecs (as well as their ancestors) to sacrifice as many as fifty thousand people a year as a gourmet source of protein for its privileged élites. In North America the idea of taming an animal, then considered an equal partner in the natural world, would have been sacrilegious. The only animals that the Incas domesticated were llamas, alpacas and guinea pigs, and whatever diseases they may have transferred left little or no legacy. While the domestication of animals in the Old World clothed its people with an amazingly diverse microbial raiment, New World people and their immune systems stood naked in more ways than one.

Upon its arrival in the New World, smallpox abided by one

of the most important but least appreciated principles of biology: the rule of invading rabbits. Take a cane toad, horse or dandelion from its home, move it across the ocean to similar terrain with good food and no predators, and the invader will multiply as fast as rabbits. Australia can testify to the calamitous truth of this principle. In 1859 twenty-four wild English rabbits, casually imported by a squatter, multiplied and stripped bare 4 million square miles of grassland before the Second World War. Smallpox was a sort of New World rabbit. When humans crossed the Bering Strait into the New World thirty thousand years ago, they left their major diseases and their immune defences behind in the cold. When smallpox discovered multitudes of humans with no predatory immune checks, it behaved like every other plant, animal and germ that clung to the Europeans and multiplied in a paradise without defences.

The first evidence of the biological catastrophe about to befall New World peoples was unwittingly provided by Christopher Columbus. After bumping into one Caribbean island after another in search of the Orient, Columbus kidnapped several Arawaks and returned to Spain with his human specimens, as well as a couple of parrots and some polished fish bone. For the Arawaks, this primitive biological experiment was a disaster. Of ten Indians only seven survived the voyage, and when Columbus returned to America to continue his search for Cathay a year later, only two remained alive. Subsequent and larger Arawak test groups died just as quickly in germ-filled Spain where "the land did not suit them."

The first recorded New World epidemic of smallpox, incubated by sick Old World immigrants, erupted in 1519 on the island of Española, now Haiti and the Dominican Republic. The epidemic raged for five years and spread to most of the populous centres of the New World, travelling up the Mississippi River by canoe and as far south as Cuzco by foot messengers on Inca roads. First on the menu were the tobacco-smoking

Arawaks. Smallpox obliterated these people so completely that the name Haiti, an Arawak word which means rugged, is one of the few reminders of their existence. When the epidemic spread to Puerto Rico and Cuba, it consumed half the Calusa with such ease that survivors fled by canoe in search of a holy healing river in Florida. According to Calusa prophets, who were already influenced by Christianity, the River Jordan possessed curative powers. The people of Florida, finding themselves smitten by unknown fevers and spots, joined in the quest. "There remained not a river nor a brook in all Florida, not even lakes and ponds, in which they did not bathe," observed one astonished Spaniard. This desperate New World search by a dying people for healing waters eventually became an Old World fiction called the Fountain of Youth.

From Cuba the epidemic travelled to Mexico in the feverish body of a black slave accompanying one of the conquests. Franciscan friar Ray Torbio Motolinía observed the germ's advance with some disbelief: "When the smallpox began to attack the Indians it became so great a pestilence among them throughout the land that in most provinces more than half the population died.... They died in heaps, like bed bugs." The epidemic arrived in Tenochtitlan just in time to save Hernando Cortez and his army from becoming a sacrificial supper. Under their leader Cuitalhuac's fearless command, the Aztecs' obsidian-wielding army had shredded three-quarters of Cortez's soldiers as they retreated from Tenochtitlan too laden with gold to effect a proper withdrawal.

Smallpox, however, prevented Cuitalhuac and his warriors from finishing the route. The epidemic's fortuitous appearance convinced the Spanish that God favoured their mission: "When the Christians were exhausted from war, God saw fit to send the Indians smallpox...." The disease first struck down Cuitalhuac, and for seventy days it burned among the city's bewildered inhabitants like a fire. "Sores erupted on our faces, our breasts, our bellies; we were covered with agonizing sores from head to foot. The illness was so dreadful that no one could walk or move. The sick were so utterly helpless that they could only lie on their beds like corpses, unable to move their limbs or

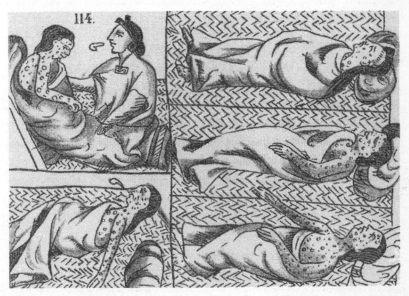

Thousands of terrified Aztecs lay on their beds and screamed with pain until they recovered or died from the "big pox."

even their heads. They could not lie face down or roll from one side to the other. If they did move their bodies they screamed with pain." The Aztecs couldn't believe that such a disease could be considered small and called it the "big pox."

After the "big pox" had thrown its deadly cloak over the citizens of Tenochtitlan, Cortez regrouped and returned with more men, ships and cannons. When the streets became so littered with dead that it was impossible to walk, the Aztecs finally surrendered after eighty days of fighting. Pock-marked warriors sang songs of sorrow: "We are crushed to the ground; we lie in ruins. There is nothing but grief and suffering in Mexico and

Talateloco where once we saw beauty and valour. Have you grown weary of your servants? Are you angry with your servants, O Giver of Life?" The Aztec lament soon became the elegy of the Americas.

Unknown to Cortez, smallpox had a secret ally in Mexico. As the most crowded region of the hemisphere, its 25 million people had created a subsistence crisis similar to the one that had strangled Europe before the Black Death. In 1505 famine prompted several thousand Aztec peasants to sell themselves into slavery in order to get enough food to eat. With too many people trying to grow maize on an eroded and degraded land, the people living in the Valley of Mexico had walked to the edge of a precipice. Food shortages combined with isolation from disease, writes historian Murdo MacLeod, made the people of Mesoamerica more vulnerable to biological assault than medieval peasants before the plague: "There is some justification for saying that if fourteenth-century Europe was ripe for disaster, then Mesoamerica was overripe."

After its conquest of Mexico, smallpox, now joined by plague and influenza, visited populous Yucatan and Guatemala in 1521. The "Great Fire" and "Easy Death" spotted and killed nearly a third of Guatemala's highlanders while the Maya in Yucatan fell like dead birds; 400,000 people (two-thirds of its population) died in less than twenty years. The pandemic continued its relentless march, depopulating Costa Rica, Panama and Nicaragua. In 1524 it ran into the heart of the Inca empire on the skin of messengers bearing news of the invasion of "bearded men." According to one Inca poet, the pestilence arrived in Quito in a box borne by a man dressed in black. Huayna Capac, the Child of the Sun, opened the box and beheld "a quantity of things like butterflies or bits of paper which spread abroad until they disappeared." When his generals dropped dead a few days later, Huayna Capac hid his feverish royal body in a stone house where he, too, rotted away. His sudden departure and the death of his heir, Ninan Cyoche, unravelled the authoritarian empire and started a brutal five-year-long civil war between two brothers, Huascar and Atahualpa. By the time Pizarro arrived in 1532 with 170 men and 40 horses, the epidemic had done the work of an army equipped with precision air force bombers. While disease had decimated Inca royalty, the civil war had consumed the empire's best warriors. With an ally like smallpox, Pizarro needed very little military genius.

In the Amazon the smallpox conquest ignited an equally amoral chain of events. Coughing and bleeding Amazonians burned pepper to keep death from their door, while the weeping of their families filled the rain forest. In the presence of plague-free missionaries, aboriginals fled or trembled like twigs. Stunned and disheartened farmers neglected to plant manioc and died of famine. Convinced that their gods had abandoned them, thousands of Amazonians took to Christianity like some kind of mysterious but useless antibiotic. One Jesuit settlement near Bahia converted 40,000 fearful Indians between 1559 and 1583, only to watch smallpox bury them. By 1580 only 300 remained. The relentless progress of Old World germs and the cultural disintegration it wrought demoralized Jesuits, who counted souls the way conquistadors counted gold: "Anyone who saw them in this distress, remembering the time past and how many of them there were then and how few now, and how previously they had enough to eat but they now die of hunger, and how previously they used to live in freedom but they now found themselves beyond misery, assaulted at every step and enslaved by force by Christians—anyone who considered and pondered this sudden change cannot fail to grieve and weep many tears of compassion."

In North America the epidemics shattered tribes, sent many people into flight and buried some cultures altogether. When Alvar Nunez Cabeza de Vaca began his epic walk across the southern United States in the 1530s, he encountered Indians on the move, fleeing the smallpox upheavals that were rewriting Amerindian history. By the time the French had invaded the Mississippi Valley, the only sun-worshipping Mound Builders of any significance left were the warlike Natchez, who wore tattoos like war medals. But by 1721 they were no more than a shadow of their former selves. Epidemics had so thoroughly wiped people out up and down the Mississippi that buffalo overran the mounds and crossed into Kentucky in the early 1800s. Pioneers on their way to Oregon later thought the ruins belonged to the lost tribes of Israel or to Vikings. When smallpox hit the region again in the 1830s, whatever was left of the Oto, Omaha and Missouri tribes merged with the Pawnee. These plague-driven unions, however, simply made the job of smallpox and measles even easier by concentrating the surviving Amerindians into bigger groups.

Although the epidemics did not begin to winnow the Indians of New England until the 1620s, the effect of the disease was equally catastrophic. When the chief sachems perished along with a third or half of their people, ambitious individuals without a community formed traitorous alliances with the invaders. One Indian, Squanto, the sole survivor of an epidemic, tried any means to amass power. To increase his own status, recorded one Puritan, Squanto convinced other Indians that the colonists buried plague in their storehouses, "which, at our pleasure, we could send forth to what place or people we would, and destroy them therewith, though we stirred not from home." It was an effective piece of manipulation.

Across the Americas, Indians repeatedly demonstrated their complete lack of experience with contagious disease. Their traditional method of healing, a good sweat followed by a plunge into cold water, only increased the mortality of febrile diseases such as smallpox and measles. Near the Great Lakes the Winnebagos tried to scare away smallpox by hanging up dead dogs in trees. In Florida the Ticuma learned a few public health tricks from shipwrecked Spanish sailors. They stopped taking the death-dealing sweats and recruited an expendable minority (transvestites) to isolate and care for the sick until the afflicted recovered. Although these efforts did not save the Ticuma from extinction, most Amerindians never achieved this kind of public health sophistication. On the Great Plains the unfortunate Assiniboine thought they could bluff the demon smallpox, a creature with eyes who could see those afraid of it. Their remedy was "to stay near those smitten with smallpox, to use the same pipe, eat from the same dish, wrap oneself in the same blanket, and to show in other ways that one is not afraid of the disease." The fearless Assiniboine almost disappeared during the great smallpox epidemic of 1837.

Dismayed by how the invaders seemed invulnerable to disease, many New World peoples tried to throw the germs back at the advancing Europeans. In Mexico enslaved Aztecs mixed infected blood into bread destined for Spanish stomachs and threw smallpox dead into wells. On the Great Plains sick Cree limped into trading posts and forts where they spat on door handles, wiped pus on window-panes and lay prostrate on the floors. "If we can only give this disease to the white man and the traders in the fort we will cease to suffer it ourselves," they said. The Cree had the right idea but the wrong germs. More than seven hundred perished during the epidemic of 1870; the traders, recipients of the new smallpox vaccine, said that wolves fought over Indian corpses.

By the nineteenth century smallpox had visited nearly every New World community from the Aleutian Islands to Tierra del Fuego. In most cases it arrived, as the Kiowa said, before the white people. In 1763 George Vancouver sailed into Puget Sound to find a smallpox cemetery of skulls and vertebrae. When Lewis and Clark trekked across the Great Plains in 1801, they found Natives with thirty-year-old pock-mark scars.

During the 1830s the painter George Catlin raced with small-pox for subjects: each time he put a chief on canvas, smallpox buried him. The Choctaw chief, He Who Puts Out and Kills, died of it and so did Catlin's friend Chief Four Bears of the Mandan. The humiliation of dying from smallpox thoroughly galled the chief, as it did most Indians: "I do not fear Death my friends, You know it, but to die with my face rotten, that even the Wolves will shrink with horror at seeing Me...."

Smallpox disrupted and dislodged traditional beliefs and spirituality with the same force as the Black Death rocked the Catholic Church. Not only did the invading virus make shamans, soothsayers and medicine men look impotent, but it also made them feel quite useless. Aztec magicians were blunt in their assessment: "O lord, we are no match for them: we are mere nothings." Aboriginal healers had no antidotes, charms or prayers that made any difference. The injustice of dying in heaps while the invaders multiplied like rabbits also convinced many Indians that Europe's Great Spirit possessed much stronger medicine. The proud and once numerous Micmacs in Eastern Canada thought that they were better than the whites in every way, but as epidemics sapped their confidence they began to suspect that "God protects and defends" the French, "his favourite and well-beloved people." This belief cast the Indians into what the writer William Styron (borrowing Milton's phrase) would call "darkness visible," a deep depression that led to mass suicides and infanticides.

In Latin America such conclusions drove Amerindians into Catholic churches in search of a new spiritual order that didn't eat the living. But in North America spiritual alienation sent aboriginals into the fur trade. Before Europeans started wearing beaver hats, most North American Indians considered humans and animals social beings that ate, smoked and danced together. In dreams people talked to the animals, and in dreams the animals answered, while shamans, like good telephone operators, solved any communication problems between the two worlds. In such a universe, hunting and all other aspects of living were spiritual and taboo-rich exercises that forbade waste and needless slaughter. Angering the beaver people or the caribou people was a serious business that could bring misfortune, misery and illness. But when smallpox and plague attacked, many Amerindians suspected that the animal kingdom had broken its faith and had declared war on native people for unspoken sins. This "conspiracy of the beasts," as historian Calvin Martin calls it, prompted many believers to abandon sacred ways and to embrace profane ones. Taboos that once made Amerindians "keepers of the game" were dropped like hot coals once animals became expendable enemies. "In an attempt to extricate himself from their morbid grip, the Indian sought to destroy his wildlife tormentors," explains Martin. "He went on a war of revenge, a war which soon became transformed into the historic fur trade."

Another architect of the fur trade emerged in New England where the epidemics that littered the woods with the bones of the Abenaki also increased the value of wampum. As symbols of personal wealth and power, these strings of white and purple shells defined prestige in New England. A gift of wampum could settle a dispute or appease a spirit, and Indian chiefs, the wampum keepers, used them judiciously. But when Europeans promised wampum for beaver tails at the same time as smallpox survivors needed wampum to re-establish some kind of social and political order, the result was disaster for animals. "Even a limited market in prestige was enough to turn Indians into the leading assailants of New England's fur-bearing mammals," says ecologist William Cronon.

History thrives on irony, and the Indian conversion to the fur trade, America's first commercial church, provided irony in spades. By killing lynx, deer, beaver and moose, the native people erased their chief means of subsistence, introduced malnutrition to their families and ultimately became more susceptible to disease. "Yea the times have turn'd everything upside down, or rather we have Chang'd the good Times by the help of the White People," concluded Connecticut's Mohegans in 1789. "For in Times past, our Fore-Fathers had everything in Great plenty....But alas, it is not so now, all our Fishing, Hunting and Fowling is entirely gone."

The massacre of New World mammals also created more space for other Old World invaders. To European cattle and sheep, New England must have appeared as a spacious paradise without predators, and by the seventeenth century the fur trade had made it easier to find a feral pig or cow in the woods than a deer. In Central America and Mexico cattle, sheep and pigs (like smallpox) also discovered rich grasslands that had never been grazed. Taking advantage of so much free grass and obeying the rule of the invading rabbit, cattle soon outnumbered Mexicans and congregated in herds as large as 150,000. These wild horned animals, which the Indians feared too much to eat, trampled down cornfields and brought famine to the smallpox veterans. The more fields the Indians surrendered to invading cows, the more the cows multiplied. Throughout Central America cattle ultimately helped to drive Amerindians from lowland fertile farms into the mountains, where to this day they reap a poor life from poor land.

Although smallpox was certainly the most lethal of all the Old World germs, it did not work alone. In North America between 1520 and 1899, 41 epidemics of smallpox competed with 17 attacks of measles, 10 influenza outbreaks, 4 waves of bubonic plague and 4 assaults of scarlet fever. The list for South America would require a chapter by itself. By the seventeenth century whiskey had reinforced these epidemics by further depressing the immune system of Amerindians. In 1699 a German missionary took a look at all of this dying and concluded that "the Indians die so easily that the bare look and smell of a Spaniard causes them to give up the ghost."

The exact number of Indians that eventually perished during the Great Dying probably surpassed the total number of casualties during both World Wars. What was 20 percent of humankind in 1490 became, after smallpox and the wars of conquest, less than 3 percent a century later. Central Mexico's pre-Columbian population dropped from a wealth of 25 million people to an impoverished and enslaved remnant of 2 million by 1568. The Valley of Mexico did not regain its gregarious character and attain a population of 20 million again until the 1940s; even then only 7 percent of this new growth was Indian. In the Andes, Old World germs whittled an empire encompassing anywhere between 12 and 30 million people down to 1 million by 1650, the nadir of the Great Dying. The devastation had been so complete in the Western Hemisphere, says Henry Dobyns, that "one Native American lived early in the twentieth century where about seventy-two had existed four centuries earlier."

All of this dying created an enormous shortage of labour at a time when the Spanish needed Indian hands to exploit the New World silver mines and sugar plantations. To replace the heaps of dead in Mexico, Peru and Española, the Spanish plucked natives from any land they could. Even the Puritans sent shackled Indians down to the West Indies. But with a population of a million people, Nicaragua became the prime raiding target. In the 1530s and 1540s slavers carried off more than 500,000 Nicaraguans and killed another 50,000 that resisted. So great was the demand for living Indians that twenty slaving vessels made 210 trips a year, each carrying as many as 350 slaves. Only half of the slaves ever survived the journey while the rest soon died in mines that resembled underground cemeteries. By 1578 no more than 8,000 Indians remained in Nicaragua.

In response to this massive depopulation of the New World, the Spanish began importing slaves from Africa. Boosters of *la*

Crowded slave ships created floating germ factories; the cargo typically arrived in port looking like walking skeletons.

trata negra argued that Indians "died like fish in a bucket" while blacks "prospered so much in the colony that it was the opinion that unless a negro should happen to be hung he would never die, for as yet none have been known to perish from infirmity."

It was a persuasive argument. One hundred years after Columbus had landed in a New World as full of people as a "hive of bees," the Spanish had already imported one million Africans to fill the empty spaces. Contrary to popular belief and textbook errors, Africans outnumbered whites in the New World until the eighteenth century.

The slave trade, however, subtracted almost as many people as it added to the New World. During the infamous "middle passage" across the Atlantic, white sailors distributed typhus, smallpox and measles among the chained slaves while the blacks shared their dysentery, yellow fever and malaria. The biological wars waged on these ships took a heavy toll on both sides. Each year nearly a fourth of the sailors died or were abandoned in the Caribbean. Smallpox claimed the most by killing up to 70 percent of the human cargo and 10 percent of the handlers. By the time a slave vessel arrived in the New World, it was as full of nasty infections as a modern-day hospital. "There is perhaps not any condition in which human nature may be viewed in a more revolting aspect than that of a crowded slave vessel with dysentery on board," wrote one British medical officer. "Of all the horrors attending the middle passage with the exception of perhaps smallpox, it is the worst. The effluvium which issues from her decks, or rather prison, is peculiar and sickening by any conception, and is generally perceptible at a great distance to leeward." The Portuguese called the slave galleys *tumbieros* or floating tombs.

When these stinking ships arrived in Cartagena, Bahia, Veracruz or Buenos Aires, they were invariably full of dead sailors, sick slaves and "the cruel disease." The slaves acted as such potent conduits for both European and African diseases that the Caribbean and coastal areas of South America eventually lost their Indian populations altogether. The New World's coastal killing fields struck great fear into port authorities, who quickly learned that whites born in the New World were not regularly exposed to smallpox and had no more acquired immunity to it than blacks and Indians had. Smallpox epidemics carried by slaves even struck New York in the eighteenth century. To save whites, strict quarantines were imposed on slave ships in the sixteenth and seventeenth centuries. Neo-Europeans ordered slaves to be lodged in the "furthermost houses of the town or in tents" while physicians carefully inspected the cargo before branding the slaves with hot irons to mark ownership.

These public health measures rarely broke up the profitable chains of infection that enriched slave-traders. The constant traffic of fresh African slaves, necessary to replace the victims of smallpox, measles and abuse, created an unending disease cycle. For every two black slaves purchased on the Guinea Coast, only one made it to the New World. During the three and a half centuries of the slave trade, the New World and the Atlantic Ocean claimed nearly fifteen million Africans. Furthermore, European diseases and a paucity of female slaves prevented blacks from becoming a self-sustaining people until the death of slavery in the nineteenth century. Abolition improved life for many. It ended the numbing epidemics that kept the slave trade in business, it gave blacks a chance to become a self-sustaining group of immigrants for the first time and it made life in America's major ports longer and healthier. In fact, the whole American abolition movement may have sprung more from an unconscious concern about biological safety for white urban dwellers living in slave ports than from intellectual notions about human rights.

While smallpox single-handedly established and sustained the slave trade, it also cleared the way for adventurous and entrepreneurial whites. In New England, Puritans built towns such as Boston and Plymouth on rotting cornfields abandoned by smallpox victims. Mexico City rose out of the ruins of Tenochtitlan. The epidemics created the illusion of so much empty space that Europeans logically concluded that God had conferred upon them divine property rights to the hemisphere. With a bible in one hand and a gun in the other, the Puritan John Cotton declared that Genesis authorized his people to "come and inhabit where there is a vacant place," without the annoyance of real-estate negotiations. Settlers in New Spain wrote to their relatives to drop everything and immigrate: "God will help us. This is as good as ours, for God has given us more here than there, and we shall be better off."

The indentured servants and convicts that replaced Indians in the New World could not believe how much better off they really were. Compared to the crowded and disease-ridden cities of Europe, the New World looked like a land of unlimited opportunities. Here Europeans not only lived longer but could eat three meals a day. Freed from the constraints of scarcity and the terror of epidemics, Neo-Europeans embarked on one of the world's greatest economic orgies. During this new Age of Exuberance they cut down trees faster than smallpox killed Indians, and exported fish, fur, sugar and silver. In looting the abundance of the New World, they also constructed the foundations of capitalism. Adam Smith marvelled at this development and proclaimed a new economic law: "The colony of a civilized nation which takes possession, either of waste country, or of one so thinly inhabited, that the natives easily give place to the new settlers, advances more rapidly to wealth and greatness than any other human society."

Smallpox shaped the character of several Neo-European countries but the scars left on Canada run particularly deep. Thanks to the great epidemics of the seventeenth and eighteenth centuries, Canada took all its economic lessons from the fur trade. The Hudson's Bay Company, Canada's first corporation, demonstrated that easy wealth comes from exploiting the wilderness: once the beaver have been exterminated in one river system, move on to the next. The ethics of the fur trade became the ethics of the nation, and after furs, Canadians skinned the land of trees, minerals and finally the power of water. The legacy of smallpox has not only given Canada the weakest conservation record of any developed country but also the least sustainable economy.

The Americans joined in this rape of the land but infused it with a new religion: the cult of the future. When smallpox erased the original peoples and their histories, the settlers of the United States designed a country disconnected from the past and wedded to the pursuit of sheer possibility and constant innovation. What began as a conquest of "wilderness" and space ultimately evolved into a conquest of the future. The American empire now behaves like a virus, valuing mobility, reinventing its identity and constantly erasing tradition. With their fast foods, blue jeans and technological wizardry, Americans have become an epidemic of modernity. Octavio Paz has no doubt that America is "a construct aimed against history and its disasters, oriented toward the future, that *terra incognita* with which it has identified itself."

Smallpox endowed Latin America with a different kind of arrogance and conceit. In contrast to Americans, Mexicans are preoccupied with the past. As a people of mixed blood and orphans of smallpox, they are forever trying to stop the flow of history in order to reconnect with a time innocent of germs. In Central America the chaotic rhythm of epidemics has engineered a culture of injustice. After smallpox the conquistadors replaced sustainable yield with unbridled looting. Central Americans have endured a succession of economic dictators such as indigo, bananas, cotton and coffee because monocultures seemed the best way to exploit both smallpox's survivors and a land too rich to comprehend. Europeans have never appreciated how aptly they named smallpox when they called it "the cruel disease."

During the grimmest days of the Great Dying in the late 1800s, Indians on the Great Plains started one of the saddest religions ever born in the New World. Tribes on the verge of extinction from California to Minnesota clasped hands, danced in circles and sang for the return of dead relatives. The so-called Ghost Dance religion began when a Paviotso Indian in Nevada had a vision about dead relatives returning from the grave. Dozens of tribes immediately adopted the prophecy and added to it. Some Indians danced for buffalo, elk and other wild game to return in abundance. Others danced for the whites to burn up and "disappear without even leaving ashes." Tribes such as the Pawnee, who had lost most of their traditional knowledge with their smallpox dead, also danced for the old ways to come back. The Kiowa Dance came with a simple chant:

> The spirit host is advancing, they say.
> The spirit host is advancing, they say.
> They are coming with the buffalo, they say.
> They are coming with the buffalo, they say.
> They are coming with the [new] earth, they say.
> They are coming with the [new] earth, they say.

The dead never did return but Indians have started living longer. It took nearly four hundred years for their immune systems to recover from the invasion of Old World germs, but as a people they have slowly adjusted. One of the first symptoms of improved health has been overcrowded reserves. Canadian and American policy-makers herded their pock-marked Indians onto small parcels of land in the 1800s with the expectation that these remnants would eventually die off. When many reserve Indians began to double their numbers after World War II, most reserves simply didn't have enough room to support hunting and trapping economies any longer. This demographic change explains why land claims are in the news and why ingenious Mohawks in Quebec and Seminoles in Florida have set up huge multimillion-dollar bingo halls—one of the few forms of economic development that Indians can squeeze onto real estate originally expected to become graveyards.

With stronger immune systems Indians have also experienced renewed political vigour. Two events in 1990 illustrated what a people can do when they are not fighting germs all the time. In Canada, a Cree named Elijah Harper used his vote in a provincial assembly to single-handedly defeat a cynical and anti-democratic constitutional amendment that ignored aboriginal rights and the aspirations of most Canadians. At the same time that Harper shook up Canada's autocrats, one million Indians in Ecuador broke the silence barrier and barricaded roads and occupied plantations for a week. They demanded the break-up of estates, money for bilingual education, and recognition of Ecuador as a multilingual country. Five hundred years after Columbus, Indians are now talking about recovery, not discovery.

Although the World Health Organization seemingly stamped out the virus in Africa in the 1970s, the smallpox conquest has not ended. Old World germs continue to consume Amerindians in the Amazon as quickly as ranchers burn trees. And new viruses such as HIV continue to kill disproportionate numbers of aboriginal people because the smallpox legacy of poor health still festers like an open wound. As the cultural and demographic losses build, the mission of the Ghost Dancers becomes more and more impossible. Alfred Crosby, the pre-eminent historian of the Old World's biological aggression, now calculates that the cattle, Europeans, dandelions and germs that trailed Columbus probably annihilated more buffalo, Yanomamö Indians and genetic diversity in four hundred years than evolution could have killed off in a million. No matter how hard aboriginals might now try, they cannot hope to recover the New World as it once was, before that spotted stranger appeared in the east.

6

SYPHILIS:

VENEREAL LIAISONS

What cannot be cured must be endured.
German Proverb

Like most Europeans in the seventeenth century, the French
wag Voltaire thought and talked a lot about syphilis. It was the
AIDS of his time, and about one out of every five French citizens had the pox. Voltaire called it the "common enemy of
mankind" and characters in his books joked and gossiped about
it and died from it. Every time Dr Pangloss appears in *Candide*,
he's lost another part of his anatomy to syphilis. The diseased
state of Europe taught Voltaire a thing or two about the nature
of power. In one short fable he argued that two sisters governed
the world: smallpox and syphilis. The elder sister, "conspicuous
in Europe from time immemorial," spent most of her time
"spoiling people's looks" and making war on beauty. The
younger, a resident of snake-infested lands in the Americas,
made "a direct attack on everything that makes beauty useful
and precious...." For five thousand years the two sisters lived

apart, each content in her own kingdom. It wasn't until the fifteenth century, says Voltaire, that they paid each other visits, "travelling by the Spanish fleets." Neither sister regretted the exchange: "For ever since that time they seem to have resolved to live together for evermore."

Voltaire's fable holds more truth than fiction. Just as smallpox became the Old World's calamitous gift to the New, syphilis was America's biological surprise for Europe. As the only New World germ that caught Europe's immune system unprepared, it took a fulsome revenge, doing the work of several plagues and then some. Syphilis also broke a lot of new epidemiological ground. Unlike the old-time microbes that caused malaria or leprosy, it actually had a recorded beginning. And unlike plague or influenza, it didn't simply fill the graveyards and leave. Syphilis arrived on the continent in 1493 with a bunch of sailors, and after rapidly rearranging the sexual map of Europe became a permanent resident. For five centuries now syphilis has meddled in the politics, wars, literature and sex lives of the civilized world. With a little help from bed-hopping aristocrats, lonely soldiers and hard-pressed whores it introduced the condom, the wig, antibiotics, and a great deal of fear to European bedrooms. Civilization and syphilization have always been one and the same. In spite of numerous and violent campaigns directed against the spirochete or its unhappy carriers, the microbe remains triumphant, if not ascendant, in the New World.

Columbus and his sailors first picked up syphilis on the island of Española or Haiti. The Arawaks were a friendly and numerous people (perhaps three million strong) who freely gave the Spanish everything they had, including tobacco and bacteria. According to a surviving Arawak myth, one of their folk heros, Guagagiona, had "great pleasure" with a woman but then had to retire to the bushes to cleanse himself of ulcers. For the Arawaks the disease was probably a mild yet common skin infection that was no more irritating than a case of scabies. Columbus's sailors, virgin soil for the germ, likely got superinfected with the spirochete because they often had sex with five or six obliging Arawak women a night. Even Columbus, who died in 1506 with syphilitic visions that he was "an ambassador of God," described the Indians as a "most loving people." After all this free and undeserved affection, Columbus and his men sailed back to Spain in 1493 with several kidnapped Arawaks. Although many of the sailors complained of rashes, headaches and unfamiliar ulcers during the voyage, most attributed their unease to the "tolls of the sea." The disease had probably reached one of its quiet stages before Columbus docked in Seville; the Admiral never mentioned it in any of his dispatches for fear of alarming his sponsors. With six sailors and six surviving Arawaks, Columbus set out for Barcelona to announce his "discoveries." In every small town people celebrated his navigational prowess and remarkable adventures with great feasts, parties and sexual orgies. Sleeping with one of Columbus's sailors or one of the friendly Arawaks was like sleeping with the New World itself.

According to the Spanish physician Ruy Diaz de Isla, syphilis flowered everywhere Columbus and his men went. The first big epidemic erupted in Barcelona in 1493. Diaz de Isla, who recorded it, knew a new disease when he saw one. As one of the fifteenth century's most skilled doctors, he treated more than 20,000 syphilitics and several sick members of Columbus's crew, including Vicente Pinzon, master of the *Nina*. He also tracked one outbreak of the disease to a public fountain where several of the Admiral's sailors had washed their infected clothing. Diaz de Isla later called the illness "the Serpentine Disease of the Island of Española" because, like an ugly snake, it "separates and corrupts the flesh and breaks and rots the bones and disrupts and contracts the nerves." He identified the disease's three stages and gave the sick a modern prescription: refrain from sex, practise good hygiene and eat well. Diaz de Isla was also the first physician to recognize that catching a bad case of malaria was the best way to arrest the disease "for as long as five years or more." He estimated that there wasn't a town in Europe with one hundred or fewer inhabitants that hadn't lost ten people to Española's serpent by the 1530s.

With piles of pre-Columbian bones, archeologists have confirmed Diaz de Isla's guesswork on the origin of the serpentine disease. Unlike other scourges, syphilis leaves behind its own calling card. The bacteria, *Treponema pallidum*, looks and behaves like a corkscrew (which is why it's called a spirochete) and bores its way into long bones and the skull. In Tennessee, Virginia, Alabama, Arkansas and any place Amerindians lived together in large numbers, scientific grave-diggers have found thoroughly diseased, enlarged and thickened tibiae. Syphilitic cranial knobs have also been identified on ancient Amerindian skulls in Florida. Bones that belonged to the great Mound Builders in the Ohio and Mississippi Valleys all bore the scars of treponema. Scientists poking around in Mexico, Guatemala and Peru have also found syphilis's imprint: worm-eaten skulls, swollen tibiae and gaping holes where the palate should have been. Because two other treponemes (pinta and yaws, both tropical skin diseases) leave the same distinct marks, scientists can't tell if the treponema that troubled Amerindians and Arawaks were spread by skin contact or sex. But there is no doubt about where Columbus encountered them. In contrast to the New World's abundant skeletal evidence, no bone with treponematosis dating earlier than 1500 has ever been found in Europe, Africa or Asia.

Columbus's sailors were ambitious couplers and by 1494 the disease had arrived in Naples just in time to meet the army of King Charles VIII of France. The king wanted to add Naples to his empire and seized the city with a mercenary army of fifty thousand men recruited from Switzerland, Germany, Russia and

France. After the usual raping and pillaging, Charles withdrew his troops and their numerous camp followers back to France. The Italians had threatened to launch a counter-attack and the king lost his nerve. At the end of the campaign Charles disbanded his army of syphilitics and sent them home to distribute the spirochete across Europe. In Paris the sight of his sick demobilized troops disgusted citizens, who were horrified by melon-sized ulcers "from which issued a villainous and infected mud which almost made the heart stop beating." Voltaire observed, "France didn't lose all she had won in this campaign. She kept the pox."

The venereal fall-out from the Naples campaign could soon be felt and heard across the world as one country after another blamed its neighbour for spreading the disease. (In this way syphilis announced the birth of nationalism.) Every country with a developing sense of patriotism took part in the name-calling. The Italians, of course, called it the "French Disease" and the French, the "Neapolitan Disease." The Germans and the English agreed for once and called it the "French Pox." The Portuguese called it the "Castilian Disease." The Poles blamed it on the Germans, and the Russians blamed it on the Poles. The Arabs blamed it on the Jews who had been expelled from Spain, and the Hindus called it the disease of the Franks (western Europeans). The Persians called it the disease of the Turks while the Turks called it the "Christian Disease." The Chinese called it the "Ulcer of Canton," the city where the Portuguese introduced it. And depending on their mood, the Japanese blamed the disease on the Chinese or the Portuguese. There are about three hundred examples of syphilitic neighbour-bashing. Gonzalo Fernandez de Oviedo y Valdes, a well-travelled Spanish historian, roared every time he heard these tattle-tales. "Many times in Italy I laughed, hearing the Italians speak of the French disease, and the French call it the disease of Naples; and in truth both would have had the name better, if they called it the disease of the Indies."

Nobody called the disease syphilis until Hieronymus Fracastorius wrote a poem about the unlucky shepherd Syphilus in 1530. It is one of the most celebrated texts in the history of medicine. (Fracastorius knew he was destined to write great things; while a baby in his mother's arms, a bad storm suddenly sprang up and struck his mother down with a thunderbolt. Only little Fracastorius survived.) The poem describes all the symptoms of syphilis and the tendency of plagues to break in and out of the darkness when people least expect them. According to Fracastorius the shepherd was the very first human consumed by "the unspeakable disease." After Syphilus cursed the sun for an intolerable heat-wave that was killing his cattle, the gods sent the uppity shepherd a good dose of the pox. "O Syphilus!" This all happened somewhere in the West Indies before the Spanish arrived. Fracastorius followed up his poem with another insightful work on syphilis called *De Contagionibus*. The name syphilis really didn't catch on until the nineteenth century when doctors liked its clinical Latin sound.

Syphilis behaved a lot more wildly in the 1500s than it does today. The Europeans offered little resistance to the unfamiliar microbe and syphilis had no shame. But in the Old World it had to change some of its habits. In humid Española syphilis could count on naked Arawaks to spread treponema by skin to skin contact. It was a lot colder in Europe and Europeans wore a lot more clothes. To survive, thin and delicate spirochetes migrated to the most hospitable environment they could find: European genitals. The disease that Europeans first recorded sometimes started as an ulcer on the mouth or sex organs and was followed by rashes, joint pains and gummy tumours the size of eggs or loaves of bread all over the body. In some cases it ate away the lips, the nose, throat and tonsils, turning the face into "foul drippings." It was not unusual for a man's bloated and rotting balls to fall off. "We saw the joints denuded of their flesh and bones, growing squalid, the face eaten away gape with hideous opening, the lips and throat giving forth but feeble sounds," says Fracastorius. In contrast to the disease's slow and well-mannered progress today, fifteenth-century syphilis turned a healthy person into a leprous-looking mess in a couple of weeks and buried him or her within a year. The German humanist and nobleman Ulrich von Hutten devoted a whole diary to the pox symptoms and spent nearly half of his life trying to get rid of the disease. He wrote about "boils that stood out like acorns, from whence issued such filthy stinking matter, that, whosoever came within scent believed himself infected." Most male syphilitics get no more warning today than an ulcer on their penis, tongue or anus, and it is even harder for women to detect the disease early.

Europeans suffered severe anxiety over "the French Disease." It looked like a relative of leprosy and appeared as contagious as plague. People caught it by kissing, a common form of greeting, and even by sharing drinking cups. The civic-minded in Germany and Switzerland banned syphilitics from entering inns, public baths and even leper colonies. As early as 1495 Emperor Maximilian of Germany issued an edict on "the evil pox" that described the new pestilence as punishment sent by God for too much cursing and swearing by commoners. Children found with syphilitic ulcers were beaten for swearing too much. In Paris local officials gave infected strangers four *sous* and ordered them to leave the city within a day or face the halter. They also forbade local syphilitics from leaving their homes until cured. In 1497 the Scots gave the syphilitics of Edinburgh two choices: retire to the island of Inch Keith until "God provide for their health" or get branded with a hot iron on the cheek. One of the few cities that responded with some compassion was Frankfurt. It offered the infected free medical care and exempted them from taxes for the duration of their treatment. This response might have had something to do with the numbers of city fathers who came down with the disease.

Venereal diseases, which health bureaucrats now call sexually transmitted diseases (STDs), take their name from the busiest of all Roman goddesses, Venus. She was beauty, love, eros, drink and mischief all mixed up in one. The VDs weren't part of her arsenal or part of Greek and Roman sex lives, but she would have appreciated their style. Like rich tourists the VDs have historically travelled in bacterial or viral safaris. Men and women that show up at VD centres don't have one wound but five or six. One of the probable reasons that syphilis saturated Europe so quickly was the prevalence of gonorrhea, chlamydia, scabies and warts of "cumbersome dimensions" on medieval genitals. Perhaps the most common medieval complaint for men was scabies, a bad itch caused by a small white mite that builds communities in forests of pubic hair. Because of scabies, most medieval men scratched their balls and bums raw, leaving open sores on penises and thighs. Any breakage of genital skin, whether by scratching or inflammation, gives other microbes a free ride into the body. The virus associated with AIDS, for instance, has piggybacked on the sores and inflammations that chancroid, chlamydia, herpes and other VDs leave on penises and vaginas. Syphilis, likewise, found swift entry into Europeans because of scabrous venereal wounds. Syphilitic rashes and scabies still do a lot of work together.

Old-time sexual diseases such as gonorrhea and chlamydia may have caused a lot of burning and infertility but little horror among medieval adults, who didn't recognize the venereal nature of the infections until much later. As both Chaucer and Boccaccio show in their bawdy tales, the Middle Ages took a casual, even ribald approach towards sex. All manner of couplings happened frequently, with or without violence. In a society where marriage did not happen until late in life (when all the necessary resources had been secured to feed a family), most young men walked around with unemployed cocks. Unmarried apprentices, soldiers, priests, journeymen and male servants lustily ogled women, married or unmarried, and bellowed cat-calls that would make most New York construction workers blush. When a sixteen-year-old girl walked past two masons in the city of Dijon in 1505, the single men yelled a familiar medieval boast: "We'll fuck you! We can fuck you as well as anybody." The envy and frustration of young males also institu-tionalized rape in many cities. Each year gangs of men no older than twenty-four raped as many as twenty women in Dijon. They burst into the homes of servant girls, young widows and priest's concubines, terrified the neighbours and repeatedly vio-lated the women, yelling obscene curses. Probably half the men of Dijon had engaged in gang rape before the age of thirty.

Public authorities, all older and married men, thought the best way to protect their wives and to control rape was to create municipal brothels. Some were small four-room cottages while others occupied twenty bedrooms or even an entire block of buildings, especially in cities with a lot of priests. Although ostensibly off-limits to married men, the brothels offered the unattached male good cheap sex with a licensed whore. The brothel owner, like a cinema manager, made most of his money by selling food and drink to his customers. Until syphilis there was no shame in being a "stew" and no shame in visiting one.

The municipal bathhouse also provided a lot of sexual enter-tainment. In the thirteenth century the Roman custom of tak-ing a bath enjoyed an all too brief revival in Europe. Frankfurt-on-the-Main had at least fifteen public baths in 1387 and Vienna had twenty-nine. Historians say that Paris had so many bathhouses that Parisians washed more often in the fourteenth century than they do now. The urban poor so valued an oppor-tunity to wash off grime, fleas and lice temporarily, that they saved or begged for "badgeld" (bath money). Whole families visited these public bathhouses and scrubbed, ate and sang together in the same tub. In Germany, people undressed at home and walked to the baths covered with nothing more than little aprons. Naked men and women often frolicked and mingled in a pool open to all classes. Many women complained that they got pregnant by swimming in tubs previously used by men enjoying themselves, and this became an increasingly common story as more and more people mixed washing with sex. Many bathhouses had more beds than tubs, and catered to the broad and unending sexual interests of priests, nobility and travellers. Indeed informal houses of prostitution gave young girls and scantily clad bath attendants a chance to start a career in whoring.

The healthy merriment, clean scrubbing and energetic coupling that made public bathhouses popular places ended very quickly with syphilis. Either authorities promptly closed the bathhouses down or the public stopped going for fear of catching the pox. There were no arguments about the civil rights of bathers, the politics of bathing or even the culture of bath and bed, because medieval society feared pestilence and valued civil-minded behaviour. By the end of the sixteenth century most public bathhouses had disappeared, and Europeans quietly embraced three centuries of dirt, lice and typhus in the shadow of the pox. Instead of bathing, people started wearing pounds of perfumes and donning underclothes to protect their costly outer clothing from dirt. Bath owners, who often moonlighted as barber-surgeons, merely converted their establishments to treat their former customers for syphilis.

Physicians openly welcomed this lower class meddling because they didn't want to treat poxy individuals. They recoiled from syphilis the same way they had recoiled from plague and every other novel epidemic. Faced with a contagion not listed in their textbooks, most doctors closed their doors, saying they would have nothing to do with an illness that "begins in one of the most degrading and ignoble places of the body." In 1532 a physician in Metz admitted that his learned peers abandoned the poor with "the distemper" to die in fields and woods, and "would neither give their advice about them nor visit them." This neglect left the job of treating the pox-ridden to barbers, surgeons and quacks, the peddlers of quacksalves or quicksilver. These pox treaters all made mercury their remedy of choice because it had long been used to treat other skin diseases such as scabies and leprosy. This reasoning did not make mercury effective or safe, but it did make quicksilver a uniform cure for the masses or "the little people."

Barbers and quacks liberally employed the toxic metal in one of two forms: as a salve or in a fumigating chamber. After mixing the mercury with pork fat, fresh butter, vinegar, myrrh, turpentine and sulphur in an iron mortar, they rubbed the unction into open sores that often went as deep as the bone. Every quack and surgeon had a different recipe and some added live frogs, chicken's blood, snake venom and human flesh to their plasters. Having greased patients in mercury, the barber or surgeon wrapped them in towels or blankets and stuck them in an extremely hot room, tub or oven. According to the prevailing medical orthodoxy, only endless salivating or sweating could expel "the excrements of evil" from the body. (Drooling is the number one sign of too much mercury in the blood.) Some surgeons insisted upon a loss of 4 pints of saliva in the first day while others calculated that 28 to 30 days of mercury rubbing and cooking should produce "112 pounds Troy of spittle" for a proper cure. Not many patients lived long enough to produce that much drool. About half died of heart failure, dehydration, suffocation or outright mercury poisoning. Many syphilitics simply killed themselves rather than cook in an oven for a month breathing mercury fumes. Ulrich von Hutten miraculously survived ten such cures but admitted that he was an exception. He also died of syphilis at forty-five years of age.

A syphilitic who was treated with mercury looked rather shabby. He walked about toothless and hairless and salivated uncontrollably like a sick dog. People with pox and mercury also lost all their red blood cells, couldn't hold down a meal,

Syphilitics often drooled or cooked to death in crude ovens, as well-intentioned quacks rubbed mercury into their sores.

sank deep into depression and complained of failing kidneys and livers. In the sixteenth century it was often hard to tell if a person was dying from syphilis or from mercury poisoning. The French writer Rabelais said that meeting a syphilitic greased in

mercury was an unforgettable sight: "Their faces shone like a
larder keyhole...their teeth danced in their heads like a key-
board of an organ or spinet under the fingers of a maestro...they
foamed at the gullet like a boar at bay in the toils of a pack of
blood hounds...." Although some physicians argued that the
treatment was "murderous," others insisted that the pox would
yield to nothing else. Syphilis, reasoned surgeons and quacks, is
never resolved "except under the influence of a medication
which imposes on the body the chastisement of its impurity and
on the soul, the punishment of its errors."

Prescribing poison to treat a new and mortal venereal disease
seems to have become part of a medical tradition. The AIDS
epidemic has generated the same kind of quackery with a different toxin. When doctors couldn't find any effective treatment
for AIDS, they experimented with a highly toxic cancer
chemotherapy called AZT. It had been shelved twenty-five
years ago because it killed both sick and healthy cells. But in a
series of hasty drug tests, now regarded as "the sloppiest and
most poorly controlled trials" in the history of the Federal Drug
Administration, scientists noted that a few people with AIDS
lived a little longer when taking AZT. In 1987 these initial
findings, which subsequent studies have disproven, made AZT
the mercury of AIDS and the pill of the hour (physicians needed something to hand out to feel useful). Like greased syphilitics, most AIDS patients can't take AZT for too long because of
the poison's side effects. The drug not only attacks normal cells
but burns out bone marrow, depletes red blood cells, stops DNA
synthesis and depresses the immune system. Other side effects
include headaches, muscle spasms, rectal bleeding and tremors.
The kidneys and liver don't enjoy AZT either. When the bone
marrow becomes irreversibly damaged, AZT patients need one
blood transfusion after another. Though the medical profession
doesn't like to admit it, AZT is probably the most toxic drug
doctors have ever prescribed to masses of people since quacks

handed out mercurial salves and pills for syphilis. The only difference between the two remedies is that mercury sometimes induced a high enough fever to cook the spirochetes and send the syphilis into remission. AZT can't claim any beneficial effect other than killing off a few bacteria.

Throughout most of the 1500s, the rich and the nobility rarely elected mercurial torture cures. While the poor generally accepted quicksilver terror as punishment for the sin of getting the pox, aristocrats didn't consider moral improvement a satisfactory treatment. They could afford "learned" physicians and milder alternatives such as guaiacum. Once ground into a juicy concoction, this hard and heavy "holy wood" from the West Indies produced a lot of sweating and did no harm. Ulrich von Hutten praised it in desperation, and the Fuggers of Augsburg filled their banks with coin by importing it. There was even a small industry hawking a counterfeit product. While nobles rubbed the Holy Wood into their sores and calmly drank their guaiac cocktails, churches hung up branches of the miracle cure for poor syphilitics to pray to.

The demand for cures, murderous or useless, was so great that quacksalvers did good business across Europe. Wherever physicians beat away the sick, quacks arrived with bags of mercurial ointments, plasters and pills. Every adult European soon learned that "five minutes with Venus" meant "a lifetime with Mercury." Because of the newness of the disease people tried every known remedy. They ate boiled ant's nest soup, stuck earthworm plasters on their sores and even bound dead chickens to their penises. Perhaps the most famous quack was a Londoner named Mr Case. Like a good pharmaceutical salesperson he excelled at promotion, littering London Town with clever pamphlets and leaflets that opened with "Good news for the sick!" He also advertised his cures with catchy couplets: "All Ye that are of Venus' race/ Apply yourself to Dr Case— Who with a box or two of pills/ Will soon remove your painful ills." Ahead of his time, Mr Case behaved like a modern doctor: he sold a lot of pills and made a lot of money.

By the late 1550s, syphilis had lost much of its immediate corruptive power and it began to settle into the life of a subtle three-stage microbe. Within two hundred years of its arrival, it became "the Great Imitator" and harder to diagnose. Adapting to long life, the treponema signalled its youth with chancres and swollen lymph glands, middle age with joint pains and hoarse throats and old age with heart attacks and insanity. After fifty years of coexistence with the disease, many syphilitics also went blind or started to walk like a drunk with a broken foot. By the 1880s doctors had recognized the bacterial safari connection, and noted that men or women who suffered herpes "are infinitely more prone to syphilis." The big variety of symptoms, however, confused even the best doctors. To this day physicians commonly misread syphilis as leukemia, hernia, multiple sclerosis, AIDS or cancer. One New York syphilitic was recently circumcised because his doctor didn't know a chancre when he saw one.

Syphilis met every class and travelled every road in the sixteenth century. Nuns, priests, eunuchs and even popes came down with it. So did peasants, beggars and kings. Puritans gossiped that Pope Julius II wouldn't allow anyone to kiss his big toe because it was just too putrid with pox. Old greeting habits such as kissing were abandoned and people started to shake hands when they met. When beggars or nobles got into an argument, they usually shouted, "A pox on you!" Reflecting the times, Shakespeare's characters delivered one poxy curse after another while Sir John Falstaff and Nell died "of the Malady of France." When not searching for a cure, people debated whether syphilis was caused by soldiers eating human flesh, men screwing horses or by French lepers sleeping with whores. Others thought wearing linen shirts, an innovation, might have upset the natural order of things. Gentlemen such as Erasmus of

Rotterdam believed that a nobleman without the pox was "ignoble and a rustic." The learned even boasted about their mercury treatments because surviving one was actually something to be proud of. The poor, who couldn't afford a fashionable disease, prayed to St Job, the former patron saint of lepers, for help and mercy. And the poets sang the obvious: "Be very prudent in your love making…. Avoid blotchy folk. And don't despise those who are loyal partners; For to keep a man's lance out of any old hole the Great Pox was created."

After syphilis, sex lost some of its spontaneity. Men started to suspect women, and women, men. D.H. Lawrence, who thought more about sex then he enjoyed it, argues that the "utter secret terror" of the disease had an "incalculable effect" on English, Spanish and American thinking. The terror was never great enough to stop the spread of the disease but it was very real. Saddling the beauty of procreation with a future of madness, paralysis and idiotic children was "a fearful blow" to sexual life. After syphilis, Chaucer's naturally bawdy tales sounded naive and fatherhood seemed dreadfully perilous to Lawrence: "The terror-horror element which had entered the imagination with regard to the sexual and procreative act was at least partly responsible for the rise of Puritanism, the beheading of king-father Charles, and the establishment of the New England colonies. If America really sent us syphilis, she got back the full recoil of the horror of it, in her puritanism."

The terror of syphilis affected male minds the most and resulted in the persecution of whores. Although homeless men carried and spread the disease, homeless women or stews usually became its reservoir. Before the spirochete, philosophers as respectable as St Augustine regarded prostitutes as angels whose wings protected other women from "capricious lust." But as soon as syphilis arrived, "the safeguarders of morals" lost their protection. During the fifteenth century one pope tried to expel six thousand prostitutes from Rome but the citizens rioted.

Municipal authorities also needed the revenue from brothels. Louis IX of France tried to exile all whores, but had he succeeded the country would have lost much of its nobility. In 1635 the French government again passed a law that called for prostitutes to be "whipped, their heads shaved and banished for life without trial." In the eighteenth century police routinely rounded up prostitutes for forced medical treatment and quackery in hospitals. At the end of the ordeal, nurses and doctors lined up to beat the whores to punish them for catching the pox. Men with the pox were rarely treated in this way.

Fashion also fell under syphilis's shadow. Pox sufferers discovered that if the disease didn't remove their eyebrows, moustache or scalp hair, mercury did. The loss of whiskers and locks among syphilitics created a sub-epidemic of "shining pates" that, as Fracastorius noted, made men "objects of ridicule." It also quickly identified a man as a pox carrier, which could ruin his love life. As a consequence, the practice of wig-wearing first took root in France in the 1570s and became an enormously popular fashion in the 1600s. Before the wig the bald-headed wore informal night-caps, hats with hair attached or skull-caps that looked as attractive as the dried scalps of hanged men. In contrast to these poor disguises, the wig allowed the male or female syphilitic to hide their condition effectively without shame or embarrassment. Queen Elizabeth I, whose hair and eyebrows had been eaten by spirochetes, wore a wig, as did the poxy Queen of Scots. Until the French Revolution wigs became the official badge of the aristocracy and the best way to hide the disease.

After a while wigs came in all shapes and sizes: the Cauliflower, the Black Scratch (it looked like a crazed cat), the Three Tier, the Wild Boar's Back, the She-Dragon, the Short Que and the Full Bottom. Judges and lawyers still wear the latter, forgetting its syphilitic origin. Barbers, who not only bled pox patients but anointed them with mercury, also made and cared for the wigs. Woven of human hair, horse hair, heifer tails, Barbary sheep's wool or white goat hairs, wigs needed constant grooming to keep the lice out. Powdering a wig also required several pounds of flour a week. Priests, who wore wigs to hide the effects of their amorous adventures, often complained that some gentlemen spent more money caring for their hairpieces than they did for charity. The only time that princes, clerics and syphilitics ever worried about their wigs was during an epidemic. During the Great Plague of 1665, Samuel Pepys, the chronic diarist, didn't dare put on his wig for fear that its hair had been shorn from the head of a plague victim.

Gentlemen who were concerned about their health wore not only wigs but "armour." Throughout the eighteenth century men donned "Cundum shields" and "machines" with the faithfulness of modern-day lovers. James Boswell rarely bedded a strong "jolly young damsel" until "safely sheathed" or "in armour complete." He didn't like wearing them but expressed "much concern" about his health if he didn't. Casanova took similar precautions and regularly rolled on the "little preservative sacs that the English invented." He also called them "English overcoats." When he didn't wear them, he got syphilis or gonorrhea. "This woman...replied with a laugh that she had only given me what she had herself, and that it was up to me to be on my guard.... I considered myself a man disgraced."

Although the invention of the condom is attributed to Doctor or Colonel Condom, the celebrated inventor led a perplexing existence. Different accounts give him different lives: he spelled his name a hundred different ways, served in one of the four regiments of the Guards or was a physician to Charles II. He may have invented the handy skin sacs in 1660 or just changed the material of sheaths from bulky linen to smooth fish skins and sheep guts. King Charles II supposedly commissioned the discovery to help keep down the number of his illegitimate children. Some accounts say that Condom was no inventor at all, but a popular vendor who sold "armour" to "the Girls of the Town." Because of the invention's bawdy notoriety, Condom may have changed his name and disappeared into a fog of embarrassment.

There is no doubt, however, about the purpose of the Englishman's innovation. The sacs were a "preservative" for good health and a "preventive" against the pox. Stores called them "implements of safety." Even physicians recommended the "Condum" as the best, "if not the only Preservative our Libertines have found out at present." By the 1750s, the device had become so popular that poets sang panegyrics to it: "All ye Nymphs, in lawless love's Disport...Hear, and attend: in Cundom's mighty Praise I sing." In London's coffee-houses doctors, rakes and aristocrats praised "the Happy Invention" which "quenched the Heat of Venus's Fire / And yet preserved the Flame of Love's Desire." Not everyone, however, shared this merry view. The Scots argued against union with England in the 1700s because it would introduce the condom and unbridled sinfulness. The clergy also feared the condom's corrupting influence as much as its fearful contraceptive properties. In 1826 Pope Leo XII banned the invention because it "defied the intentions of divine Providence, namely to punish sinners by striking them in the member with which they had sinned." By not lifting the ban, the Catholic Church today still protects the soul of treponema and the sanctity of procreation.

Condoms and wigs were required attire for Europe's syphilitic aristocrats in the eighteenth century. The continent's kings and queens changed beds almost as quickly as modern-day movie stars and politicians. Every prince had a bevy of mistresses and serving maids as well as a much neglected wife. The Marquis de Sade didn't have to invent sexual perversity; he simply sat in the French court and took notes as princes and princesses seduced each other and dabbled in incest and sodomy. In France the "little people" made up ditties about their poxy rulers: "For having haunted the Bordeaux, Your features with the chancres go. And nothing's left of nose or face/ But two small nostrils in their place."

All of this promiscuity and philandering didn't make the nobility any happier or healthier. Francis I of France was as cavalier as any courtier until syphilis sprang three leaks in his bladder. Henry VIII of England and his syphilitic exploits condemned the Tudor line to extinction. Ivan the Terrible of Russia lived up to his name by boiling, burning, flogging and skewering his enemies in great numbers. Treponema finally ended his insanity with a brain seizure during a game of chess. Trying to find an aristocrat without syphilis before the French Revolution was like looking for a needle in a haystack.

Next to royalty, mercenaries and soldiers were syphilis's best allies. Men without women, particularly men who could drop dead at any moment from a cannonade or bayonet wound or typhus, generally didn't worry about normal sexual conventions or diseases. Nor did women without food, shelter or men to protect them. The great armies of Wallenstein and Napoleon crisscrossed Europe with a rag-tag band of wives, whores and children in tow. Until authorities outlawed camp followers from marching with soldiers in the 1850s, these women cooked, sewed, washed, nursed and fought. Homeless and transient soldiers carried syphilis like guns into the camps and joked about "the merry disease" as just another part of the campaign. "Depend upon it," said Voltaire, "when 30,000 men engage in pitched battle against an equal number of the enemy, about 20,000 on each side have the pox."

Syphilis, which can take a real toll on an army's fighting ability, quickly became a crude biological weapon. When English and French troops besieged Philip V in Madrid, the king calmly allowed the city's starving prostitutes to sleep with the enemy. Although half of the soldiers came down with the pox, Philip had expected syphilis to do all his work for him and

Madrid fell anyway in 1706. The Prussians encountered similar biological resistance when they invaded Paris in 1871: French authorities simply stopped treating their prostitutes for the disease. But for most armies syphilis has always been more of a self-inflicted wound. In the 1860s, venereal diseases put more British soldiers in hospital (about 37 percent of all hospital admissions) than any other ailment. Each day an average of 586 men out of a fighting force of 60,000 lay in bed with headaches, swollen joints and mouths full of sores. Treating syphilitics also cost about a hundred pounds a soldier, not including lost service to King and Country. During World War I, venereal diseases predictably accounted for nearly a third of all hospital visits, and infected nearly half a million British soldiers. Decent housing, better pay, and soap and water all eventually helped to break but not beat treponema's preference for homeless men facing death.

While Europe's nobility was crazed with syphilis, the pox helped define the continent's emerging middle classes as a virtuous alternative to syphilization. No disease has better defined class differences and values than syphilis has. While aristocrats inquired about each other's mistresses, merchants and civil servants asked after each other's wives. Marital fidelity might have seemed ridiculous to kings and queens, but bankers and accountants valued it as much as free trade. At the same time the rich celebrated Don Juan and Casanova, the bourgeoisie read novels about Miss Sara Sampson and other young girls who fell from grace into the lap of syphilis. It was obvious to all classes that aristocrats begat stillborns and deaf bastards with flattened faces, while the bourgeoisie produced robust "little women" and wholesome "little men." It didn't take much imagination to guess where morality resided and where power belonged.

Ever since the triumph of the middle classes in the nineteenth century, syphilis has signalled moral degeneracy. The discovery of hereditary syphilis broadened the conviction that the disease represented an outright threat to the family and the development of society. Victorians, who tried to be as virtuous as the nobility had been profligate, viewed syphilis with such horror that they stopped talking about it. For nearly fifty years, until the great public health campaigns in the 1920s and 1930s, the word syphilis was banned from English and American newspapers. Prince Morrow, an anti-syphilis crusader, generally found it was "a greater violation of the properties of life publicly to mention venereal disease than privately to contract it."

Syphilis has always found a good home in civilization because civilization has never failed to shelter it. Treponema needs homeless people, roving soldiers and affluent bed-hoppers, and history seems to produce these groups with some regularity. Single men (sailors) brought syphilis from the New World and single men (soldiers) energetically spread it. Aristocrats with more time than sense proved that, after syphilis, sexual revolutions will have biological consequences. Immigrants, slaves and conquered peoples have always been easy targets for treponema because they are usually homeless, uprooted and demoralized. The high rate of syphilis found among blacks and Amerindians today is a tribute to the way slavery shattered the African family and the way the smallpox conquest rearranged Amerindian communities.

Wherever technology or capitalism dismembers families, syphilis and the other VDs invade like a pack of happy hyenas. In the general scheme of things, syphilis is no more than a sign or warning that human politics, economics or war have concentrated a lot of homeless and unhappy men or women in one place.

Campaigns to eradicate syphilis in these groups have been highly inventive. During World War I, the American navy removed all the doorknobs from its ships, believing that the knobs spread the pox as effectively as sex. During World War II, officials practised "shoe leather epidemiology" and traced the

Second World War propaganda typically assigned women the blame, but men have always been the most efficient carriers of venereal diseases.

infected partners of soldiers until they found the source. Military posters warned that, "You can't beat the Axis if you get VD." Plays with titles such as "Spirochete" scared the living daylights out of people in big cities. Only two solutions were lacking in the fearmongering campaigns: condoms and the age-old art of washing genitals with soap and water after "a bit of grumble and grunt." In the 1940s, many doctors championed penicillin as the perfect bullet to eradicate syphilis. The drug helped put *The American Journal of Syphilis*, and even most public health campaigns, out of business in the 1950s. It did not, however, wipe out syphilis. The durable pox, in fact, helped coin "the laws of failure through success" in public health: "As a disease-control program approaches the end-point of eradication, it is not the disease, but the program, which is the more likely to be eradicated."

One of the things that both Voltaire and Fracastorius really understood about pestilence was that it ebbed and flowed like a river. Although Voltaire harboured revolutionary illusions about stamping out the pox, Fracastorius, the canny epidemiologist, knew better. He reasoned that plagues operated on their own rhythm and schedule, and he didn't think it strange "that new and unaccustomed diseases should appear at certain times" like crocuses in spring. The philosopher-physician also predicted that syphilis would pass away only to experience a "resurgence, to be seen by our descendants." Because he respected the mercurial habits of epidemics and the equally surprising behaviour of human beings, Fracastorius knowingly accepted the durability of sex and venereal microbes, and unknowingly predicted the emergence of AIDS. Although very few people now know who Fracastorius was, there are very few sailors, soldiers and homeless men who do not know syphilis, civilization's abiding shepherd. If Fracastorius were alive today, he wouldn't be dismayed by these realities. Nor would he change his prognostications. Like every keen syphilologist, he knew that the pox would only disappear when civilization no longer took it to bed.

7

The Irish Famine:

A Blighted Fable

I ventured through that parish this day, to ascertain the condition of the inhabitants, and although a man not easily moved, I confess myself unmanned by the extent and intensity of suffering I witnessed, more especially among the women and little children, crowds of whom were to be seen scattered over the turnip fields, like a flock of famished crows, devouring the raw turnips, and mostly half naked, shivering in the snow and sleet, uttering exclamations of despair, whilst their children were screaming with hunger. I am a match for anything else I may meet with here, but this I cannot stand.

Captain Wynne, Inspecting Officer, West Clare, 1846

Although the potato and its favourite fungus have largely shaped modern Irish history, the New World vegetable invaded the island without much fanfare. Nobody knows exactly when or how the root got to Ireland from Peru, or even who cultivated it first. But shortly after the 1580s, it seemed spontaneously to fill Irish cooking pots and dominate Irish cuisine. The Germans believed that the pirate Sir Francis Drake first introduced the potato to the continent ("millions of people who cultivate the earth bless his immortal memory"), but the English believe that Sir Walter Raleigh or one of his relatives brought the plant from Virginia (where it didn't grow) to Ireland. Other potato legends say that Irish peasants retrieved potatoes and other loot from hulks of Spanish ships washed up against the west coast of Ireland after the defeat of the Spanish Armada. Whatever its portal of entry, the potato had become so tied to the island's identity by the mid 1600s that even Americans forgot the vegetable's true origins and soon called it "the Irish potato." After 1845, Americans and Europeans added the same national prefix to the word famine.

Plant epidemics from ergot to wheat rust have long poisoned or starved populations, but none has been quite as dramatic as the potato blight of 1845 to 1848. By wiping out Ireland's single food supply, the fungus, *Phytophthora infestans*, sent millions of the Irish to Old World graves or New World ghettos. Much of America's exuberant and corrupt political culture should give a nod to the fungus as well as to typhus and other microbial infections. England's inept response to the epidemic also reaped the kind of lasting hate that still recruits young people into the Irish Republican Army. Ever since the Great Famine, the Irish have lived by the rules of a post-fungus culture, keeping their numbers steady and constant. Even today the population of Ireland is only half of what it was before 1845. Fintan Lalor, an Irish patriot, wasn't exaggerating in 1847 when he described the famine as "one of those events which came now and then to do the work of ages in a day, and change the very nature of an entire nation at once."

Prior to the 1500s, the Irish ate great quantities of beef and tended some of Europe's largest cattle herds. Like the Masai of Africa, they even drank cow's blood and added it to milk and porridge. But after the Irish had endured nearly one hundred years of constant and bloody warfare with the English Tudors, the great herds grew thin and the peasant diet became meatless. Oliver Cromwell, a modern military thinker, always thought the best way to "extirpate" the Irish was to destroy their food base. Because of the savagery of Cromwell's armies and of his equally ruthless predecessors, Spanish visitors to Catholic Ireland complained about meagre Irish meals in the 1600s: "They do not eat oftener than once a day, and this at night; and that which they usually eat is butter with oaten bread. They drink sour milk for they have no other drink; they don't drink water, although it is the best of the world. On feast days they eat some flesh, half cooked, without bread or salt."

In such an environment the potato didn't need any splashy marketing campaigns. For a bloodied nation of starving cattle drivers, the root simply arrived in the right place at the right time. Having watched their oats, turnips and wheat being trampled, burned and raided by English armies, the peasants recognized the potato as a vegetable that could be cultivated and stored in secret—a food, in short, that could endure the malevolence of the English. The vegetable also adapted admirably to conditions on the home front. It fit nicely into the great iron cauldron or crock that traditionally served as the Irish kitchen. Potatoes could be carried, washed, cleaned, boiled and served in it. Pigs, chickens, milk cows, relatives and children could all dig into one crock heated by a small peat fire. So the potato rolled into Irish domestic life as effortlessly as a ball into a school yard.

Because it only required about three months of work, the vegetable, like the cow, left a lot of time for people to pursue traditional interests. In between seeding, harvesting and eating potatoes, the Irish talked, fiddled, danced, argued, attended weddings (a frequent event) and got drunk at wakes (whiskey or poteen appeared about the same time as the potato). The starchy root and its easy cultivation even gave the Irish lots of free time to leave home and meet in bogs and glens. Here the potato-eaters formed secret societies and planned the assassination of English landlords and informers. The potato not only nourished gangs of Oak Boys, Ribbon Men and White Boys but helped shape a political genius honed on backroom deals, midnight calls and biblical revenge. The Irish learned how to conceal their thoughts as well as their potatoes.

Ireland's geography offered the potato a pleasant residence. The New World root took advantage of the cool weather and deep crumbly soil to thrive like a weed. The moist climate and west winds also kept aphids, greenflies and viral diseases to a minimum. Peasants initially encouraged the multiplication of the root as an ideal winter food. After selling all their surplus corn and oats to pay for the rent of their land, people had little left for the crock by Christmas. But once they realized how well potatoes filled the pot, the vegetable became a year-round mainstay. No other crop, grown on an acre of land, could feed a man, his wife and six children the way the potato could. But the real secret of the potato's success in Ireland, says the vegetable's eminent historian Redcliffe Salaman, was its ability to relieve the misery of the English conquest immediately: "The disruption of the whole complex and routine of normal peasant life opened wide the door to a food which, though peculiar in its cultural requirements, strange in appearance and taste, offered the people a sporting chance of warding off the famine and pestilence which hammered at their doors."

Irish peasants adopted the potato nearly a century and a half ahead of the rest of Europe. Their continental brethren took one look at the bulbous food, compared it to disfigured relatives smitten by leprosy and forever associated the two; they didn't want the foreign root in their kitchen. In Switzerland, peasants accused the potato of spreading scrofula, and in Prussia, typhus. Herbalists also had their doubts and suspected that the plant might be poisonous because it belonged to the same family as deadly nightshade. Evangelical Protestants, finding no reference to the potato in the bible, denounced it as the devil's food. To erode these prejudices (hungry peasants were hard to govern), aristocrats wore sprigs of potato blossoms and even served the tubers at state banquets. Others ostentatiously planted gardens of potatoes and placed them under armed guard; at harvest they removed the guards and let curious peasants help themselves.

Although politicians valued the root as a stomach-filler and famine-fighter, intellectuals such as Diderot still complained that the starchy and insipid root caused flatulence. "One blames, and with reason, the potato for its windiness; but what is a question of wind to the virile organs of the peasant and the worker?" In spite of the windiness factor, the medical faculty of Paris declared the potato a safe dish for all classes by the 1800s. To promote the famine-fighter, agriculturalists championed Ireland as a land free of leprosy and full of fertile farmers who often begot twins. When Europe's peasants finally started to dig and hoe potato patches, they did so for the same reason the Irish did: as a proven defence against rampaging armies.

Within a hundred years of its introduction, the potato was crowned Ireland's king and the peasants bowed down before it. Its roots extended into every aspect of life and its fruit determined life and death. The Irish had more names for the potato than the Inuit have for snow. What the Incas originally called *papas*, the Irish called pratie, prata, pratata, fata, Murphy, or taters, and when none of these suited the occasion, they attached personal names like "Gleeson's potato" or "O'Brien's potato." Even some family names, such as Croker, became another word for potato. Over time, people diced, chopped and blended the potato in daily rituals. Good Catholics planted "pratie" on Good Friday (after the priest had sprinkled the root with holy water), and mounded them on St John's feast day. July and August, the months when the old praties had been eaten and the new ones had not yet been dug, were called "blue months," and when the first pot of new praties finally appeared on the table, people said, "May we all be alive and happy this time twelve months." Every time the skin of a potato turned red, the Irish said a child had died and been taken away by the fairies. The potato even changed memories and currencies. Women forgot how to cook other meals and let their thumbnails grow long for skinning taters. When the potato became Ireland's most important commodity, beggars asked for potatoes, not money. After a while the Irish even called themselves "praties with a bone."

The potato had no trouble supporting this new culture. Rich in vitamins B1 and B2 as well as a host of essential minerals, the root kept the poor alive and well-nourished. Its ability to store vitamin C even ended scurvy on the island. Although potatoes lack vitamins A and D, milk doesn't and the Irish readily mixed the two together. "Milk and potatoes" was breakfast, lunch and dinner in Ireland. Well-fed, with little else to do but hoe potatoes, peasant girls married at sixteen and boys at seventeen. Arthur Young, a travelling agriculturalist, concluded that the Irish diet of milk and potatoes made women extremely fertile and was just as healthy as an English meal of bread and cheese: "When I see the people of a country in spite of political oppression with well formed vigorous bodies, and their cottages swarming with children, when I see their men athletic, and their women beautiful, I know not how to believe them subsisting on an unwholesome food."

The English helped entrench Ireland's peculiar potato culture by enacting so many sanctions and taxes against the wild and rebellious country that growing or eating anything other than potatoes wasn't economical. After slaughtering five-sixths of the population by the 1650s, the English followed up with the Penal Laws. Edmund Burke compared these laws to a "machine as well fitted for the oppression, impoverishment and degradation of people...as ever proceeded from the perverted ingenuity of man." The Penal Laws not only outlawed Catholicism, the national religion, but also forbade the export of all native commodities. In closing down Ireland's famous woollen industry, the English put thirty thousand people out of work and on the potato patch. The only ships allowed in Irish ports were English ones. The flooding of the country with cheap English imports forced Irish merchants to become smugglers or growers of "Irish apples." With a third of Ireland's land rents going to England, peasants started to bank praties and spend them like coin.

English land reform made the situation worse. Protestants were given the best land and Catholics were left with smaller and smaller patches. Travelling through the Emerald Isle in the eighteenth century was as cheerful as travelling through Lapland, said Jonathan Swift. "The Families of Farmers, who pay great Rents, living in Filth and Nastiness upon Butter-milk and Potatoes, without a Shoe or stocking to their Feet; or a House so convenient as an English Hog-sty, to receive them. These, indeed, may be comfortable Sights to an English Spectator who comes for a short time, only to learn the Language, and returns back to his own Country, whither he finds all our Wealth transmitted."

When the English did visit Ireland, they observed but never acknowledged the effects of their bloody-minded sanctions. They ridiculed the culture of "the lazy root" and drew cartoons of Irish people with potato heads. Most agreed with tourist Thomas Dineley that potatoes grew a poor and slovenly people inclined to produce more poor and slovenly people. "They have certain concomitants, nastiness and laziness, wherefore having enough beforehand to furnish them with potatoes, milk and tobacco, which they toss from one another in a short pipe with this word 'shaugh,' sitting upon their hams, like greyhounds in the sun, near their cabins, they'll work not one jolt but steal...."

One of the many signs that the potato could betray its slaves occurred during the famine of 1727 when the oat crop failed. The poor consumed their winter stores of potatoes two months early and, having nothing left to eat, starved. That year Jonathan Swift made his ironic "modest proposal" on how to deal with the swarms of young beggars occupying streets, roads and doorways: "I have been assured by a very knowing American of my Acquaintance in London; that a young healthy Child, well nursed is, at a Year old, a most delicious, nourishing and wholesome Food; whether Stewed, Roasted, Baked, or Boiled; and, I make no doubt, that it will equally serve in a Fricassee, or Ragout....A child will make two Dishes at an entertainment for Friends; and when the Family dines alone, the fore or hind Quarter will make a reasonable dish....I grant this Food will be somewhat dear, and therefore very proper for Landlords...."

In 1740 Ireland got another preview of the Great Famine when a bad frost killed most of the country's crops, including corn and potatoes. Although there were plenty of oats and barley, people couldn't eat them because they needed these crops to pay high rents to absentee English landlords. Paupers and beggars flooded local towns in search of potatoes and engulfed what few relief programs existed. Because the Penal Laws had prevented Ireland from developing any kind of economy, most towns didn't have or couldn't afford the soup kitchens, public works projects or charitable workshops needed to avert famine. The crowding of hungry beggars and peasants into towns, however, gave typhus and dysentery ("fevers and fluxes") epidemic opportunities. Together with outright starvation they killed about 300,000 Irish men, women and children.

Sometime around 1780, in the absence of any major famines or epidemics, Ireland's population started to grow faster than a well-fertilized pratie. From a base of 2 million potato-eaters in 1780, the Irish multiplied to 5 million by 1800 and more than 8 million by 1841. When the potato blight began to steal food from Irish mouths, the country had topped 9 million peasants. At the time, Europeans regarded the island as one of the most densely populated places in the world; Disraeli even thought the number of peasants working arable land was denser than in China. The potato, wrote Alfred Smee, another English tourist and surgeon, "had begotten millions of paupers who live but are not clothed, who marry but do not work, caring for nothing but their dish of potatoes."

As Ireland grew richer with people, its land was divided into smaller and smaller plots. By 1845, half of the island's land holdings were less than five acres. Farms were so small that eight or ten could be harrowed in one day with one rake. On rundales or ancestral plots shared by their peasant owners, the division of property became as ridiculous as a play by Samuel Beckett. In some rundales peasants owned thirty-two patches of land, no bigger than a few square yards, in thirty-two different locations. When three people owned a horse, each claiming a leg, the fourth went unshod. When the blight arrived in 1845, six or eight families were living on land that could only feed one family. For peasants in Tyrone the solution was half-boiled potatoes: "We always have our praties hard, they stick to our ribs and we can fast longer that way."

The more people were supported by potatoes, the more emaciated Ireland's potato culture became. Milk disappeared from the diet and raising pigs became the sole source of income and rent payment. In the parish of West Tullaghobegly, Patrick M'Kye, a teacher, catalogued potato's brand of "hunger, hardships and nakedness," adding that he had seen nothing like it, even in the Americas. Among 9,000 peasants he counted 1 cart, 8 saddles, no clocks, 3 watches, 1 priest, 20 spades, 7 table forks, 1 national school, 3 turkeys, 2 feather beds, 243 stools, no boots, no carrots "or any other garden vegetables."

In 1845, the first thing the Irish noticed about the blight was its stench. The fungus rotted a potato the way armies of bacteria eat a dead man, turning the pratie into blackened and "wet putrifaction." First it spotted the leaves purple and then ate the root. Because of the awful odour, peasants even called the disease "potato cholera" and gangrene. It blasted more than half the crop of 1845, totally wiped out the crop of 1846 and returned again in 1847 and 1848. In the *Gardener's Chronicle*, botanist John Lindley announced the bad news: "We stop the Press with very great regret to announce that the potato Murrain has unequivocably declared itself in Ireland....Where will Ireland be in the event of a universal potato rot?"

Phytophthora infestans has been a benign companion of the wild potato for as long as potatoes have grown in the Andes. Both fungus and vegetable still live together there in harmony. But after the potato crossed the Atlantic and was bred to produce new varieties such as Lumpers, Cups, the Rock and Irish Apples, the relationship between plant and microbe changed. To the fungus, the fatter domesticated breeds began to look more and more like a genetically defenceless tribe of Indians that had forgotten its evolutionary script. Two hundred years of domestication, in fact, had undone all of nature's work and had upset the balance. The fungus, which faithfully trailed the potato everywhere, inadvertently caught up with it in the 1840s and became a murderer. It not only ate the plant but choked it at the same time. One scientist later said it was possible to imagine the plight of Ireland's potato plant by thinking of a man "with growths of some weird and colourless seaweed issuing from his mouth and nostrils," as well as roots "destroying and choking both his digestive system and his lungs."

The potato blight wasn't the first fungus to cause European peasants a lot of grief. In cold, wet weather the ergot fungus flourished but it preferred rye, which farmers grew to make a heavy dark bread. Until this century a person could always tell what class a European belonged to by the colour of his or her bread: the rich have always preferred white loaves. Whenever a peasant community ate too much mouldy rye, the people started convulsing, hallucinating or losing limbs to gangrene.

Sometimes whole villages dropped their hoes and started dancing like whirling dervishes on LSD. (Ergot contains lysergic
acid, the ingredient that middle-class students refined in the
1960s and 70s in order to behave, unwittingly, like possessed
peasants.) Outbreaks of ergotism were known as "Holy Fire,"
"St Vitus's Dance," "St Anthony's Fire" and "Tarantism."
Peasants foamed at the mouth, talked to God and generally
behaved like a mass of Timothy Leary clones. Between the fourteenth and sixteenth centuries, people attributed these dancing
manias and fits of epilepsy to witchcraft. Midwives knew better
and used five to nine grains of blighted rye to induce abortions.
The dancing and hallucinating didn't stop until farmers started
to grow wheat and potatoes in the eighteenth century.

Like ergot, *Phytophthora infestans* needs very specific weather
conditions to reproduce itself, and in 1845, Ireland amply provided all the congenial dampness the fungus required. After a
good sunny spell it rained "one continued gloom" with low temperatures for several weeks in July. Record-breaking dampness
and moisture spread the blight spores over the largest crop of
potatoes the Irish had ever grown. Presented with this large
food supply, the fungus obeyed the rule of invading rabbits and
began an orgy of eating that sucked the life out of both the
potato and its cultivator.

While the Irish started to eat seaweed and nettles, English
plant lovers argued about the cause of the blight in the pages of
the *Gardener's Chronical* and the *Horticultural Journal*. In the latter, Rev. Miles Berkeley, an expert on fungi, asserted that a fungus and only a fungus had blighted the potato. Dr John Lindley
correctly dismissed Berkeley's single-actor theory as simple-
minded. He believed that the potatoes had grown rapidly in
good weather and had then drunk too much water when the
rains and gloom came. The fungus, he argued, merely took
advantage of the plant's bloated physiology. "As soon as dimin-
ishing vitality took the place of customary vigour, all sorts of

parasites would acquire power and contend for its destruction. It was so with all plants, and all animals, even man himself. First

As the potato dominated the economy and set off a fatal population avalanche, ragged Irish children became a familiar sight in the 1800s.

came feebleness, next incipient decay, then sprang up myriads of creatures whose life could only be maintained by the decomposing bodies of their neighbours. Cold and wet, acting upon the potato when it was enervated by excessive and sudden growth, would cause a rapid diminution of vitality; portions would die and decay, and so prepare the field in which mouldiness could establish itself."

The scenario described by Dr Lindley also appeared among the Irish people. Without potatoes, peasants quickly lost their vitality and became prey to microbes such as rickettsia, the bacterial ingredient in typhus. It kills about a third of those it infects and is as generic to filth and squalor as cold is to the Arctic. Outside Ireland typhus made great history by defeating armies (camp fever), dogging vagabonds (road fever), emptying jails (jail fever) and cleaning out passenger ships (ship fever). Typhus had become such a regular feature of Irish life by the 1740s that the Irish called it "black fever" while English landlords predictably called it "Irish fever." Typhus swelled and darkened faces before driving sufferers mad or killing them with high temperatures, delirium and coma. The disease, always a good barometer of poor health, waxed and waned on the island depending on how dirty, undernourished, overcrowded and stressed out the people were. Excreted in the feces of the body louse, typhus flourished best during cold weather when lousy peasants rarely washed and huddled together in mud cabins for warmth. During the Great Famine it worked its way through Ireland the same way it culled inmates in a lousy poorhouse. The winter of 1846–47, one of Ireland's coldest, escorted typhus on its rounds like a slavish hospital intern.

Typhus wasn't the only microbial looter to take advantage of so many decaying and starving Irish peasants. With no potatoes in the crock, scurvy returned and people's teeth fell out. Dysentery assaulted crowds of skeletal beggars and many of the Irish literally shat themselves to death. Throughout the country children went blind with xerophthalmia from lack of milk and vitamin D. All in all, the famine and its ascendant microbes reduced the Irish to the same state as their blighted potatoes and restaged the horrors of the Black Death. Starving children aged so quickly that they grew hair on their faces and looked like decrepit old men or monkeys. Beggars lost their voices, walked on their knees and held up their dead children to passers-by as "feed me" signs. Thrifty peasants even designed special coffins with trap doors in order to bury dozens of dead relatives from the same box. Other famine victims gave up on coffins altogether. Whole families dragged themselves to cemeteries, dug their own graves and lay down, as wide-eyed English reporters found them, in "the arms of death" or the "jaws of starvation."

All of this dying happened just a few hours' sail from the world's richest Empire. But the English hemmed and hawed, insisting that accounts of the blight were exaggerated. They also didn't think a government should interfere with either Providence or food markets, forgetting that the only market in Ireland was blighted. As in 1740, the Penal Laws had prevented

So many Irish peasants died during the Great Famine that only the lucky corpses were carted off to cemeteries.

the creation of any emergency relief agencies, and workhouses designed to feed the unemployed and hungry were predictably too small and disorganized to do much good. Subsidized imports of corn arrived late and were inadequately distributed; many Irish women didn't even know how to cook corn. To the English, a people that lived by the potato deserved to die by the potato. In fact, economists feared that the famine would only kill a million Irish peasants and that such a death rate "would scarcely be enough to do much good." Although the English Treasurer Charles Trevelyan eventually organized soup kitchens for three million people by 1847, he still thought spending English money on the dying Irish was a poor investment. "The great evil with which we have to contend is not the physical evil of the famine, but the moral evil of the selfish, perverse and turbulent character of the people."

Blighted by both the fungus and the English, thousands of "praties with a bone" elected to emigrate. Abandoning their traditional fears about leaving home, they boarded leaky and rotten ships and endured eight weeks of more starvation and disease crossing the Atlantic. Short on food and water, these "coffin ships" incubated typhus and dysentery and smelled no better than slave ships. Many vessels buried as many as half of their passengers in the Atlantic before vomiting their "cadaverous," "feeble" and "wretched" charges ashore into Canadian quarantine stations. On Grosse Isle in the St Lawrence River and in Montreal's "fever sheds," thousands of emigrants found what they had tried to escape: fever and death. Peasants who buried their children and spouses on Grosse Isle using shovels for crosses kept their hate: "By that cross, Mary," vowed one husband, "I swear to avenge your death. As soon as I earn the price of my passage home I'll go back and shoot the man that murdered you, the landlord." Those who survived their New World passage took their grudges against the English and walked as fast as they could to the U.S. border because Canada was only "a second edition of Ireland with more room." In those days it wasn't hard to find a dead Irish immigrant on Canadian roads leading to New York or Buffalo.

In the United States, the slaves of the potato became children of the slums. Irish immigrants routinely ignored advice to go West because they were too weak and emaciated to travel any farther. In New York, Albany and Boston they built "Paddy towns" and "Irish Channels" where nobody else would live. They rented out the dampest and darkest one-room cellars for families of twelve and a couple of pigs. Unskilled and uneducated, they took the foulest kind of jobs as bone boilers, horse skinners, street cleaners and glue makers. Much to the horror of urban officials, they also nursed typhus and tuberculosis wherever they settled. For most of the nineteenth century, diseased Irish people constituted a class of leprous immigrants that healthy Americans tried to avoid. Many Bostonians feared that the Irish would turn their city into "the moral cesspool of the civilized world." But when politicians discovered that Irish made good voting blocks, they enlisted the newcomers who, in turn, infected American politics with a whiskey cynicism and a club-wielding enthusiasm for settling disputes—just the sort of values that oppression, fungus and typhus nurture well over time. After several generations of living in basements and gerrymandering elections, the descendants of famine survivors became respectable American citizens by joining police forces, building financial empires and, like Henry Ford, making cars.

For every Irish pauper that sailed to America, another poorer cousin emigrated to England or Wales. Thanks to the potato complex, Irish workers had already fuelled the Industrial Revolution by working for potato wages. But the new famine immigrants, often blind and sick, sank into the ghettos of Liverpool and Manchester. Scorned and beaten, the Irish became Europe's unofficial "niggers." Health officers often complained that Irish potato paupers didn't even know how to properly use "domestic appliances instituted for cleanliness and decency in town." Long before the appearance of the IRA and random street bombings, the English regarded the Irish as a beggarly and sickly race of misfits, an image that still influences politics between the two peoples.

By 1851, famine and fever had buried two million Irish people and sent another two million overseas. The survivors that remained on the island learned a sharp lesson about potatoes, fungi, typhus and English imperialism that they never forgot. Although Irish peasants continued to eat potatoes, they exercised a new prudence in bed. Like France's peasants after the Black Death, the Irish postponed marriage until the age of thirty or forty when enough land became available to support a new family. Only one son could inherit the land, which meant that other offspring either emigrated or became nuns and priests. The Catholic Church reinforced this post-blight ethic with tirades against the evils of the flesh and edicts on the sacredness of marriage. As a consequence fewer people live in Ireland today than did in 1800. If people are part of everything they have met, no matter how small or tragic, then *Phytophthora infestans* and rickettsia are as much a part of Irish culture as fairies. This conclusion is not malicious flattery or thundering moral commentary but just another peculiar sign of how the superorganism insinuates itself into human history.

8

TUBERCULOSIS:

CONSUMPTIVE REVOLUTIONS

There is a dread disease...in which the struggle between soul and body is so gradual, quiet, and solemn, and the result so sure, that day by day, and grain by grain, the mortal part wastes and withers away, so that the spirit grows light and sanguine with its lightening load, and, feeling immortality at hand, deems it but a new term of mortal life; a disease in which death takes the glow and hue of life, and life the gaunt and grisly form of death....
Charles Dickens

Romancing tuberculosis was a popular pastime among writers in the eighteenth and nineteenth centuries. The disease had become Europe's number one killer, and artists, along with the poor ("the meaner kind" and "the common sort"), were falling before what John Bunyan called "the Captain of all men of death." It never occurred to the scrofulous Irish living in dank Manchester cellars that glorifying death might brighten a dull career, but that's exactly what many artists did. Glassy-eyed and sad with consumption, they started the "graveyard school of poetry" and introduced Europe to the Romantic mood. Graveyard writing featured weepy landscapes surreally dotted with languorous women, stone tombs and falling leaves. It also portrayed early death as both a special grace and a unique spiritual enterprise. In 1819, John Keats, an original graveyard poet, wrote, "Youth grows pale, and spectre-thin, and dies." Two years later, the 26-year-old poet proved his romantic credentials by coughing himself to death.

The graveyard school drew some fantastic deductions about TB. Its members added up all the rattling "lungers" in their midst and concluded that tuberculosis had something to do with genius. The tie between intellect and TB became so strong that even healthy writers such as Alexandre Dumas pretended to be frail in order to look tragically hip. Dumas, who peopled his novels with consumptives, didn't care much for the fad but knew "it was the fashion to suffer from the lungs" and "to spit blood after each emotion that was at all sensational." Edmond and Jules de Goncourt, popular French social critics, even advised Victor Hugo to abandon his good health if he wanted to be "a greater poet." The two brothers argued that a writer needed to experience crucifixion by consumption in order to "render the delicacies, the exquisite melancholies, the rare and delicious phantasies, of the vibrant cord of the heart and soul."

In this unhealthy critical environment, peer pressure among artists to get sick or die of TB was intense. In the 1800s, most writers and composers of any merit seemed to be coughing their way to fame and an early grave. Frederic Chopin had to fight off chills and coughing fits in order to finish composing the Preludes. Niccolo Paganini, who had both syphilis and TB, looked as gaunt as an AIDS cadaver when he played the violin. The budding ecologist Henry David Thoreau stopped taking walks because of TB, but still concluded that "decay and disease are often beautiful, like...the hectic glow of consumption." When tuberculosis didn't consume all of Robert Louis

Stevenson's energy, he wrote "The Strange Case of Dr. Jekyll and Mr. Hyde." Speaking through a tubercular haze, the poet Elizabeth Barrett Browning praised a "butterfly within, fluttering for release" while Katherine Mansfield became the gleam "on the plant that the frost has laid a finger on." Frederich Schiller, Anton Chekhov and Franz Kafka also wrestled with bouts of consumption. The list of nineteenth-century artistic types with TB is almost as long as Toronto's phone book. Consumption became such a popular way to die that even lesser poets developed a sense of humour about feverish exits. While gasping for air night after night, the French writer Paul Scarron wrote his own satirical epitaph:

> Pass, O friend, with footfall light,
> Lest he wake—t'would be too bad
> Should you break the first good night
> Scarron ever had.

There are many reasons why artists died of consumption in the 1800s but genius is not among them. Like industrial factory workers, many poets and writers chronically overworked, ate poorly and lived in damp, airless quarters. In pursuit of beauty, truth and other abstract goals, artists manufactured the same kind of conditions to which industrialization exposed the working class every day. The genius theory supported artists' egos, but ignored the biological realities of the Industrial Revolution and its coarse assistant, the great tuberculosis epidemic of the nineteenth century. The crowded and bustling cities of the industrial age threw coal dust, tubercle bacilli and homeless migrants together in a new kind of chaotic poverty. Not a family in Europe escaped being touched by the capitalistic economics of mass production or the tubercular politics of mass consumption. The peculiar and sentimental illusions about TB held by artists simply reflected its prevalence and its new-found influence on human society.

More than 70 percent of all Europeans were infected with TB at one time or another during the 1800s. But only about one person in seven died from the disease. Most of the dead were immigrants, industrial workers or the homeless—the same sort of people who die of TB today in Bombay, Nairobi and Manila. Industrialization helped the bacillus achieve a killing peak among Europeans in the 1820s and 1830s when poets such as Shelley were writing about "melancholy days" and "pestilence stricken multitudes." This was also the Industrial Revolution's most intense phase of city building in Europe.

There is nothing romantic about dying from tuberculosis. Irish factory workers gave up the ghost with their mouths open, hungry for air, without a falling leaf or languorous woman in sight. Painters and writers died the same way, but refused to admit it because it didn't rhyme with romance. Artists still cling to the fanciful deceit, and to this day people mistakenly think of writers and composers as frail and sensitive (they are usually neither). The AIDS epidemic illustrates that many artists still entertain tubercular thoughts. Anyone reading the entertainment pages could logically conclude that only dancers, actors, writers and stage directors now die of AIDS. These articles almost always imply that gifted middle-class youths have fallen victim to a tragic disease of genius. Most Africans with AIDS know better, as do most Third World poor suffering from TB. The idea of the graveyard school is purely a white middle-class conceit.

René Dubos was the first medical ecologist to recognize the social nature of tuberculosis and its rather unique industrial ecology. His first wife died of the disease and his second, Jean, also had TB. Understanding the bacillus became one of Dubos's passions. Together with Jean, in 1952, René wrote *The White Plague*, TB's most magisterial biography. The Dubos were not fooled by the germ theory (that idea that one germ equalled one

Belching soot and smoke, nineteenth-century industrial cities such as Manchester incubated tubercular germs in revolutionary numbers.

disease) and recognized that the tubercle bacillus wasn't a mass murderer on its own. They concluded that bad housing, poor wages, foul air and overcrowding demoralized people to such an extent in the 1800s that they died more easily than was normal, artists included. Tuberculosis, an unexpected by-product of early capitalism, merely looted the immune systems of people who were displaced, poisoned and uprooted by machines. The epidemic, say the Dubos, was "perhaps the first penalty that capitalistic society had to pay for the ruthless exploitation of labour."

Tuberculosis, like its half-brother leprosy, belongs to a 300-million-year-old germ family called mycobacteria. Without knowing it, modern city-dwellers eat and breathe mycobacteria every day. These ubiquitous germs live in tapwater, grass, mud, hay, rubber tubing and oil deposits. Sooner or later all species bump into mycobacteria, and it would have been difficult for the poor and the homeless to avoid the germ during the Industrial Revolution. Most mycobacteria don't produce disease unless the host lives in ghetto-like conditions. Cattle herded too close together are more likely to get TB than wild cows are and the same idea applies to pigs, birds and fish. Almost any type of mycobacteria, it seems, can cause TB in the wrong kind of crowd. Aside from the leprosy germ, the two strains that humans have irritated and provoked the most are *Mycobacterium tuberculosis*, which spreads from person to person via coughing and spitting, and *Mycobacterium bovine*, which jumps from cows to humans in milk and other beef products.

It seems that TB appeared seven thousand years ago after humans tamed cattle and herded too many of the animals into small spaces, including their own houses. After sleeping next to their cows, drinking milk and cooking beef, people eventually developed their own strain of TB. It has appeared in epidemic form whenever humans, in wave after wave of migrating peasants, have packed themselves into cities, changing their diet, shelter and work habits all at once. City builders such as the Greeks and Romans wheezed and hacked aplenty, and call the ailment *phthisis*. Hippocrates thought it was the most fatal and common disease of his time.

Socializing with one form of mycobacterium can either give people immunity to other kinds or make them hypersensitive. Children who drank unpasteurized milk in the eighteenth century often got mild forms of bovine TB that protected them from the human strain. Lepers, however, develop TB very fast and die quickly. Losing immunity to local mycobacteria can also be hazardous. Before the arrival of Neo-Europeans, the Sioux and the Cree on the Great Plains grew accustomed to a buffalo-type TB. When the buffalo disappeared, so did their "natural vaccine." This might explain why Plains Indians died faster than England's tubercular working class after white people herded Indians onto small, crowded reservations.

Mycobacteria can fill in for one another like members of a football team. When *Mycobacterium tuberculosis* started to disappear in the 1900s, other mycobacteria took its place in the same kind of people that TB normally afflicts, producing exactly the same kind of fatigue, emaciation and lung damage. About 50 percent of all AIDS patients are riddled with mycobacteria, including TB. That's because immuno suppression can activate dormant organisms the way the opening of a can of dog food can awaken a pet. AIDS is also common among TB's favourite terrain: the homeless and undernourished. Their health profile wouldn't much differ from that of gin-drinking Irish consumptives in nineteenth-century Manchester. Depending on the health of the host, mycobacteria can destroy any human organ. During the Middle Ages tuberculosis appeared as inflamed and disfiguring bumps on the neck, a condition known as scrofula. Peasants with scrofula lined up before kings to receive the favoured cure: "the royal touch." TB migrated to the lungs during the Industrial Revolution because foul air had so battered and smoked the breathing apparatus that germs thrived on its damaged cells. In strong industrial workers, the disease cantered; in the weakest victims, particularly women and children, it galloped. People with galloping consumption became spectres as well as literary subjects very quickly.

With so many mycobacteria around, TB watchers have always wondered why one person gives the germs no foothold while another becomes a virtual incubator for tubercles. In the late 1950s, Glasgow researcher David Kissen discovered that grief was an important ingredient in TB's nurturing broth. He arrived at this conclusion after asking his patients to describe their life histories before he tested them for TB. Out of 267 patients examined, one-third were consumptive. More than half of these TB patients said they had suffered "a break or serious threat of break in a romance, engagement or marriage"; only one-quarter of the non-consumptives had this kind of bad luck. Kissen kept on gathering stories and discovered that TB patients on the mend suffered relapses after being crushed by another emotional loss. In later studies, Kissen also noted that consumptives needed more attention than other people; they said that they hadn't received much love as children. Kissen concluded that a "threat to personal and family relationships" made people more vulnerable to tuberculosis.

There have been few threats to the family as grave as the Industrial Revolution. In one generation the machine and the city devoured and dismembered the large rural peasant family, reducing the survivors to nuclear units of wage slaves. The divisions created between husband and wife, father and son, and mother and child still haunt the family today. Working twelve-hour shifts in gas-lit, noisy factories, family members never saw the sun and rarely saw each other. Subsisting on potatoes and laudanum, most labourers died at the age of seventeen in Manchester and fifteen in Liverpool. Gentlemen in the west end of town lived twice as long. Stunned by how Blake's "Satanic Mills" alienated the family and subverted fatherhood, men drowned their grief in gin. Alcoholism, consumption and fathers were such inseparable companions in the nineteenth century that consumption became an occupational hazard for pubkeepers and barmen, who found it hard to avoid the spittle and coughs of their grieving clients. Like a perpetual source of grief, the Industrial Revolution robbed millions of people of "the emotional satisfactions" that make life bearable. The millions of consumptives now living in São Paulo or Bombay all tell the same story.

In industrial Europe, poverty was nothing new to most rural families, but city living came as a grievous shock. Before 1750, England had only two cities with more than 50,000 people. Capitalism's new factories, however, needed crowds of cheap workers and emptied the countryside of people as if they were sacks of grain. By 1801 England had nine great cities, and by 1851, twenty-nine metropolises with over 100,000 people. These architectural deserts had no trees, no promenades and no public squares. There was no lighting or water. City air filled immigrant lungs with coal dust, cotton fibres, sulphur dioxide and lead. These pollutants were as new an experience for the lungs as living in crowded, airless tenements was for the senses. In the new industrial slums, workers also ate less meat in 1850 (35 to 40 pounds a year) than they did in 1500 (200 pounds a year). (Meat and cheese eaters are less likely to catch TB. Scientists suspect that it's only a matter of nutrition but certain beef products may contain mycobacteria that act as natural vaccines against disease.)

Europe's smoky, damp and smelly cities (immigrants could smell Berlin six miles before they got there) may have filled industrialists' coffers, but they put a damper on tourism. When curious Americans visited England to see the genius of the Industrial Revolution in the 1850s, they choked on smog, and gagged at rivers that smelled of dye vats. Everywhere they walked they saw "squat houses" in wretched streets of brick, "kennels to sleep and die in." In narrow alleys and dusty yards they met the "pale, lank, narrow-chested, hollow-eyed ghosts" that the communist Friedrich Engels described. Most American tourists, like Hyppolyte Taine, couldn't wait to go home: "Every day that I live I thank Heaven that I am not a poor man with a family in England."

Family grief, overcrowding, bad food and foul air knocked out working-class immune systems so effectively in the nineteenth century that it's almost a surprise *Mycobacterium tuberculosis* didn't kill more people than it did. Those from greatly dismembered families seem to have suffered the most. All 78 boys and 91 of 94 girls slaving away in a Kent workhouse had consumption in 1844. At the same time, half of the children in a Berlin orphanage died of it. Blacks working far from home on

British ships spat blood while Irish immigrants boiling bones in New York and Boston were twice as likely to die from TB as their relatives were back in Ireland. When peasants poured into Vienna in the 1800s, the number of consumptive deaths rose from 500 to 800 per 100,000 people. The story was the same across Europe. Refugees of the Industrial Revolution, children without parents, parents without children, families without homes, and immigrants without roots all walked into the arms of tuberculosis. Whenever the middle classes intercepted these waves of grief and tubercle bacilli, they also got TB. But, well-fed and comfortably housed, most spontaneously recovered.

TB wasn't the only germ that flourished during the Industrial Revolution. Scarlet fever was "scarce anything" in the 1700s but a pain in the throat, yet in the 1800s "throat distemper" became a fierce killer of children. So did diphtheria, another bacterial infection that attacks the larynx. Measles took a fatal turn in the 1800s and started killing adults. In European cities where the poor daily drank water contaminated with animal and human shit, cholera, a tiny bacillus native to India, appeared on the continent for the first time. By dehydrating paupers like prunes before they died, cholera shook "the firmest nerves" and inspired dread "in the firmest hearts." Glasgow was still a fairly healthy place in the 1700s, but by the 1830s, industrialization had left people working in cesspools and sleeping in cupboards along with cholera and typhus. Surviving in Europe's harshest industrial nightmare required tough knuckles and an even tougher immune system. Between 1848 and 1854, cholera killed a quarter of a million poor in Great Britain. The Industrial Revolution may have favoured TB, but it also provided cholera and other germs with gainful employment.

In the New World, Neo-Europeans introduced TB and other urban germs when they industrialized Amerindians, destroyed their food supplies and stuck them on reservations (rural slums). TB started to eat two thousand Sioux prisoners of war in 1880 and by 1913 had reached epidemic rates ten times higher than those present in Europe. Native Indian life didn't favour the spread of TB; nor did eating buffalo meat. But confinement in an open air prison with only wheat and sugar on the table did. Because grieving New World people weren't suffering from air pollution, TB attacked their bones, spines, brains and stomachs. In the 1850s scrofula "was the curse of the New Zealand race" and killed 22 percent of Maori as recently as 1939. The Bantu of South Africa had no dealings with TB when they lived in their native kraals surrounded by friends and relatives. But once they started migrating to white Johannesburg, TB became their most frequent companion.

Through the ages the rich and the poor have chosen very different remedies for consumption. Peasants considered drinking goat's milk or ass's milk wise, and breast-feeding even wiser (breast milk is one of the world's best immune boosters). Sitting in a barn inhaling cow vapours also seemed to work miracles for the rural poor. The rich, who have never liked any animals except horses, preferred travel and rest. Not surprisingly, most of the world's great tourist routes follow old tubercular paths. The Greeks, like Cicero, took long sea voyages to Rhodes, and the Romans sent their coughers to Sicily or Egypt. In the nineteenth century, English doctors rated destinations according to the stage of consumption: sea voyages for early coughers and Madeira or Pisa for the wan and emaciated. Skiing and horseback riding were also recommended for those who could afford it. While American "lungers" vacationed in Albuquerque and Tucson, British and German "pale face invalids" flocked to the Mediterranean Riviera, considered the "last ditch of the consumptive" a hundred years ago. Today it is the first ditch of the idle middle-class tourist: before Club Med, there was Club TB.

Until the single-minded German scientist Robert Koch found the tubercle bacillus in 1882 swimming under a microscope, most physicians regarded TB with "professional nihilism." They believed that "the treatment of tuberculosis was but a meditation on death" and let patients take sea voyages or sit in their barns. Younger and bolder doctors tried bleeding, phosphoric acid, ether, digitalis, carbolic acid (inhaled for eighteen months) and boa-constrictor excreta. But this kind of experimentation didn't become popular until Koch gave physicians a visible target. Armed with pictures of the tubercle bacillus and indoctrinated by Pasteur's germ theory, doctors launched a fearsome offensive. In this new war they pricked consumptives with Koch's tuberculin vaccine (a grand failure), cut out ribs, collapsed lungs, performed countless x-rays and injected gold salts (which ruined the stomach and killed the liver). When not tormenting their patients, doctors organized international congresses and formed unions against the microbe, making it the first germ in history to be so honoured. Between TB conventions, TB specialists wrote for the *Tubercle* and the *American Review of Tuberculosis*. But the only remedies they didn't write about or prescribe were better housing, good food, clean air and a respect for the role that families play in nurturing health. Such a prescription would have ended the physician's first professional disease monopoly.

In their campaign against TB, doctors also subverted the noble idea of clean air, peace and rest with the sanatorium, a sort of updated leper colony. Between 1900 and World War II, just as the disease was disappearing from Europe, doctors helped to implant these institutions across the industrialized world. Sanatoria for the poor looked and functioned like military hospitals where people had to ask permission to go to the bathroom. Habitually understaffed and poorly heated, a tuberculosis sanatorium for the poor offered road repair work and ditch digging, hours of jigsaw puzzles and four rectal temperature-takings a day. (At least leper houses required fewer undignified examinations.) Sanatoria for the rich, however, served as early models for the modern middle-class vacation. The earliest and most famous of the TB resorts appeared on Swiss mountaintops where wealthy consumptives ate huge meals, shopped for expensive clothes, played cards, read novels, gambled nightly and flirted with other consumptives. Drinking lots of cognac also helped to kill time. The TB patients that invaded Davos, St Moritz and Samadan changed the nature of the Swiss economy completely. According to tuberculosis historian F.B. Smith, wealthy coughers and wheezers gave the country's infant drug business a steady income and helped establish Switzerland's famous banking industry. The rich, with or without TB, had peculiar and secretive financial needs that the numbered bank account answered. When the menace of TB receded, retreats for consumptives simply became skiing resorts. Thanks to the popularity of TB, Switzerland's pharmaceutical corporations and banks prospered.

The sanatoria also had a remarkable effect on interior design. The doctors and architects made sure that germs and dust could gather nowhere, and as a consequence many sanatoria for the poor looked like early "cold storage warehouse cubes." Ceilings lost their mouldings and windows their ledges. Paint replaced smelly and germ-filled wallpaper, and miles of linoleum covered the floors. Advertising flyers even told prospective consumptives that linoleum prevented TB germs from hiding in floorboard cracks and awkward joints. They also said that "impervious" linoleum made it easier to wipe up messy balls of sputum. As the germicidal properties of linoleum gained fame, the material rapidly became required flooring in every house in the 1920s and 1930s. No home was safe or complete without it.

Although sanatoria complemented if not influenced the Bauhaus school of architecture (the sterile square box boys), they had no effect on the control of tuberculosis. No more than 11 percent of TB patients ever stayed in them, and most people were diagnosed too late for a régime of food, air and work to do them any good. To improve their records, many sanatoria didn't accept TB patients who had one foot in the grave. Even when research showed that people who stayed at home died at the same rate as consumptives removed from their families, doctors continued to champion their TB colonies until the 1950s; then they renewed their attack on tuberculosis with drugs and the BCG vaccine. But the vaccine interfered with the natural resistance that local mycobacteria created, and the magic bullets lost their magic. In the United States consumptives now appear in hospitals with TB that can withstand and defeat combined doses of isoniazid, rifampin and streptomycin. Perhaps the medical profession's greatest achievement is that it has made a superior, far more lethal and drug-resistant germ than the tubercle bacillus and the superorganism could ever have made on their own.

Tuberculosis began a remarkable disappearing act in the mid 1800s. When immigrants had adjusted to the demands of urban living and capitalists had provided their wage slaves with better food and shelter, TB retired and found employment in Hong Kong, Jakarta, Mexico City and São Paulo. In 1845 consumption killed 500 out of every 100,000 Europeans; by 1950 the mortality rate was down to 50 per 100,000. It lingered among Irish and Amerindian groups, people that had been the most displaced, but in general it returned to the ubiquitous mycobacteria fold. Doctors had little say in the transition. The slow decline began before Koch discovered the tubercle bacillus and continued during the sanatoria campaign. By the time antibiotics entered the picture, TB in cities such as New York had already fallen to eleventh place as a cause of death. The coughing and spitting had stopped with hardly a doctor in sight.

TB wasn't the only infectious disease to wane, doctorless, at the end of the nineteenth century. In fact, the mortality graphs for most of Europe's fatal crowd diseases took amazing and uninterrupted dives before antibiotics had been invented.

Whooping cough killed 1,400 children out of every million in 1850. But one hundred years later and long before doctors started pushing a controversial vaccine, whooping deaths had fallen to less than 10 per million. There are no kinks in the whooping cough graph: the line goes straight down. Scarlet fever behaved the same way. Its death line coasts downhill like a child on a toboggan, bottoming out before doctors arrived with antibiotics. Measles, typhus, pneumonia, dysentery and polio all share similar histories. Smallpox was the only disease that doctors and a vaccine played any role in controlling. The sudden retreat of these epidemics had a dramatic impact on the European population, which grew from 118 million in 1700 to 187 million in 1800. By 1900, in spite of the immigration of some 50 million peasants to the New World, Europe's population had tripled to 321 million. The continent had lost its natural population check: infectious disease.

There are as many explanations for the great demographic revolution as there are for the origins of World War I. Stronger immune systems, better food and the invention of the toilet probably all contributed to longer life and fewer epidemics. After centuries of unfriendly encounters there is no doubt that humans and microbes eventually signed a natural, ecological truce without interference from drugs or vaccines. In some cases the microbe became less virulent (measles and diphtheria) or the human host more resistant (tuberculosis). This peace could not have been possible without better nutrition. As maverick British physician Thomas McKeown argues, people who don't eat well generally don't offer much resistance to disease. He notes that measles or diarrhea are harmless and short-term ailments among well-fed children, but are often lethal for the slum dwellers of Mexico City. When the Industrial Revolution ended the old famine and epidemic routine that dominated European history by finally putting more beef, potatoes and milk on the table, epidemics started to disappear. The germs didn't actually

The figure of Epidemic, popularly depicted as a blind skeleton on a dragon, heralded sudden and public death.

retreat or go away (most Europeans still tested TB-positive in the 1940s); they just didn't cause disease in well-fed people.

At the same time Europeans started to eat more regularly, they also began to haul cartloads of germs away from their homes. The Great Sanitary Awakening began in the 1800s when members of the middle class realized that if they didn't scrub down their cities and the working class, they were going to die of TB and cholera as well. The movement was led by eccentric physicians who were not yet indoctrinated by the germ theory, who believed that it was their duty to "remove from around our habitations the putrefying recrements of organized bodies." They waged campaigns to widen streets, plant the dead outside of town, remove night soil, ventilate hospitals and jails, and wall-in sewers. They were aided by such nonmedical innovations as windows and cotton garments. The window allowed sunlight to kill a lot of germs, including tubercles, while cotton clothes put an end to typhus. Unlike wool, dirty cotton could be boiled to kill lice and still keep its shape. Panes of transparent glass and cotton underwear did more to increase the average life span of nineteenth-century Europeans than all the world's patented drugs and medical graduates combined. If the truth were known, cities might have more statues commemorating windows and cotton briefs than bronze idols celebrating Pasteur and Koch.

The social changes created by better food and clothes were so startling that humans still haven't figured out the implications of life, marriage and death without TB or cholera. Before the epidemics retreated, two births produced only one adult European, and only three out of ten adults ever celebrated their fortieth birthday. Dying was as accepted and public a part of life as shopping is today. Having a picnic in the cemetery wasn't considered morbid, and funerals gave mourners the chance to gossip, do business and eat well. People also didn't fear something as unpredictable as death; it was a rare day when an eighteenth-century worker or peasant didn't spy a dead man floating down a river or find a dead child rotting in a garbage heap. Even infants made a street game of their easy mortality:

Grandmother, Grandmother,
Tell me the Truth
How many years am I
Going to Live?
One, Two, Three, Four....

The omnipresence of early death receded in the late 1800s, when children started to live past the age of five and adults started celebrating their sixtieth or seventieth birthday. Instead of suddenly vomiting or coughing to death from TB, pneumonia, diphtheria or typhus, people took slow and lingering exits with heart disease and cancer. German historian Arthur E. Imhof doesn't consider this necessarily a fair disease exchange. He notes that death by epidemic disease was generally quick and public. The sick didn't suffer too long or burden their families for untimely periods. Heart disease and cancer have none of these blessings. Death by cancer takes a long time and usually arrives in a leper-like and "hidden" institution, far from relatives, friends and lovers. These chronic diseases also force the sufferer to struggle with a creeping and incurable loss of health, and all kinds of accompanying sorrows.

The exit of TB and cholera also changed the state of marriage. In the age of plague and smallpox, men and women married at different times, some at seventeen and some at thirty-five. For peasants, the age of marriage was usually determined by the random and pestilential death of the farm owner. People didn't marry for sex or looks; they carefully chose a partner for his or her ability to outlive an epidemic and feed a family. For affection and intimacy men turned to male friends, often made in childhood. Women leaned on the shoulders of female neighbours, relatives and friends for love and support. The randomness and suddenness of death simply made it unwise to invest too much emotion in a single person. Consequently a good marriage wasn't necessarily based on hugs, flowers or candle-lit dinners. And if a marriage didn't work out there was generally no need for a backdoor exit such as divorce. If a woman didn't like her husband, she simply patiently waited for tuberculosis, typhus, or some fever to do the job, praying that she and her children wouldn't be swept along with him. Men also counted on death to do the parting.

Because TB and plague ensured that widows and widowers were as numerous as divorcees today, an old farmer and a young girl didn't make an unusual couple. Second marriages with perilous clutches of accompanying children happened regularly. Grimm's fairy-tales talk openly about dead parents and the terrible tensions of reconstituted families. Hanzel and Gretel were abandoned in the woods because the stepmother didn't want to feed them during a famine. Little Brother and Little Sister begins with a timeless lament of children: "Since our mother died, we haven't had a happy hour. Our stepmother beats us every day...."

In contrast to the golden age of pestilence, most people now marry at a standard age for standard reasons: sex, affection and intimacy. As the divorce rate of the Western world demonstrates, "love marriages" often don't last very long. Expecting one individual to carry the heavy burden of friend, confidant, income earner and sex expert is not a gamble our pestilence-ridden ancestors would have chosen. Without germs to relieve them of the strain of romantic love or an unpleasant spouse, modern men and women have done the next best thing: they have marched *en masse* to the divorce court. There were no more than four divorces in all of England and Wales in 1857 when tuberculosis ruled the mortality tables. Today there are 160,000 a year. Waiting for someone to die of heart disease takes too long. In North America, half of all marriages fall apart sooner than the incubation period for AIDS. Not surprisingly, the divorce epidemic has merely returned marriage to its traditional short length. Although most couples filing for divorce don't know it, they've found a legal substitute for tuberculosis and typhus.

With the Fourth Horseman as a constant companion, our ancestors lived more diverse lives. They didn't all marry at the same time and they didn't all die at the same age in the loneliness of hospitals. People respected the elderly because reaching old age was an epidemiological achievement and a natural marvel. Our ancestors didn't have to worry about the boredom of suburban living or the horror of a private death. Death to them was only a passage to eternal life and a long vacation with God. In spite of the hazards of eighteenth-century life, and there were many, the scrofulous and lousy peasants of old attained an enviable dignity. Their folk tales and songs accommodated dying children, short lives and even shorter marriages. Every pestilence had a place, and there was a place for every pestilence.

With the retreat of tuberculosis and other scourges, we have inherited the mixed blessings of long life and lingering death. Life without constant pestilence is such a radical departure from the scheme of things that we remain lost and confused in its absence. As our divorce rates show, we clearly don't know how to enjoy the challenge of marriages uninterrupted by meddlesome germs. Death, now an unfamiliar and unwelcome apparition, terrifies us, and in our abuse and abandonment of the elderly, we cling to the absurd vanity that death and aging are not part of life. The graveyard school of poetry had some crazy notions about consumption, but at least it accommodated death with a fine verse or two. Our struggle to accept longer lives and slower deaths keeps us from romancing their uncertain challenges.

9

Influenza:

Viral Waves

Flu?
If we but knew
The cause of flu
And whence it comes and what to do
I think that you
And we folks, too,
would hardly get in such a stew.
Do you?
Illinois Health News

Most city dwellers have never worried too much about influenza. In comparison to a killer like rabies or a disfigurer like smallpox, "the influence" looked like no more than a delightful nuisance. Getting wretchedly sick and not dying was such a blessed relief hundreds of years ago that the flu-smitten alternately named their brief debilitator "the new delight," "the jolly rant," "the gentle correction," "the blue plague," "the new acquaintance" or "the grippe." Influenza actually had a lot to

recommend it. It didn't pock the face, rot the genitals or cripple
the legs. It appeared mostly during the winter when people
crowded indoors, and caused little more than a sorry collection
of aches and pains. Although it often killed children and old
people with pneumonic complications, the influence never
stacked corpses outside a cemetery the way plague or cholera
did. It also didn't spoil the fortunes of trade or sex, two unfor-
givables in any human disease vocabulary. In fact, the flu was
just what the doctor ordered ("everybody ill, nobody dying")
and exactly what the plague-ridden needed: a familiar and
short-lived ailment that gave both peasants and kings something to sneeze and complain about.

Until the Great War, influenza remained a "homey" pestilence with little clout and even less meaning. But in the spring
of 1918, the flu abruptly turned on adults and buried more than
50 million people in eighteen months. The death rate stunned
physicians. It took the battlefields of France four years to kill 15
million men but the flu did the same work in much less time. In
the United States alone more people died of the flu (550,000
adults) in 1918 than the U.S. military lost to combat in both
World Wars, Korea and Vietnam. In Alaska, whole Indian villages disappeared while India lost more than 12 million people.
Adults with flu finished a poker game or army drill one minute,
only to drop dead the next. Although the epidemic initiated
the biggest plague die-off in world history, it is remembered,
when it is remembered at all, as no more than a gentle correc-
tive. People will cite leprosy and plague with awe before they
implicate "the influence" as an inspiring grave-digger.
Sometimes familiarity breeds a mysterious indifference, even for
germs.

Although microbe hunters didn't discover the flu virus until
1933, the flu germ has been an international globe-trotter for
thousands of years. The first epidemics of sneezing and coughing likely began when farmers tamed the horse, pig or duck.

These barn animals are proven flu carriers while the duck's stomach is probably the world's best flu factory. Flu pandemics (outbreaks occurring over a wide geographical area) didn't really erupt in a major way until cities started to grow like cancers in the eighteenth and nineteenth centuries. As a highly social organism, the flu virus has always sought out crowds and paced its activity with the discordant rhythm of urban people. When humans travelled by foot, horse or sailboat, the flu germ moved slowly. With the introduction of the steamship and the train, the flu gathered speed and saw more of the world. Today, the flu virus usually flies, economy, on a 747 jet. What might begin as a sneeze in Hong Kong can arrive in New York in just twelve hours as an epidemic. As a general rule, bigger cities and faster planes invite more flu outbreaks, both local and global.

According to historians and virus experts, flu pandemics have personalities as distinct as comedians and as evasive as politicians. They usually arrive in annoying waves of varying intensity like swarms of bees. Depending on the weather, a pandemic may rapidly bed between 25 and 50 percent of the population with a notorious blend of aches, fevers, chills and weariness. Less than 1 percent may die. Every century experiences at least three to five pandemics, which appear with the irregularity of prophets. Unlike most infectious diseases, which favour the poor, flu pandemics never discriminate: they take a little bit of health from everyone. The only other sure thing about a flu pandemic is its brevity; like an offensive tourist on holiday, the flu obnoxiously flaunts its stuff and then disappears. Theophilus Thompson, a nineteenth-century flu watcher, was so enamoured by the flu's special properties that he believed there was "a grandeur in its constancy and immutability superior to the influences of national habits."

During the eighteenth and nineteenth centuries, horses usually got "catarrh" or "distemper" two months before people went to bed with the flu. "Horse colds," for example, preceded epidemics of "knock-me-down-fever" or "the new acquaintance" in 1732, 1762 and 1775. In the latter year, one English doctor reported that "the horses had severe coughs, were hot, forebore eating, and were long in recovering." In Prussia, cattle and horses also suffered "catarrhal and rheumatic affections" before the epidemic of 1837. While these accounts are numerous, the association shouldn't come as a surprise. Before the car, people depended on the horse to get around and stabled great numbers of the animals in every neighbourhood. Many virologists now suspect that many of the flu outbreaks before World War I may have been the result of a viral exchange between riders and their mounts. When the horse lost its prominence in human society, pigs and ducks picked up the viral mantle.

The unique nature of flu pandemics is a true reflection of viral genius. Flu viruses, like all members of the viral club, are small and highly mobile creatures. The herpes clan takes the shape of spheres, while others, like the influenza virus, look like a spiked transparent ball with a worm inside. As simple bits of genetic information, viruses have no active life until they take over a cell and use its parts to reproduce themselves. Viruses are very specific invaders. Cold viruses target cells in the nose and throat, hepatitis B aims for the liver and polio is partial to the gut. The influenza virus goes for what doctors call "the human respiratory tract." Unlike bacteria, viruses are also incredibly drug resistant. You can't actually kill a virus without killing the cells it has invaded. Destroying the "respiratory tract" to disable a flu germ has never struck even the most committed microbe hunters as a laudable practice. This makes the flu virus and thousands of its airborne cousins very hardy organisms.

The ability of the flu virus to mutate and change shape every ten to fourteen years (the interval is not always this predictable) also makes influenza invincible. Scientists have looked hard for the strain that caused the epidemic of 1918 but have never found it because the flu virus has two special molecules on its outer surface that act as cell thieves; they provide whatever tools a virus needs to kidnap a cell, whether a cellular key, hammer or credit card. But every time a virus reproduces itself, a small part of these surface molecules is incorrectly copied, and over time the molecules change their arrangement like chess men. After generations of mutations, antibodies from the immune system can no longer identify the rearranged outer shell of the virus, and a new flu is born. Rapid mutations account for the disappearance of some viral strains and the emergence of new ones. They also explain why vaccine makers are always a step behind flu viruses.

Whenever viruses mutate unexpectedly, animals or humans usually die in heaps. In 1983 in Pennsylvania, a bird virus that normally lived in chicken lungs altered its proteins and started to eat chicken brains. The fowl plague temporarily raised the price of chicken on American menus and buried 17 million broilers and layers at a cost of $70 million. Because the chickens were raised in concentration camp conditions and had been bred to grow like Frankenstein meat monsters, the mutant had a much better feed than it would have had on wild birds. Even so, scientists still compare the vulnerable birds on Pennsylvania's chicken farms to the world's population. "There are millions of us 'chickens' just waiting to be infected," say virologists. The survival of the human species, they add, is not assured. The 1918 flu strain was just one mutant reminder of the facts of life.

When flu viruses aren't mutating or knocking off birds, they reshuffle their genes by mingling with other viruses. Exchanging bits of genetic material happens most often when ducks, pigs and humans live together. For centuries, Chinese farmers have fed pigs on duck turds, and fertilized pools of fish with pig shit. Ducks and other wild birds harbour a lot of the world's flu viruses, but they can't pass them on directly to people. Their edible turds, however, can infect pigs, which sneeze on humans and vice versa. Throughout Southeast Asia, hogs have inadvertently become a "mixing vessel" for bird and human viruses by bouncing different flu strains off all three species until a new upstart virus starts an epidemic. It's no accident that three important influenza waves flew out of China in 1957, 1968 and 1977. Many scientists now recommend that people not sneeze on ducks unless they are intent on making a new strain of flu.

The epidemic of 1918 or one of its viral strains probably started in Asia and quickly arrived at a pig farm in Iowa. At the turn of the century, the midwestern state was a corn-fed pig factory and had twice as many porkers as its neighbours. After the annual Iowa Cedar Rapids Swine Show in September, a mysterious ailment gripped its porkers. The show's prize-winners returned to their barns only to sneeze, cough and walk like arthritic cripples. Millions of hogs fell ill and thousands died. Pig farmers, who also got the chills, said they had never seen anything like it. At the same time the pigs got sick, Canadian hunters found moose and elk with flu. The virus also hit bison and sheep.

It took a scientist from Iowa and a man familiar with pigs, Richard Shope, to propose an entertaining theory about swine flu nearly a decade after the pandemic. At a New Jersey laboratory, he discovered that Iowa porkers normally carried a parasitic lungworm that also sheltered the flu virus. It wasn't the 1918 strain (that one's gone forever), but it was influenza nonetheless. The life cycle of both lungworm and virus worked in such a way that the flu bug seeded the lungworms in the spring and appeared in the pig's respiratory tract by fall. The pigs also had loads of Pfeiffer's bacilli, a normally harmless freeloader that can cause pneumonia. The presence of all three parasites in a pig didn't necessarily produce sickness. Shope speculated that the virus needed a trigger, and he poured buckets of cold water on the animals in the same way that Iowa's fall weather does. Shope's pigs immediately started to sniffle, weaken and even die. Shope concluded that the pandemic began on an American pig farm, which explains why it became known as the "swine flu." But most virologists now suspect the virus spread from man to pig and not vice versa. Shope was right about one thing though: the flu of 1918 was a viral and bacterial cocktail.

The first wave of the epidemic engulfed Americans with the tell-tale headaches and fevers during the spring and summer. The only portent was the number of young people dying from pneumonia. Most flu epidemics have U-shaped death graphs. The young and old, exhausted by the flu, simply lose their ability to fight off a variety of bacterial pneumonias like Pfeiffer's and die. But in the summer of 1918, the flu graph looked ominously like another letter of the alphabet: W. More healthy twenty-year-olds than usual seemed to be catching pneumonia and giving up the ghost. Doctors didn't recognize the trend until the fall. By then American troops had already introduced the flu to war-weary Europe. Coughing Germans called it "the Blitz Katarrh" while feverish English soldiers named it "Flanders Grippe." American troops added to the confusion by calling it the "Spanish Flu" or "Spanish Lady." Spain, a neutral power, didn't censor its news during the war, and flu, which eventually killed half a million Spaniards, was already making headlines.

After the first wave hit Japan as "wrestler's fever," the pandemic's second and most mortal wave overwhelmed Camp Devens outside of Boston. The overcrowded military cantonment housed 45,000 men where only 35,000 were intended. The first case of "fulminating" flu appeared on the first of September and by the eighteenth had multiplied to 6,674 cases. Many of the soldiers, men in the prime of health, turned blue, bled from the nose and died in forty-eight hours, struggling for air. One physician called it the most vicious type of pneumonia that he had ever seen, and reported that "mahogany spots" spread over the face "until it was hard to distinguish the coloured man from the white." Within a week, eight thousand sick dough-boys crowded into a hospital designed for only two thousand patients. Exhausted nurses couldn't offer the dying anything more than tender loving care, a blanket and food. When ninety men died in one day, army pathologists opened their chests and found that the lungs of the dead looked more like "red currant jelly" than breathing apparatus. A healthy lung will normally float in water, but the flu-riddled specimens sank like lead. One pathologist solemnly concluded that "this must be some new kind of infection."

The army doctor was only partly right. A strain of flu that singled out twenty- to thirty-year-olds was indeed a new acquaintance. But the bacterial infections that caused the pneumonia, such as streptococci and Pfeiffer's bacillus, were old and seasoned microbes. The only real novelty of the pandemic, as in Iowa's hapless pigs, was the way the flu virus and various bacterial allies performed together like kick boxers. The virus delivered the first hard blow by provoking a hyper immune response in healthy adults that was so violent fluids flooded the lungs. Having had no previous experience with the 1918 swine strain, the adult immune system simply overreacted. All of this inflammation and water allowed wandering bacteria to deliver the mortal kick with lung-dissolving infections. Crowded barracks, fetid trenches and sealed troop ships guaranteed that there was no shortage of meningitis or staphylococci to stalk soldiers. There was also no penicillin in 1918. By the end of October, one in five U.S. servicemen had the flu.

When the pandemic rolled into American cities, it spread like lottery fever and then abruptly collapsed all social services with the weight of the dead. In Philadelphia, the flu silenced the telephone exchange after disabling most of the operators. Streets went unpatrolled as more than five hundred cops stayed in bed. Firefighters and garbage collectors also didn't show up for work. Children, who had lost both parents to this flu, wandered the streets as flu orphans. The dead lay on kitchen tables for days until taxis, the flu hearses, picked them up. In one week alone, the city's flu dead totalled five thousand people, more than local grave-diggers could handle in a month.

The confusion and grief that accompanied the killer flu struck every major city in North America. In Chicago, one flu-crazed father announced he had found a cure for the disease and cut the throats of his children. Catholic nuns found the heavy hand of pestilence crushing so many Boston families that they reported the abnormal as the routine: "Well, the Mother had died, and there were four sick children in two rooms, and the man was fighting with his mother-in-law and throwing a pitcher at her head."

As the flu circumvented the earth, it left a repetitious trail of quick deaths. India lost nearly 4 percent of its population to the flu, which was that nation's greatest die-off in any plague. Two months after the pandemic, visitors to Central Africa found villages of three to four hundred families "completely wiped out, the housing having fallen in on the unburied dead." In the South Seas, the death rate reached 20 percent and among Alaska natives, 8 percent. So many people died in Tahiti that trucks rumbled day and night "through the streets, filled with bodies for the constantly burning pyres."

Because there wasn't much that doctors or nurses could do other than care for and feed the survivors, civilians tried the usual assortment of remedies to intercept the Spanish Lady. Some authorities banned gatherings while transport workers disinfected buses and trolley cars with sprays. One small town in Arizona made it a criminal offence to shake hands. Every morning the U.S. Army forced its recruits to gargle with vinegar and water; the men then drilled twenty yards apart. In many places, people seized upon the imagined flu-fighting properties of vegetables; some tied cucumbers to their ankles while others put a potato in each pocket. One Oregon mother even buried her four-year-old girl neck-high in onions. The more scientific-minded added sulphur to the soles of their shoes.

Perhaps the most popular protection against the flu was a white cotton mask, For a short time it became almost as ubiquitous as today's condom advertisements. In San Francisco, public health officials started a cotton craze by passing an ordinance

Although officers ordered U.S. Army recruits to gargle daily with vinegar and water, the popular anti-flu tonic did little more than freshen the breath.

that forbade people from appearing in public places without a mask over their nose and mouth. The jeans manufacturer Levi Strauss even offered to make masks for most of the city's inhabitants. The only place people didn't have to wear masks was at home or in a restaurant while eating. At the beginning of the epidemic, the mask had such appeal that frightened newlyweds wore gauze even when they made love. Voters went to the polls looking like sterile bank robbers, and public-minded citizens in San Francisco even celebrated the end of the war with flags, bonfires and masks. But after a month of flu fashion, interest in the uncomfortable and unpleasant pads waned. When civil libertarians and smokers eventually formed an Anti-Mask League, the police arrested thousands of mask-slackers. Whether masks actually kept the city's death rate low (cotton is not an effective virus barrier) will never be known. However the masks did cause a sharp decline in diphtheria, measles and whooping cough. During the flu's hit-and-run on San Francisco, the city coped with 50,000 flu cases and buried 3,500 dead.

By April of 1919, the third wave of the flu had crested and the pandemic had passed. The Treaty of Versailles was signed by world leaders who were wearied, confused and depressed by the flu. While scientists demanded funds to go on microbe hunts and set up viral surveillance systems, the average citizen quickly forgot that the pandemic had killed more humans in a couple of months than any other scourge in history. After the war, writers ignored the flu's short drama and historians omitted its dead. The disease historian Alfred Crosby refers to this "inaptitude for wonder and fear" as just one of the "peculiarities of human memory." But the absence of emotion and interest probably illustrates how integrated a member of civilization the virus has become. The flu's impeccably modern persona (brief, global and anonymous) made it a simple event to accept. A quick and easy death is a twentieth-century ideal and the flu, so familiar and so fast, performed to expectation.

Influenza didn't recur on such a large scale until 1957, when a variant dispatched 70,000 people in the United States alone. A predicted killer epidemic in 1976 never materialized, and a potentially deadly Italian strain simply refused to go global in 1989. Edwin Kilborne, a research professor at New York Medical College and perhaps the world's leading authority on influenza, now predicts that a pandemic worse than 1957, but not as bad as 1918, is imminent. Given that many of the bacterial free-loaders that accompany influenza have acquired multiple resistance to antibiotics, "We are in a more vulnerable position now than we were in 1957," says Kilborne.

Most scientists, including Kilborne, believe that the next pandemic will likely start on a Chinese duck pond. Although Latin America and India could also hatch a global "jolly rant," they aren't being watched as closely by viral surveillance teams. China is considered a hot zone because it has long favoured agricultural practices that encourage viral leapfrog. On many Chinese farms ducks and wild waterfowl, a key flu reservoir, mingle freely with pigs, a reliable flu carrier. The close association of ducks, pigs and peasants creates ample opportunities for influenza viruses to jump across species and to recombine in variations inimical to people. Given such ecological realities, influenza certainly hasn't exhausted its possibilities.

10

AIDS:

Faltering Defences

I am sick of guys who moan that giving up careless sex until this
blows over is worse than death. How can they value life so little
and cocks and asses so much? Come with me, guys, while I visit
a few of our friends in intensive care... Notice the looks in
their eyes, guys. They'd give up sex forever if you could promise
them life.
Larry Kramer

AIDS is an old-fashioned epidemic caught in the neon glare of
sex, drugs and rock and roll. Like most plagues, it is a scourge of
the poor and of people in poor health. Most of the 15 million or
so humans now infected with the human immune deficiency
virus (the microbe associated with AIDS) don't own cars or use
microwave ovens. Most also don't eat very well. Contrary to a
lot of media hype, this aspect of the epidemic will not change.
AIDS has never really threatened well-fed, white middle-class
couples who shun promiscuity and avoid invasive medical treatments, and is not likely to. Perhaps the only constant in the
epidemic's overwrought history has been its preference for well-

defined groups of sick people. Puerto Rican coke addicts, Manhattan gays, London hemophiliacs and Thai prostitutes all have one thing in common: before AIDS they all suffered from ailing immune systems. Although the reasons for their poor health differ, the consequences of habitual drug abuse, blood transfusions, venereal diseases, bathhouse sex and inadequate food are basically the same around the world. Battered immune systems can only take so much abuse before one or more members of the superorganism go looting. As an epidemic of faltering immune systems, AIDS is just another microbial warning that more than one disturbance has taken place among the poor in health.

Although AIDS may not be a new plague, it has certain novel features. To begin with, it has two disparate geographical centres: the United States and Africa. On each continent the syndrome appeared as a surprise. The "gay plague" confounded New York homosexuals in the 1970s just as "slim" bowled over Kinshasa prostitutes. Although many scientists and gay activists still blame Africa for AIDS, most of the epidemiological evidence does not support their finger-pointing. AIDS, in fact, appeared in isolated cases in the United States long before it erupted in central Africa. American men were dying of AIDS-like diseases in the 1950s, and probably much earlier. If the epidemic had started in Africa, Europe (its former colonial boss) would have been swept by AIDS long before the United States. The record of the dead suggests otherwise.

Two distinct viruses, HIV-1 and HIV-2, play important roles in the epidemic. HIV-1, a truly global citizen, seems to be the most virulent and lethal of the two. HIV-2, which calls West Africa home, moves more slowly, and appears to be less infectious. American scientists suspect that HIV-1 may have sprung from apes and note that HIV-2 bears a close resemblance to an African mangabey virus. But European scientists believe that HIV-1 may be a human parasite with no animal reservoir that has travelled with the species for a long time. They also suspect that HIV-2 was actually spread to apes by humans and not vice versa. Nobody knows for sure, but the historical record supports European hypotheses more than it does the American ape theories.

Contrary to popular belief AIDS is not an African export. Like syphilis, AIDS seems to have a genuine New World stamp on it. There is no doubt that gay American males incubated the epidemic when they adopted promiscuity and Third World hygiene standards as badges of liberation during the 1970s. From gay ghettos, the plague spread to black and brown ghettos where injected drugs offered a new escape from poverty. American sex tourists, American blood products, American medical technology and American drug habits then swiftly introduced AIDS to immuno-suppressed people in Japan, Brazil, Haiti, Australia and the Netherlands. European strains of the virus bear a much closer resemblance to New York samples than to African ones. These truths don't appear in North American newspapers very often. Americans will talk about any aspect of AIDS except its parenthood.

The parallel and spontaneous eruption of the African AIDS epidemic can be traced to completely independent, unAmerican calamities. Since World War II, Africa has witnessed faster city making than England during the Industrial Revolution, more famines than pre-revolutionary France, more forced migrations than the eighteenth-century slave trade, more wars than Central America and greater population growth than China. That Africa began to seduce its people with the sirens of modernity at the same time that America began to experiment with drugs and sex as never before is one of history's more remarkable coincidences. As a consequence, "the disease of the century" speaks uniquely to each continent. For Africa, the epidemic is another biological marker of too much unchecked urbanization, malnutrition and homelessness. But for the

United States, AIDS is the latest symbol of a culture that does-
n't respect limits of any kind. In a hurry to break taboos and
cross new frontiers, Americans and their technological toys triggered a viral surprise of fatal proportions.

As the history of epidemics illustrates, each era conscripts a
different germ to add drama and death to everyday life. The
Middle Ages had leprosy; the Renaissance, syphilis. The
Industrial Revolution elected TB. AIDS, however, is a non-
conformist. It has always been more than one disease or germ.
In fact, AIDS represents one of the wildest smorgasbords of
opportunistic infections ever assembled in medical history.
According to the U.S. Center for Disease Control, AIDS consists of twenty-five different diseases or some combination
thereof. Because of this complexity, doctors refer to AIDS as a
syndrome rather than a disease. Rarely have so many members
of the superorganism or its viral helpers been employed by one
epidemic.

Dying from AIDS is like reliving every past epidemic all at
once. AIDS patients typically succumb to pneumocystic pneumonia (a microbe found in most human lungs), Kaposi's sarcoma (a rare cancer), tuberculosis (the galloping kind), cryptococ-
cal meningitis (a fungus), toxoplasmosis (a brain parasite carried by cats), diarrhea, candida (a yeast infection), lym-
phadenopathy (swollen lymph glands), cryptosporidiosis (an
intestinal parasite), herpes, dementia, cytomegalovirus (another
herpes virus) or loads of mycobacteria. Shingles, salmonella and
an army of bacterial infections may also bring on death. For
women, the killers are wildly different and include cervical cancer and pelvic inflammatory disease. Africans claim TB, strep
and salmonella as their AIDS markers. Many of these infections
do not kill healthy people and are called "opportunistic"
because they prefer individuals whose immune systems are
weak. When mixed and shaken like a disease cocktail, the
AIDS-related infections make for a horrible and painful death.

Poets have already tried, but no one will likely succeed in romancing such a cruel way to die.

According to the orthodox explanation for this strange collection of infections, AIDS is caused by a nasty slow virus that belongs to the notorious retrovirus family. This old tribe of microbes generally produces benign lifelong infections, but it has a track record of crippling animal immune systems. Visnamaedi, for example, causes wasting and shortness of breath in sheep, while another retro cousin produces swamp fever in horses. Although cancer researchers have long suspected that the retros can bake a good human cancer, they have had trouble finding the recipe. In the 1970s, discouraged microbe hunters almost gave up looking for the cancer link. But just as scientists began to adopt a kindly perspective on retros, Bernie Poiesz at the National Institutes of Health in Bethesda, Maryland, finally discovered one associated with a rare lymphoma cancer in 1980. Robert Gallo, the chief of the lab and a long-time believer in the cancer-retrovirus theory, hailed his associate's find as one of "the most exciting discoveries of twentieth-century biology," and quickly attached his name to it. He also named the new microbe HTLV, the human T-lymphoma virus. Japanese scientists later connected the virus with a type of leukemia that has now been located in the Caribbean and Africa.

At the same time that retroviruses regained their appeal in scientific circles, doctors reported that young men in North American cities were dying of an unusual cancer (Kaposi's sarcoma) and deadly pneumonia. When hemophiliacs and the hapless recipients of twelve or more blood transfusions also started to die with similar symptoms, scientists suspected a virus at work. Seeking greater fame, Robert Gallo immediately indicated that the offender might be HTLV-1. While Gallo wasted two years trying to prove that his leukemia virus caused the new syndrome, French scientists pursued another microbe. In 1983, Drs Françoise Barre-Sinoussi and Luc Montagnier at the Pasteur

Institute in Paris identified one more human retrovirus that would soon be named HIV. Although Gallo claims to have detected HIV simultaneously, several scientific investigations have proven otherwise. There is no dispute, however, that Gallo was the first scientist to boldly announce on television (on April 24, 1984) that a retrovirus was the sole cause of AIDS. Given the hysteria and concern that had so far accompanied the epidemic, Gallo's HIV theory became one of the most rapidly accepted dogmas in the history of medicine. As pure and simple germ theory, it implied that high-tech cancer drugs or vaccines could quickly solve the problem.

According to Gallo and the AIDS scientific establishment (it models itself after the professional TB careerists), HIV disarms the immune system by infecting helper T-cells. The T-cells lead the attack against foreign microbes in the body by giving chemical orders to other immune system defenders: T8 suppressor cells and B-lymphocytes. When T-cells get knocked out of commission, the immune system collapses and bacteria, viruses and fungi run riot. Scientists admit that they don't understand the disease mechanism at work because at any given time only a fraction of T-cells appear to be infected by HIV. They know that their diagnosis is purely a matter of guilt by association. But the HIV club still insists that the virus is the only agent neutralizing or suppressing the immune system. Robert Gallo is adamant about the HIV theory: "Every individual with a pathogenic strain [of HIV] will die with this virus, but fortunately not all strains are equally pathogenic.... HIV would cause AIDS in Clark Kent, given the right dose and the right strain of the virus...alone and of itself."

Since 1984, HIV theory has begun to look as simplistic as the medieval belief that comets or Jews set off the Black Death. Most critics now agree that HIV is involved in the epidemic, but they question its primacy. Among the doubters is Luc Montagnier, one of the HIV's French discoverers. He recently found that a small dose of tetracycline stopped HIV from killing T-cells in a petri dish. This remarkable discovery implied that another microbe was doing the killing and prompted Montagnier to speculate that HIV needed a partner to become an immune-cell terminator. Together with Dr Shyh-Ching Lo of the Armed Forces Institute of Pathology, Montagnier now suggests that the accomplice may be a mycoplasma. A distant relative of bacteria, mycoplasmas are the smallest, simplest and most common independent organisms in the world. About 20 percent of all pneumonias are caused by mycoplasmas and can be effectively treated with tetracycline. Both men suggest that mycoplasmas and HIV can work together to poke holes in immune defences.

According to Montagnier, repeated antibiotic abuse among gay males encouraged the growth of rare strains of mycoplasma in the urinary tract. Under antibiotic pressure these emerging strains changed their life cycle. In addition to living as filaments the mycoplasmas abruptly developed the ability to become microspheres or tiny particles. These microspheres then entered human T-cells, a novel achievement for any kind of bacterium. Once in the cell the mycoplasma helped HIV, a confirmed T-cell break-and-enter expert, by providing it with proteins the virus doesn't have. In short, mycoplasmas serve as boosters of HIV replication, thereby setting the course for the autodestruction of the immune system. Many AIDS patients do indeed show strong evidence of mycoplasma infection. Montagnier believes the present epidemic may well represent an alliance of American mycoplasmas and a virulent strain of African HIV.

Cofactor theories such as Montagnier's are not the only ones now infecting scientists. After ten years of fruitless HIV dogma, researchers have implicated herpes, hepatitis B, cytomegalovirus and even another retrovirus linked to autoimmune disorders as partners in AIDS. In Africa scientists have also inducted leprosy, syphilis, malaria and schistosomiasis—all radical immune suppressors—into the AIDS pantheon. Modern medicine knows very little about the biological consequences of such disease cocktails. But in animals, disease overloads tend to launch civil wars in the immune system.

One of the reasons scientists are now pursuing cofactors so rigorously is because HIV has never caused disease in healthy animals. The well-known Berkeley biologist Peter Duesberg has routinely reminded the HIV club that a germ cannot be accepted as a health hazard until it reproduces similar symptoms in guinea pigs, rats or monkeys. Researchers have pumped chimpanzees full of HIV, but they have never developed Kaposi's sarcoma, candida or even pneumonia. Only monkeys injected with distinct monkey retroviruses have gotten sick, but not with the same wild variety of diseases. Duesberg has also noted that the epidemiology of AIDS doesn't support HIV theory. Five percent of AIDS patients never develop any HIV antibodies, and less than half of all AIDS patients are ever tested for the virus. (Weak strains of HIV probably account for this anomaly and some individuals may even have a natural immunity to HIV.) As the HIV club's first and most persistent critic, Duesberg also doesn't understand how one virus could cause so many different infections in so many well-defined groups. "If the HIV/AIDS hypothesis were true, it would be a truly revolutionary break with all previous scientific experience." AIDS specialists, however, have called Duesberg a "charlatan," and many of his more extreme pronouncements are indeed ridiculous. Duesberg, for instance, does not think sex has anything to do with AIDS.

Other scientists who question the HIV-only hypothesis note that many AIDS conditions such as dementia can and do have origins other than HIV. Dementia can steal patients' memories or otherwise reduce their faculties. It occurs in about half of all AIDS cases. But in many patients neurosyphilis, not HIV, appears to be the culprit. Several scientists have now noticed that many AIDS symptoms read like classic third-stage symptoms of the old French Disease: headaches, aching joints, weight loss, impaired vision, swollen glands and patchy hair. People who have been labouring under the influence of syphilis for many years can also develop meningitis, Kaposi's sarcoma, tuberculosis and pneumocystic pneumonia. Several AIDS patients have even been found with large genital abscesses packed full of treponemas, exactly what Fracastorius saw among European syphilitics in the fifteenth century.

The syphilis epidemic, now masked by the AIDS epidemic, is really the product of improper medical care, a lot of unprotected screwing around and much homelessness. For twenty years, European physicians have warned their American peers that established penicillin dosages for syphilis don't kill all of the treponemes. Even a treatment of twenty-five days may miss a couple of spirochetes, which normally reproduce every month during their third stage of life. The penicillin used in North America also doesn't penetrate brain or eye tissue, where treponema often retreats. In both America and Germany doctors have systematically stripped many AIDS patients of dementia and other symptoms by giving them continuous intravenous doses of penicillin, sometimes for a year. New York physician Stephen Caiazza, who recently died of AIDS, achieved remarkable success with this cheap treatment. One of his AIDS patients, a vice-president of a savings bank, couldn't remember the day or month, let alone go to the bathroom by himself, before he started taking the antibiotic Doxycycline. Six weeks later, he returned to work.

Kaposi's sarcoma, the skin cancer that served as the epidemic's red flag, can also make an appearance without HIV. Although AIDS specialists have consistently blamed the retrovirus for spotting gay men with leper-like lesions, researchers have now concluded that the microbe at work is an unknown venereal disease. Fourteen gay men with no evidence of HIV infection but lots of KS proved the point. So did an epidemic of KS among heterosexuals in central Africa in the 1960s. Medical records also show that young men and children have been dying of Kaposi since the 1870s. Some of the very first cases of KS appeared in Vienna and Naples, popular gathering places for homosexuals in the nineteenth century. Blood transfusions, syphilis and pneumonia have also been associated with KS for a long time. (HIV, it should be noted, can cause some cancers.)

Another great weakness in the HIV-only theory is that it blithely ignores the obvious. Almost every group infected by AIDS has been exposed to an unhealthy variety of immune suppressors long before HIV became the virus in vogue at medical labs. Six years ago Robert S. Root Bernstein, a clever physiologist at Michigan State University, examined the health profile of various AIDS patients from junkies to gays and added up the number of immune-destroying agents at work in their bodies. The long list contains some surprises: it includes heroin, cocaine, nitrates, semen (in male rectums), malnutrition, amoebas, bacteria, viruses, chronic use of antibiotics, blood transfusions and the indirect health-stealing properties of drug addiction, poverty and anorexia. He doesn't think that any of these agents (with the exception of massive blood transfusion, prolonged intravenous drug use and severe malnutrition) are powerful enough to cause AIDS by themselves, but he does believe that "a combination of several of them would certainly be sufficient."

Coke addicts, for example, attract immune busters the way magnets pull iron. In the process of ritualistically marking their arms as many as twenty-four times a day, addicts share needles, blood and germs. The average junkie carries a hefty disease load of hepatitis B, C or D, cytomegalovirus and tuberculosis. To support their habits, many addicts sell sex and collect cash, coke or venereal diseases. By spending money on drugs rather than food, many drug users eat no better than African famine victims or nineteenth-century Irish immigrants. Malnutrition, of course, is one of the world's most ancient and effective immune destroyers. A 1982 American study found that heroin addiction put a perilous weight on the immune system when HIV wasn't even in the neighbourhood. About 24 percent of the addicts had declining numbers of T-cells at a time when only 12 percent of them tested positive for HIV. For decades, men and women on junk have complained of a litany of AIDS-like fevers, night sweats and swollen lymph glands.

Hemophiliacs also defy the myth that HIV is the sole cause of immune suppression. Long before the AIDS epidemic, bleeders recorded the same kind of T-cell losses that define AIDS. Because hemophiliacs (most are men) lack the molecule that clots blood, they often spend their lives running to and from the hospital for blood transfusions. These large and repeated transfusions keep bleeders alive but tax the hell out of their immune systems and have the same jolting effects as an organ transplant. Unknown blood, like an alien kidney or liver, activates the immune system and mobilizes antibodies. For most of this century, the average life span of a hemophiliac was thirty-three years.

During the 1960s, a revolution in blood products changed the brotherhood of hemophilia. Instead of making Factor VIII (a blood-clotting protein) from single blood donations, blood factories created a new and more powerful concentrate from two thousand to twenty thousand donors. Although Factor VIII immediately lengthened the life span of hemophiliacs to fifty-five years, it also increased their risk of catching more than one virus during a transfusion. The more donors used to make a batch of Factor VIII, the more alien microbes the batch will contain. Today it's hard to find a hemophiliac without hepatitis B or C, cytomegalovirus or Epstein-Barr virus (another microbe associated with immune suppression). Even by itself, a transfusion of foreign proteins like Factor VIII acts as a powerful immune depressor. After years of receiving the blood of other people, a hemophiliac's exhausted immune system may suddenly self-destruct or go haywire. AIDS in hemophiliacs is very much connected to age and the number of immune-numbing transfusions received.

Contaminated Factor VIII products and penny-pinching blood banks ensured that three-quarters of North America's hemophiliacs became HIV-positive in the 1980s. Even though the blood banks knew their stocks were polluted with HIV in 1983, they decided not to heat the concentrates and kill the germ until 1985 because of the cost. In the interim, the United States ("the OPEC of blood products") exported 20 percent of its Factor VIII to Japan and Western Europe—it didn't even charge extra for the HIV component. But the fact that only 6 percent of the hemophiliac population has gotten sick with AIDS again indicates that more than one microbe is at work in the epidemic. Not surprisingly, most hemophiliacs only develop the syndrome following a good shock to the immune system by radiation, surgery, blood transfusion or a super infection of cytomegalovirus (CMV). HIV is not a loner.

During his research of AIDS, Bernstein also leafed through the historical literature on opportunistic infections. He found that they had a habit of popping up in young males between the ages of twenty and forty, who suffered numerous and inexplicable infections. Cytomegalovirus, for instance, was first identified in a 36-year-old man in 1925. The literature reports that this normally peaceful virus has gone on killing sprees only after a person has had surgery, received blood or abused drugs. Probably three in ten adult cases of CMV before the AIDS epidemic would have fit the current AIDS definition nicely. Thirty of sixty cryptococcosis cases a year prior to 1966 would also have qualified as AIDS today. Pneumocystic pneumonia, which normally follows in the wake of immune bruisers like venereal disease and hunger, shares a similar history. Not surprisingly, most of these opportunistic infections started to increase by leaps and bounds before AIDS exploded into the headlines in the 1980s. Bernstein concludes that their parallel and exponential growth suggests that AIDS has been consuming immuno-suppressed people for a long time: "You can't prove it's AIDS, but people were dying of things like AIDS, minus the fact that we didn't know whether they were HIV-positive or not, more than a century ago."

The long history of these infections suggests that HIV has been floating around America and Africa for several hundred years. Some researchers say the virus may even have been present for a millennium. According to retrospective blood tests, the first American to die of AIDS was a 28-year-old male from Tennessee whose body surrendered to pneumocystic pneumonia and cytomegalovirus in 1952. Nobody knows what kind of sex he enjoyed. In 1968 a 15-year-old St. Louis black melted away with chlamydia and Kaposi's sarcoma. He had never travelled, but was a young male prostitute. The first known European casualty was a British sailor in 1958. He expired after being besieged by multiple infections and suffering a host of now-familiar symptoms including fatigue, weight loss and pneumonia. All known therapies failed to ward off death. Convinced the hapless sailor had died from an "unknown viral disease," an enterprising physician preserved some diseased tissue in paraffin. After it lay in storage for thirty-one years doctors finally remembered the sample and put it through a polymerase chain reaction test. This innovation allows scientists to detect gene sequences in a virus. The sailor's sample was packed with HIV.

Another early casualty, a Norwegian, also did a lot of globe-trotting. This seaman travelled to Africa, picked up more than one venereal disease and brought them home in 1966. Before he died of the usual pot-pourri of infections, he passed on his germ legacy to his wife, who died of leukemia, leg paralysis and dementia. One of his daughters became the first known case of

AIDS in a child. Although the blood of all three subsequently tested HIV-positive, an accomplice such as syphilis or immuno-suppressive medical treatment probably contributed to this family tragedy. The identity of the first African to die is predictably unknown, but tests of blood specimens indicate that the virus or a relative was swimming in the blood of a few Africans as far back as 1959. It was also present among healthy Indians living on the banks of the Orinoco River in Venezuela in 1968. Nobody knows what it was doing there or why it wasn't killing them.

So, long before the epidemic, HIV was likely everywhere, sleeping in healthy people and acting up in the unhealthy. What changed in the 1970s was not the prevalence of HIV, but the number of new immune-destroying agents that Americans and Africans entertained in their homes and cities. The disposable plastic syringe was one of these innovations. Before its introduction in the 1970s, drugs were primarily swallowed or inhaled. Shooting galleries were rare because steel or glass syringes were neither cheap nor convenient. But the disposable needle or "works" was to the drug addict what styrofoam was to fast food. It escorted heroin and cocaine out of the shadows and served them efficiently in the streets. Between 1960 and 1973, the number of heroin addicts alone jumped from 45,000 to 100,000 in the United States. Similar social changes occurred among other people destined for the AIDS camp. For hemophiliacs, it was the explosive growth of Factor VIII consumption (12 percent a year). And for gays it was sexual promiscuity.

Dr Joseph Sonnabend has argued for this scenario since the beginning of the epidemic. He is a New York physician who has done a lot of lab work with viruses. He treated New York's first AIDS cases and made the very first recommendations on "safe sex." Trained to look at the whole patient including his or her environment and behaviour, Sonnabend believes that social upheavals in America and Africa have shaped the outcome and boundaries of the epidemic more than HIV. He regards the virus as no more than a potent signal of an immune system that has been overloaded by drugs, blood, semen or CMV. The real, social causes of AIDS, including drug abuse and poor living, merely trigger the latent retrovirus to life, he says. "Doctors like their drugs and they like their germs. They don't like social factors."

Given the revolutionary changes in sexual behaviour that took place among American gays in the 1970s, Sonnabend is not surprised that the AIDS epidemic appeared in New York and San Francisco first. Having all kinds of sex with lots of different men is a highly efficient way of pumping immune suppressors into the body. "When promiscuity becomes a means of transmitting everything that can be transmitted between people, there are biological consequences," says Sonnabend. The question is not one of behaviour but of scale. One or two naked people can cavort safely in a pool but a hundred will eventually pollute the water. "It's a critical mass thing. I know it's not new."

Promiscuity has long been a hallmark of gay culture. Men have sought out other men for anonymous dalliances in parks and public rest rooms ever since Christianity condemned homosexuality as a "sin against nature." (In the Bible, St Paul actually speaks out against promiscuity and prostitution, not homosexuality.) Prior to the 1960s these brief affairs were largely discreet; sodomy laws and public disapproval of homosexuality restricted the amount of cruising and coupling going on. In 1948 homosexuals told the famous sex researcher Alfred Kinsey that they might go for months or even years without sex. But in the 1960s these constraints began to erode. As middle-class youth grew more tolerant of sex for sex's sake and of homosexuality, gays started to couple more often. A 42-year-old Los Angeles man boasted to health officials in 1962 that he had had sex with 1,500 men in 15 years, or about a 100 men a year. He said he had been touched by gonorrhea only once. He would not have had this kind of luck in the 1970s.

The gay liberation movement began with a riot outside the Stonewall Inn in Greenwich Village in 1969. Long harassed by police, the bar's patrons simply had it out with their harassers. The street battle marked the beginning of a new pride and boldness that gay men hadn't shown since the Weimar Republic. In this great awakening, all aspects of gay culture were brought out of the closet, including promiscuity and what the poet James Boughton called "silliness, sassiness and sissiness." With the motto "so many men, so little time," many gay liberators redefined gayness as sex, sex and more sex. The more men a man screwed, the more gay and politically correct he was. Gays who preached monogamy were sneered at as wimps and hopeless heterosexual clones. Gay liberators promoted anonymous couplings as a noble fast food that was quick, wholesome and easy. Across North America gay businessmen, who were often gay leaders, catered to "the quest for the holy male" by building fast sex shops in every major city; sex became as impersonal and handy as ordering a hamburger. By the mid 1970s, a $100-million sex industry made it possible to buy gay sex in dark rooms in bookstores, sex clubs, bars and bathhouses, all day and all night.

The most famous of these fast sex establishments had names like the Continental, the Toilet Bowl, the Glory Hole, the Mine Shaft, the Jaguar and the Bulldog. Many of the bathhouses resembled Roman spas while others had a San Quentin look, complete with iron bars, cells and guards. In the Mine Shaft, a Greenwich bar, health inspectors found sex aids like gym horses, crucifixes and whips. Many establishments also had "glory holes" in the walls for liberated gays to stick their penises through for fast fellatio. In the musty and salty darkness of the fast sex joints, men rarely talked; sex just happened the way mice do it: without words or an exchange of names. The only thing that counted in a bathhouse was the length of a man's penis, his Marlboro looks (or lack of them) and the shape of his buttocks. Ugly gays sought sex in the darkest corners of the baths nicknamed "Pigs Alleys." Gay writers and scholars such as Dennis Altman thought they had discovered some kind of higher political ideal in the fast sex outlets: "The willingness to have sex immediately, promiscuously, with people about whom one knows nothing and from whom one demands only physical contact, can be seen as a sort of Whitmanesque democracy, a desire to know and trust other men in a type of brotherhood." It can also be seen as a form of biological suicide.

Before the fast sex establishments made urban gays sex junkies, one New York doctor estimated that maybe a thousand men had sex in New York bathhouses and parks every night. But as the institutional opportunities increased, so did the numbers. The same sort of explosion occurred in Toronto, Vancouver and San Francisco, a homosexual mecca for 100,000 gay immigrants. The gathering of so many gay men in one place is a historical first. Thanks to the new theology of promiscuity, many San Francisco gays needed calculators to figure out how many men they had had sex with in a year. The first white middle-class gay males to die of AIDS averaged 1,100 anonymous partners in their lifetime. The U.S. Center for Disease Control mistakenly labelled them "healthy young men," an illusion under which many AIDS researchers still labour.

In the "democratic" palaces of promiscuity, new and exotic sexual practices appeared with a Dionysian vigour. One of the most fashionable was fist-fucking. It required one man to stick his hand or arm up his partner's asshole. Licking and sucking another man's anus (rimming) also became popular. *The Joy of Gay Sex* advertised rimming as a "prime taste treat in sex" while gay newspapers glorified it as a "revolutionary act." Men often performed these sex acts while high on cocaine, Quaaludes or "poppers." The poppers (butyl and isobutyl nitrates) relaxed muscles and made it easier to stretch the anus. By the mid seventies, 70 percent of the gay community were inhaling sweet banana-smelling nitrates.

Not all gays revelled in their new drugged-out, sex-crazed culture. San Francisco journalist Randy Shilts complained that gays had achieved the opposite of liberation by enslaving themselves to sex devoid of affection and sentiment. By focusing solely on positions and orgasms, gays had developed a never-ending appetite for kinky sex because "the experience relied on heightened sensory rather than emotional stimulation." Perhaps the only thing revolutionary about promiscuity, fist-fucking or rimming was that they exposed gay men to more blood, feces, bacteria, protozoa and viruses than any peasant encountered in Bangladesh.

The immune-weakening consequences of this lifestyle became apparent very quickly in VD statistics. Although gays account for probably no more than 8 percent of the male population, they account for more than 50 percent of all syphilis cases in North America. Rates of syphilis doubled during the 1970s because of the bathhouse culture. The prolific coupling of gay men also helped rocket gonorrhea cases from 259,000 in 1960 to 600,000 in 1970 and more than 1 million in 1980. Denver gay men, who averaged 2.7 sexual bathhouse encounters a night, had a 33 percent chance of walking home with syphilis or gonorrhea. In addition to the traditional VDs, gays picked up other sexual infections like new clothes. One study of 4,179 gays found that they supported an amazing diversity of microbial life: 37 percent had the clap, 66.8 had crab lice, 18 percent had venereal warts and 17 percent had scabies.

Perhaps the most common sexual infection to appear during the gay sexual revolution was hepatitis B, a virus borne by blood and semen that slowly suffocates the liver in half of those infected. Prior to the gay sexual revolution it appeared mostly in blood recipients, drug users and the odd patron of tattoo parlours. After Stonewall and the gay liberation movement, two-thirds of gay men suffered from the disease. Randy Shilts notes that a gay man had one chance in five of catching hepatitis B "within twelve months of stepping off the bus into a typical urban gay scene." By 1979, 60 percent of 3,816 homosexual men in five different US cities showed evidence of hepatitis B. The rate among straight men was less than 10 percent.

Another immune suppressor that more and more gay men encountered was semen. Prior to the 1960s, homosexuals played defined sex roles. One man was what squeamish health officials called "the insertee" and the other "the insertor." But in America these distinctions evaporated in the 1970s as more and more men voted for "receptive anal intercourse." In the rectum, semen puts the immune system on full alert by working as a powerful suppressive, especially if it enters the bloodstream through torn rectal tissue. Antibodies to semen can quickly pit working members of the immune system against each other, causing a variety of auto-immune disorders. Many physicians suspect that promiscuity helped semen to play an important background role as a subtle immune subversive among gays.

The bathhouse culture also introduced gays to a variety of Third World parasitic gut infections. Shigellosis is a bacterial disease that causes the runs and comes with fever, vomiting and cramps. It's the kind of ailment doctors expect to find in Mexico City or Manila where poverty and poor hygiene deposit human feces in food, water and milk. When white middle-class males started sharing fecal matter in the bathhouses, shigellosis became an undeclared partner in the sex trade. In the 1970s, 69 percent of Seattle's gays who ran to the toilet with shigellosis had had sex in a bathhouse. Other Third World stomach problems like amebiasis (the world's third deadliest parasitic disease after malaria and schistosomiasis) and *Giardia lamblia* (another protozoan that can cause prolonged diarrhea) also colonized gays. The U.S. Center for Disease Control reported that the number of amebiasis cases jumped from a constant level of less than 2,500 in 1972 to more than 7,300 in 1982. About 30 percent of all gays in New York and Los Angeles now harbour amoebas that, if hungry enough, can eat their way through the intestinal wall into the liver, where they can build large deadly abscesses. By 1969 one astounded doctor wrote that Manhattan gays already had the disease profile of "a tropical isle."

The so-called "Gay Bowel Syndrome" created another health problem: malnutrition. Unchecked protozoa have a habit of dining on the intestines so regularly that the gut loses its ability to absorb nutrients. Chronic diarrhea also doesn't give a person a chance to absorb or digest food, no matter how nutritious. Giardiasis, for example, puts a number of key enzymes out of commission. Like AIDS, malnutrition depresses the immune system and lowers the number of helper T-lymphocyte cells. During the 1970s, the gay ideal, the willowy young man, got thinner because of parasites and chronic malnourishment.

At the beginning of the epidemic, it dawned on some gay doctors and a few gay leaders such as Larry Kramer that the new urban gay lifestyle had a deadly character. But whenever Sonnabend spoke unequivocally about promiscuity being a "considerable health hazard," gays shouted him down. Some even responded that "gays are once again allowing the medical profession to define, restrict, pathologize us." Others wrote that they refused to avoid casual sex "to blight my life in order—supposedly—to preserve it." Except in San Francisco, most bathhouses never closed, liberal-minded public health officials closed their eyes and the obituary columns filled with the names of young middle-class men who thought they could defy biology. Sonnabend has always suspected that many gay leaders and doctors uncritically rallied behind the HIV theory because it somehow absolved promiscuity and let many gay leaders off the hook for promoting an ideal whose deadly consequences well-educated men could have predicted with a little thought.

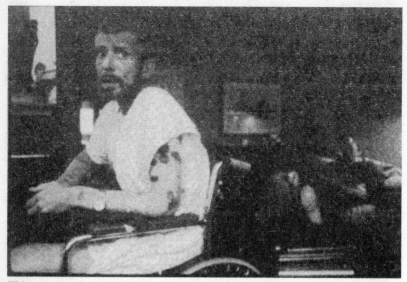

The most visual manifestation of AIDS, Kaposi's sarcoma predominantly spots gay men, and may very well be a distinct venereal disease.

Mirko Grmek, an AIDS historian, now describes the epidemic's heart with this sobering thought: "Homosexual promiscuity with transcontinental networks functioned as a veritable culture medium for the AIDS virus. The historical novelty certainly does not reside in homosexuality itself, but in the extent and degree of promiscuity."

While Americans discovered that new sex and drug frontiers led to unexpected risks, Africa invented an equally unique terrain for its AIDS epidemic. Here AIDS has almost nothing to do with homosexuals or drugs; instead it has everything to do with the poverty of uprooted peoples and the sexual habits of homeless men in crowded cities. AIDS is very much an urban problem in Africa. Although western observers initially predicted massive die-offs for Africa, AIDS is not a Black Death. It hasn't yet matched the power of malaria or tuberculosis. By the time the epidemic wanes, most epidemiologists now predict that

AIDS will have killed several million Africans (1 to 5 percent of the population), forming a small blip on the continent's astounding growth chart. Nations will not perish, but hundreds of thousands of prostitutes, truck drivers, migrant labourers and their children will.

Although AIDS is not a "slate wiper," it is a compelling sign that all is not well in Africa. Population upheavals have a way of unsettling microbes, and the continent has been changing at an unsettling rate recently. With or without AIDS, Africa has the world's fastest-growing population. The forty-two nations that lie below the Sahara desert are home to 512 million people, who are reproducing at a rate three times faster than the rest of the earth's population. By the year 2000 they will number a billion very hungry citizens.

Like medieval European peasants in the fourteenth century, Africans are producing more and hungrier citizens on a blighted landscape of eroding soils and disappearing forests. Although the number of Africans at the dinner table has increased by 30 percent in the last twenty years, food production has dropped by nearly 20 percent. Good sources of protein have also disappeared. To feed more people, farmers have replaced traditional legumes and millet with irrigated monocultures of rice (bringing more malaria). With nearly a quarter of the land now drying into desert, famine and malnutrition have taken up residence in one in every four households. The thymus, home of those important T-cells, atrophies in hungry women and children, and children with starving thymuses usually fall victim to viral infections and AIDS-like diarrhea.

At the same time that Africa's countryside has become less fertile, its cities have become progressively denser. About one-third of all Africans are now urban dwellers. As during the Industrial Revolution in England, this great marathon from farm to factory happened quickly. In 1891 Nairobi, the capital of Kenya, was only a few tents full of Europeans, but by the

1920s it was a multi-racial city. Today, with a population of a million that grows by 8 percent every year, it is a slum-infested metropolis with 400,000 unemployed workers.

For most of this century, venereal diseases have accompanied city building in Africa like troops of European engineers. Africans have never been sexual prudes and for most men "grazing" has been an accepted part of life. For many tribes, polygamy is a happy ideal. In this scheme of things, making children has always counted more than making marriages. City living, however, added a new dimension to African partner swapping. During the colonial era, men outnumbered women in most African cities by six to one. Migrant workers and miners left their wives on the ancestral farm and often couldn't afford to return to their families for a year. Lonely and desperate, they sought out prostitutes, often the only job available to women in African cities. Visiting prostitutes became part of the African way of life and remain a well-established practice in many cities. About half of all the workers in Nairobi still keep their wives outside of town, and about half of the city's prostitutes, who each entertain an average of 963 men a year, have syphilis or gonorrhea. These facts explain why 7,000 out of every 100,000 residents of Nairobi (and Kampala) hosted gonorrhea in the 1980s. (For the city of London, England, the rate was 310.) Before AIDS, the incidence of syphilis, genital warts and even Kaposi's sarcoma grew as fast as Africa's population.

Perhaps the most important venereal partner for HIV is chancroid. It's an ancient bacterial infection that African men mistakenly call "the woman's disease" or "the wound." It's a painful, dime-sized ulcer that appears on the penis or clitoris. Long associated with prostitution and war-time, chancroid is now most common in tropical countries where men go uncircumcised. In true venereal piggyback tradition, the chancroid ulcer can carry a good batch of syphilis and a huge amount of HIV. Several Canadian researchers who have been battling venereal diseases

in Nairobi for more than a dozen years now conclude that uncircumcised men with chancroid are three times more susceptible
to HIV infection than circumcised men. The virus thrives best
in African and Asian countries where men go uncircumcised and
carry chancroid sores on their foreskins.

It's no accident that Canada's largest outbreak of heterosexual AIDS has occurred in Newfoundland, a province with high
STD rates and where most men are not circumcised. AIDS is
out of control in India, a country where 80 percent of men
retain their foreskins. By contrast AIDS has moved very slowly
through Nigeria in spite of that country's thriving prostitution
trade. The reason: all ethnic groups practise circumcision.

Uganda was one of the first hotspots for the African epidemic, for similar reasons. The battered country illustrates how
much HIV favours people with faltering immune systems. After
twenty years under the rule of the despot Idi Amin and a bloody
guerrilla war, Uganda was simply anemic. By 1986, less than 20
percent of the people had access to clean water, and one out of
four children looked at the world through hungry eyes.
Tuberculosis, measles, malaria and diarrhea have stalked this
terrain like big game hunters. And roving soldiers have spread a
large and deadly arsenal of STDs. Few Ugandan men are circumcised and many support chancroid.

AIDS in Africa has been largely a female disease linked to
big-city prostitution. Only seven African countries have the
same number of men and women who are HIV positive. For the
remaining nations of central and western Africa, women have
been dying much faster than men. In countries such as Ghana,
only prostitutes or their pimps have AIDS because they have
come home to die from the red-light districts in the Ivory
Coast. Felix Konotey-Ahulu, a Ghanaian doctor, has noted
these and other peculiarities that the HIV theory doesn't
answer. Bed-hoppers who confine their activities to their own
remote villages usually don't come down with "slim." Nor do

rare pockets of African homosexuals. The only exception is young men who work in international hotels and drop their pants for American dollars. Konotey-Ahulu suspects there is "something" that the city sex trade is spreading that village prostitutes don't. That something happens to be chancroid and other VDs. He also notes that, like hemophiliacs, many HIV-positive Ugandans suddenly develop AIDS after immune-jolting experiences such as surgery, pregnancy or even gynecological examinations.

In addition to urban prostitution, and explosive VD rates, modern medicine probably gave African AIDS a helping hand. More than one epidemiologist has noted that AIDS appeared in Africa at the same time that the World Health Organization eradicated smallpox on the continent. This is not a coincidence. During the 1970s members of the World Health Organization studiously vaccinated young people in central Africa with live smallpox vaccine. The smallpox fighters sterilized needles over the flame and reused them forty to sixty times during their thirteen-year campaign. As a general rule, AIDS patients do not tolerate vaccinations very well. An American soldier, who was HIV-positive, developed AIDS immediately after a smallpox vaccination and died. Live vaccine directly provoke the immune system and can awaken other sleeping giants such as viruses. In his thoughtful history of AIDS, the germ historian Mirko Grmek asks a good question: "Might the massive introduction of vaccinia virus, into the heart of a seropositive but disease-free population, have 'awakened' the HIV and triggered the epidemic?" The smallpox issue is just another AIDS unknown that scientists cannot fathom and that the WHO is understandably reluctant to discuss.

Grmek also suspects that AIDS is occupying a niche once filled by tuberculosis. Most scientists forget that the success or failure of one disease directly influences the fortunes of other infections. Grmek looks upon disease as an onion with endless layers: peel away one and you reveal another. When tuberculosis beat a temporary retreat in the middle of this century, it began to unmask AIDS. Having been the world's major killer to date, TB "made sporadic cases of AIDS invisible and prevented the dissemination of the disease." In other words, before AIDS had a chance to flaunt its wares, TB finished off the victim. But as vaccines, sanatoria and antibiotics took a steady toll on TB, AIDS started to break through this disease barrier. No longer confined to isolated sparks of infection, HIV was now ready to blaze. Blood transfusions, promiscuity and intravenous drug use merely provided the match. And once ignited, AIDS has had the synergistic effect of reviving TB to the extent that the incidence of consumption is fifteen times greater in HIV-infected individuals than in the general population.

What both the American and African experiences ultimately say about AIDS is that the unique nature of HIV and its complex biology are rather unimportant to the growth of the epidemic. "The soil is much more important than the seed," notes William Cameron, director of the HIV clinic at Ottawa General Hospital. "It's the host population that determines the progress of the epidemic."

Kinshasha prostitutes, San Francisco gays, Thailand's sex workers and New York street youth all share similar experiences and behaviours. These core groups are promiscuous, tend to be saturated with sexual diseases, are immuno suppressed and pass on their infections to uncircumcised men rather effortlessly. Wherever these conditions exist the growth of AIDS has been explosive and constant.

In Africa, as in America, the public health answer to AIDS is to "love carefully," try "zero grazing" and wear a condom. But if AIDS is a combination of immune-busting forces and HIV a mere sexual looter of wounded immune systems, then these safe-sex goals look rather narrow-minded. People addicted to fast sex or involved in the sex trade need more than condoms.

They also need to know that promiscuity introduces people to a common market of immune-wearying microbes. Drug addicts need to know that clean needles will not protect them from the immune-destroying powers of addictive lifestyles. An effective AIDS education program might also invite doctors to relearn the immune-suppressive properties of blood transfusions, vaccinations, antibiotics and anti-viral drugs.

A society that recognizes AIDS as a "constellation of circumstances," as opposed to the nefarious workings of one virus, might also have to admit that anti-viral drugs and vaccines will not stop an epidemic fueled by different cocktails of sex, drugs and blood. In fact, the only way to answer an epidemic driven by sex and sustained by faltering immune systems is to remove, one by one, the underlying social and economic suppressors at work. In North America, the only way to slow the epidemic is to spend billions of dollars on urban renewal, drug counselling and job creation. People with homes, good jobs and a sense of self-worth usually respect their immune systems. If gays want to survive as a distinct group in North America, they will have to abandon promiscuity as a badge of identity. In Africa, plague priorities must include agricultural reform, an end to rampant militarism, and the dismantling of the sex trade. For African women, it also means challenging the sexual behavior of African men. "The customary and legal rights of males to unlimited numbers of partners according to their wishes" can no longer be "an unassailable facet of African culture." Without radical political reforms, Africa, like medieval Europe, will feed one epidemic after another with its teeming, malnourished masses.

Until governments and doctors treat AIDS as a sign of genuine disturbance in human culture, the epidemic will remain as durable as syphilis. We can then expect four hundred years of surprising deaths, new fashions, quack medicines and an extensive condom iconography. In preparing for a long viral fad in medicine, doctors have already concealed their traditional impotence by plying strange cancer drugs and fantastic theories that avoid any mention of poverty or promiscuity. The profession has also established half a dozen journals on AIDS, and now regularly socializes at HIV congresses and conferences. Tuberculosis established a tradition of building medical careers, and AIDS is another opportunity for ambitious drug pushers and microbe hunters. Once AIDS retreats on its own schedule, nonplussed by the frantic conference life of doctors, another plague will arrive as surely as tomorrow. All the lessons of leprosy, syphilis, tuberculosis and AIDS will be conveniently forgotten amidst the shrieks of the dying, the furious finger-pointing and the mystic fog of germ talk. No matter how hard the superorganism tries or the Fourth Horseman rides, humans are not ready to take responsibility for the biological consequences of their actions.

Nor, as Grmek writes, are we prepared to face the uncomfortable truth that AIDS is a virulent bastard of technological progress. "Blood transfusion is a medical success, but also a vehicle of the virus," notes the historian. "Elimination and control of diverse infectious diseases were great victories, but they opened the door for AIDS. Thus the situation is a corollary of what Edward Tenner calls the revenge theory: 'Technological progress has changed our world, but the world seems bent on getting even, twisting our cleverness against us.'"

11

THE BACTERIAL RENAISSANCE:

UNDYING GERMS

"We have organisms now proliferating that never existed
before in nature. We have selected them. We have organisms
that probably caused a tenth of a percent of human disease in
the past that now cause twenty, thirty percent of the disease
that we're seeing. We have changed the whole face of the earth
by the use of antibiotics."
Mark Lappe

Let us call him Pablo. He lead a real life with a real family and
died a few years ago with a finality that accompanies all death,
bacterial or human. But he left this world as a biological time
bomb.

When Pablo walked the streets of Buenos Aires he did so as
a cosmopolitan millionaire, a robust 49-year-old and the father
of five children. Like many North and South Americans he regularly consumed antibiotics. Faced with a fever or an annoying
sniffle Pablo voted for convenience and treated himself with

drugs that he bought over the counter at the local pharmacy. Antibiotic prescriptions aren't needed in Argentina or many other countries for that matter. Pablo reasoned, correctly, that his doctor would simply have prescribed a pill, so why waste time. Annoying sore throats and irritating coughs were unnecessary when the miracles of tetracycline or ampicillin were but a short walk away.

But one day a fever struck Pablo and like an annoying relative it wouldn't leave. Despite generous courses of several different antibiotics, Pablo couldn't end his latest tango with another damnable microbe.

Disturbed by the failure of his miracle drugs, Pablo sought professional advice. His physician noticed that Pablo looked a little pallid and found tiny red spots on his arms and legs. A blood test yielded a serious diagnosis: acute leukemia. Taking advantage of his class and position, Pablo quickly flew to Boston for treatment.

A ten-day course of chemotherapy went well but with one minor complication: Pablo's fever and high white cell count persisted. The doctors told Pablo that *Escherichia coli*, an intestinal bacterium, was colonizing his bloodstream. They pumped him full of antibiotics, but to no avail. Then they tested the *E. coli* and made a sobering discovery: it proved resistant to eight antibiotics, including all the so-called miracle drugs that Pablo had abused over the last ten years: ampicillin, cephalosporin, gentamicin, tetracycline and other potent microbe killers.

In the end the good doctors rid Pablo's bone marrow of leukemia, but twenty-two days after his treatment the wealthy businessman succumbed to the ravages of *E. coli*. This germ is a normally benign creature whose popularity among research scientists makes it the lab rat of the microbial world. But repeated antibiotic use transformed a quiet rat into a fearful raptor, making Pablo a veritable biological hazard. Resistant strains have a history of travelling, and when they appear in a hospital or nursing home they can quickly undo life and mock medical miracles. The deadly strain that Pablo carried in his gut, in fact, had the potential to neutralize many powerful drugs in communities around the world. Pablo's pill popping not only killed him but made of the Argentine a petri dish incubating an untreatable disease.

The transcendent rise of drug-resistant bacteria is raising hairs and quickening pulses around the globe. It is easily the most tragic and dramatic medical story of this century. With the exception of treponema, the cause of syphilis, every bacterium can boast resistance to one or more drugs. Although not as sexy as the fearful Ebola, the new epidemic of microbial resistance has the potential to do more harm to more people over time and at greater cost than any of the emerging viruses now making headlines.

The basic facts read a bit like a Stephen King novel. Just forty years after the discovery of antibiotics and just a decade after arrogant declarations by the medical community that the era of infectious diseases had ended, the superorganism has counterattacked. Faced with the re-emergence of nature's hardiest grave-diggers including tuberculosis and cholera, all in multi-drug resistant flavours, humbled doctors now speak quietly of "the post-antibiotic era." While modern medicine's pill arsenal is all but spent, the illusion of a pestilence-free existence persists like a bad piece of virtual reality. But around the world hospital interns and family practitioners have returned to nineteenth-century futures where common and often fatal infections such as pneumonia, dysentery, gonorrhea and meningitis defy treatment or are but one drug away from being untreatable. Not only are more Pablos dying but they are actively growing germs that won't die. "This is a serious public health problem and one of our own making," declares Julian Davies, chief of microbiology at the University of British Columbia. "We have killed the goose that laid the golden eggs."

Killing the goose is what Dr Stuart Levy, one of the world's foremost authorities on bacterial drug resistance, calls "the antibiotic paradox." For nearly two decades the Boston researcher and founder of the Alliance for the Prudent Use of Antibiotics has warned that high antibiotic consumption encourages the selection of rare strains of bacteria or "super germs" capable of "destroying the miracle." In other words, the more humans use antibiotics for medicine or animal feeds, the more we select for immortal microbes. And because hospitals, nursing homes and day-care centres maintain high antibiotic use, they have become, as one American report noted, "prime sites for the emergence of microbial threats to health." They work, in fact, like straws that suck up resistant genes from the globe's teeming communities of bacteria and introduce them to the greater human community.

Since Levy started sounding the alarm bells, the vulnerability of the so-called drug miracle has become all too clear. Pneumococci, the microbes that can in suitable terrain cause earaches, sinus infections, pneumonia, meningitis and bacteremia, don't worry much about penicillin anymore. They've also overcome erythromycin, chlorampernicol and other penicillin-like drugs. (The cell structure of these drug-resistant strains look so different from the average pneumococci that some scientists wonder if they shouldn't be considered a separate species.) In the city of Atlanta, just outside the gates of the Center for Disease Control, 40 percent of all white children under six years of age with pneumococcal infections now carry strains resistant to penicillin. In parts of Spain, too, the resistance approaches 40 percent. The consequences are obvious: higher treatment failures, greater medical costs and more human-made pestilence. "A bacterial pathogen resistant to all chemotherapeutic agents is no longer science fiction," says Alexander Tomasz, a prominent American bacteriologist.

Shigella, the diva of dysentery, now comes so well armed

that it can defeat as many as four to six antibiotics anywhere in the world. In 1969 thousands of Guatemalan children perished from shigella when a mutant strain defied all the existing antibiotics of the day. Physicians were so startled by the event that they at first fingered an amoeba as the cause of so much bloody diarrhea. As you read this sentence hundreds of people throughout Africa are now evacuating their bodily fluids because standard antibiotics hold as much medicinal value as jelly beans. Nor are shigella's resistant ravages confined to Africa. Not long ago a middle-aged Hopi woman bred a strain of shigella impervious to seven antibiotics after she had been repeatedly drugged during a history of urinary infections. Her singular creation has become a deadly community problem. More than 20 percent of all shigella infections among aboriginals in the southwest are drug resistant and claim ancestry to this super germ.

Yet shigella is just one guerrilla in the great bacterial resistance movement. *Neisseria gonorrhea*, once treatable with a single shot of penicillin or tetracycline, may soon beat all available treatments. Tuberculosis, still the deadly king of infectious diseases, is virtually out of control in many parts of the world, thanks in part to new antibiotic-resistant strains. TB's remarkable renaissance simply awes Donald Low, a Toronto doctor specializing in bacterial resistance. He soberly recalls how his father required surgery to treat TB in the 1950s. That standard treatment was swiftly followed by antibiotics, such as streptomycin and the wholesale emptying of sanitoria where patients had rested in soulful isolation. Today, TB patients are once again being confined in special rooms where they typically hack away with untreatable strains. "That's all happened in forty years. That's not a long time."

To understand how antibiotics upset the natural order, consider the case of children's earache, the most frequent reason for visiting a doctor in North America. Strep pneumonia or

Haemophilus influenzae are involved in most of these painful episodes. Prudent treatment consists of a warm hot-water bottle and a change in diet (dairy products are a major cause of ear problems among children). But North Americans and their doctors like their technological fixes. So drugs such as amoxicillin or ampicillin, both penicillin derivatives, are doled out. They end the earache quickly (although in most cases temporarily) but also rearrange the child's biological fauna and flora. They do so by reducing colonies of healthy bacteria and by wiping out truly beneficial troops such as gut huggers like lactobacillus. This in turn impairs the child's digestion. Acting as indiscriminately as a shotgun blast, the drugs kill or wound all varieties of strep including the harmless strains that keep the bad actors in check. Last but not least, the drugs select germs resistant to the penicillin family, which explains why so many children never shake their earache and become chronic drug consumers—a grievous cycle that ends with surgical intervention.

The persistent and unnecessary drugging of children for earaches now means that truly life-threatening infections caused by strep, such as meningitis, can defeat most antibiotics. So miracle drugs refashion the bacterial make-up not only of the individual but of the greater bacterial community as well. Ultimately antibiotics do to the human body what pesticides do to the land: they kill some creatures while giving others the opportunities to run riot.

Scientists had early warnings of these developments. Alexander Fleming, the discoverer of penicillin, the world's first true "magic bullet" (if one excludes the sulpha drugs developed in the 1920s), issued prescient words of caution as early as 1945. After cultivating in his lab mutant strains of bacteria highly resistant to penicillin, the natural product of a bacteria-killing mold, Fleming made a stark prophecy: "The greatest possibility of evil in self-medication is the use of too small doses so that instead of clearing up infection, the microbes are educated to resist penicillin and a host of penicillin-fast organisms is bred out which can be passed to other individuals."

The subsequent hoopla about penicillin, which people could buy as readily as candy after the war, buried this warning. Oversold and overused, penicillin and its sister antibiotics quickly acquired an untouchable status in the medical community. That's because the drugs answered a strong technocratic desire among many researchers, including the German scientist Paul Ehrlich, to conquer infections with chemicals. Antibiotics, in fact, answered Ehrlich's quest for "charmed bullets which strike only the objects for whose destination they have been produced."

The initial success of antibiotics, however, killed a more ecological approach to health that sought to boost the body's immune system naturally in the face of bacterial threats. The promoters of this creed, mostly French and Russian biologists, understood that the terrain, the health of an individual or a community, had more to say about which germs might go looting than the germ itself. Poorly fed or battered terrain made good quarry, they said. Dousing this terrain with chemicals might kill a germ but it didn't answer why the terrain had become so vulnerable to bacterial attack. But their multifaceted approach got lost in all the pharmaceutical propaganda that soon flooded doctor's offices.

From the beginning, antibiotics were really a consumer fetish, the hula-hoops of medicine. People popped them for absurd reasons, including colds (a viral inconvenience untreatable by antibiotics), cancers and headaches. Nevertheless, physicians placed their confidence in the new technology and boldly declared the end of syphilis, staphylococcus and meningitis. "Penicillin above all, and for ever," they shouted. The discovery of other antibiotics including cephalosporins and tetracyclines in the following two decades merely cemented the myth of "miracle drugs." It also embedded the illusion that there is a pill for every ill and the technological bluff that cures can be achieved without effort or any sense of the greater world around us. And so the import of bacteria faded from the public imagination and pharmacies eventually halved their research on antibiotics.

Bacteria, however, don't believe in miracles. They merely respond to chemical threats by uniting as a community in order to locate and share the best means of resistance. The first germ to honour the accuracy of Fleming's prophecy was, of course, staphylococcus. This bacterium, which lives in the human body along with 100 trillion other organisms, remains the most common cause of skin, wound and bloodstream infections among hospital patients. Faced with extinction in many hospitals fifty years ago, staph, the eternal scourge of soldiers and burn victims, put in a call to the great bacterial gene pool, where it located a plasmid that could eat penicillin for breakfast. Plasmids are small bits of self-replicating DNA that bacteria swap and trade like baseball cards. Staph located a penicillin-resistant plasmid in colonies of soil bacteria where mold is a foe to be battled every day. Under the do-or-die pressure of penicillin, the genes moved through the bacterial world into hospitals. Thanks to this elaborate bacterial internet, strains resistant to penicillin rose from 14 to 59 percent in staph infections in London hospitals in the five years after the war. By the 1960s and 1970s these strains had entered the general community making penicillin an unreliable treatment. Today, 95 percent of the world's staph is penicillin resistant.

The next warning the bacterial world issued to the medical community came from Japan. In 1955 a middle-aged Japanese woman came down with a stubborn case of the runs. Curious about the cause of her discomfort, doctors isolated shigella as the cause. This didn't alarm Japanese scientists, but their finding that this particular bacterium was unfazed by sulfa, streptomycin, chloramphenicol and tetracycline did.

The world's first recorded case of multi-drug resistant bacteria caused a lot of grief in Japan. Four years after its identification, it was still causing epidemics and had picked off any number of hospital patients. Baffled Japanese scientists looked for a reason for the resistance and found it in the stomachs of the afflicted. Here *E. coli* also showed resistance to the same four drugs. Tomoichio Akiba, a wise microbiologist at Tokyo University, then concluded that shigella had passed on its resistant genes to *E. coli* through conjugation. Bacterial conjugation, which remotely resembles human copulation, takes place when two bacteria touch and exchange plasmids with the help of a filament-like protein. Akiba had discovered something truly frightening: before an antibiotic or group of antibiotics could effectively destroy a germ, it might have already passed on its "knowledge" of resistance to other bacteria, like a true guerrilla. The Japanese also learned that microbes as genetically different as a buffalo is from a horse can and do regularly exchange drug-busting information and other chatter. At the time few scientists paid attention to these facts.

While Japanese scientists doggedly unlocked the mystery of multi-drug resistant bacteria, American scientists discovered that antibiotics made a great growth promoter. By adding a mash that contained a residue of an early antibiotic, chlortetracycline, to chicken feed, scientists witnessed the unbelievable: within twenty-five days the chicks grew at almost three times the rate of other birds that had only been given vitamins. When it became known that small doses of antibiotics could speed animal growth by 50 percent, the pharmaceutical industry immediately began to push the unnecessary, and a host of drugs started appearing in pig, cattle and chicken feeds around the world. Given the totalitarian nature of modern technological advances, farmers were never given a choice in the matter. It was drug or fail in the marketplace. In the United States alone the animal husbandry industry now digests about 20 million pounds of antibiotics a year or twice the amount ingested by humans. In any given year 6 billion animals in the US are raised for dinner and almost all receive antibiotics in one form or another. With the exception of some Scandinavian countries, farmers around the developed world have become pharmacists while their animals have become part of an uncontrolled experiment with antibiotics.

After forty years of drugging animals, including fish (the salmon industry alone gobbles 55 million pounds of drugs), scientists still don't know why antibiotics make them grow so fast. They guess that all young animals come naturally burdened with bacteria that may slow growth if not knocked out by miracle-laced feeds. But by fooling with Mother Nature and liberally polluting animal food with antibiotics, humans have unwittingly given bacteria another free market in which to select resistant genes.

It doesn't take much imagination to figure out the selection pressures now working on many farms. Stuart Levy estimates that an average cow dumps one hundred times more dung than a human does in a day. If old Betty has been fed antibiotics since birth, her feces will likely contain drug resistant germs. Generous cow pies add large amounts of super germs to the environment. In fact, if you want to know what animals are eating in your neighbourhood just test their handlers; the intestines of farmers and their families typically harbour high levels of bacteria resistant to the antibiotics used on the farm.

This transfer of drug-resistant bacteria from animals to humans has been documented in a number of incidents. A salmonella outbreak in England that killed several people was eventually traced back to a similar epidemic among calves induced by a multi-drug resistant strain. In a more recent case in the former East Germany, farmers started feeding their pigs a new antibiotic, streptothricin. No resistance to the drug then existed. But within six months, a resistant gene had been acquired by bacteria abiding in the guts of pigs. Within two years the resistant gene had found its way into colonies of *E. coli* in the farm workers and their families. Soon one percent of all urinary infections in the area claimed the gene too.

Although many scientists, particularly those employed by the $40-billion antibiotic industry, say that the evidence for animal–human transfers is still inconclusive, the facts suggest otherwise. A team of researchers at the Florida College of Dentistry have even demonstrated that antibiotic-resistant gum disease is acquired by eating beef tainted by tetracycline feeds. Bacteria aren't always killed by cooking, as every hamburger aficionado knows, and resistant genes can pass easily to humans through leaking gums. Because the resistant genes in both cattle and humans shared a 99 percent similarity, the team concluded that "the genetic transfer of drug resistance between species is possible."

It is not only possible but happening every day. It might also explain why bacterial resistance has recently taken on the speed of a freight train. After defeating "the wonder drug" penicillin, staph took ten years to mobilize the genes it needed to develop resistance to penicillin's replacement, methicillin. But it's only taken enterococci (an ubiquitous intestinal bacterium) two years to beat vancomycin, the antibiotic of last resort. "That's frightening for an organism that can cause serious disease," says Low.

Drug-resistant genes aren't a new development. A number of fecal studies have shown that people in Borneo and the Solomon Islands, not to mention wild animals in Africa, carried resistant and transferable genes in extremely low doses long before the introduction of miracle drugs. Because most antibiotics are made of natural substances, genes capable of resisting them have always been available in the bacterial world. But medicine's abuse of antibiotics has antagonized the bacterial world to such a degree that the superorganism has been forced to bring resistant genes to the fore in fantastic numbers and at ever quickening speeds.

The mechanisms that bacterial hordes apply to defeat antibiotics are ancient, sentient and sophisticated. To get drug-busting genes from A to B bacteria not only conjugate, but transpose, transduct, transform and mutate. Genes can be exchanged by insertion, jumping ship or even the invasion of bacterial viruses. "A kind of social behavior, comparable in some ways to that of social insects or humans, appears to be exhibited in the bacterial world," notes Montreal physician Sorin Sonea. "The binding force among bacteria is one of constant exchange and permanent choice of information bits, principally genes." These genes allow bacteria to build stronger cell walls, to digest antibiotics or even pump an antibiotic out of the cell faster than it can accumulate. Ingenuity is the grand signature of the bacterial world.

The efforts expended by bacteria to neutralize an antibiotic can be "as eloquent as an opera." After a community of enterococci acquire eight resistance-fighting genes or transposons, it can sense the presence of vancomycin, break down its old cell walls and reconfigure a new impenetrable curtain. "There are strains of enterococci that can only live on vancomycin. You know you are up against an incredible foe when they have these kinds of resources to draw on," says Low.

Nor do bacteria stop when they have found the genetic tools they need to disarm one drug. When assaulted by tetracycline over a period of weeks *E. coli* will summon up a Hydra-like resistance not only to the aggressor but to seven other antibiotics as well. "It is almost as if bacteria strategically anticipate the confrontation of other drugs when they resist one," says Levy.

The abuse of antibiotics is not just a case of knee-jerk pill popping; it is also a matter of inappropriate medicine. According to Levy, approximately half of all antibiotic prescriptions are unnecessary or inappropriate. They are simply the wrong drug in the wrong dose for the wrong germ at the wrong time. Most hospitals, for example, have no protocol for treating outpatients with infections, so that different doctors will give different amounts and even different drugs to treat poorly monitored diseases. Patients compound matters by rarely following their prescriptions. Bacteria thrive on this kind of inconsistency and irrationality. As American physician Jeffrey Fisher writes in *The Plague Makers*, the purpose of antibiotics is simple: "they are supposed to be used to treat documented bacterial infections, ones in which the causative organism has been properly identified. But we have moved so far from this axiom, it's almost as if it never existed. Instead, doctors treat more and more disease empirically, either without waiting for or ignoring laboratory results of cultures of blood, sputum or other body fluids."

But physicians aren't the only culprits. In a technological society the biological consequences of one's actions take a back seat to rights of access and convenience. Most people today demand drugs the way three-year-olds demand Halloween candy. Our addiction to antibiotics is not only illogical but dangerous; but rather than lose a patient, most doctors will succumb to an appeal and produce the desired prescription. Yet the day will come, warns pathologist Mark Lappe, when doctors will have to recognize "that the best possible treatment for the patient may not always be the best possible treatment for the hospital, the community or the next generation of patients to come."

Profligate drug taking is a more serious business in the Third World, where pharmaceutical makers often give physicians or pharmacists monetary incentives to sell their antibiotics. Even toxic concoctions like chloramphenicol used to treat typhoid fever (the drug can cause leukemia) are available over the counter in countries such as Chile. Some public events feature massive antibiotic handouts. To spare 100,000 pilgrims to

Mecca the inconvenience of encountering cholera, the Indonesian government dishes tetracycline "out of vats like coffee beans." (Such actions explain why 50 percent of all cholera strains are now tetracycline resistant.) Whenever plague or other microbial eruptions threaten parts of India, the government immediately doles out antibiotics. In Africa small children sell potent antimicrobials on the street as cures for impotence and nightmares. In the United States pet store owners sell antibiotics under the counter. And so on. "Every country is a culture of bacteria," notes Dr Levy, "and the drugs consumed by that culture affect selection pressures and ultimately the public health."

A recent study of healthy children in Boston, Caracas, Venezuela and Qin Pu, China, illustrates this truth. None of the children had received antibiotics, making them a rare group that probably represents less than 10 percent of all kids today. Yet the E. coli of children from China and Venezuela had large numbers of resistant or multi-resistant genes to eight different antibiotics. The children in Boston, where antibiotics are better regulated, had resistant genes but only in low numbers. The researchers suggested that individuals should strive to maintain the healthy bacterial ecology they acquire as children so as to keep levels of bacterial resistance low.

Antibiotic abuse has also had the effect of changing disease patterns. One of the consequences of the persistent annihilation of bacterial communities in humans has been an amazing growth of fungal infections. By killing off good bacteria and suppressing immune systems, antibiotics have transformed *Candida albicans*, a relatively innocuous yeast present in the gut, into a serious and even life-threatening infection among cancer and AIDS patients. Once dismissed as a nuisance, fungal infections now account for 40 percent of hospital-acquired infections. They can cause blindness, heart failure or even a sudden clotting of the blood. Not many drugs are good at knocking out fungi and the small arsenal that exists is already encountering formidable resistance. The so-called "emerging fungal threat" is completely man-made.

In the microbial world what goes around comes around. Drug-busting genes, bred in either American hospitals or Third World slums, quickly take out global citizenship. A strain of strep, resistant to thirteen antibiotics, appeared in South African hospitals in 1977 killing several children. Yet scientists eventually traced this super germ back to a strain that had emerged ten years earlier in Papua New Guinea. The world's resistant strains of gonorrhea initially surfaced in Saigon brothels where American officials tried to keep whores "free of disease" with daily doses of penicillin. The technocrats, however, merely created a monster germ that costs more to treat today than it did twenty years ago, and with no guarantee of success. Trying to find a strain of gonococci not resistant to one or more drugs today would be as difficult as locating a seventeenth century aristocrat without syphilis.

Most of the worst epidemics of microbial resistance to date have occurred in hospitals. A bellwether outbreak of multi-drug resistant staph shook medical authorities in Melbourne, Australia, just two decades ago. Often called "golden staph" because of its distinct colour, this germ regularly gives patients skin, brain, urinary or ear infections they didn't have before entering the hospital. (Staph is a rather stubborn colonizer of all kinds of medical devices ranging from heart valves to catheters) After dozens of patients started dying from untreatable infections in hospitals throughout Melbourne, clinicians identified the culprit as a strain of staph that resisted all frontline antibiotics. Antiseptics also couldn't kill the germ.

The outbreak terrorized patients and medical personnel alike. Even ambulance drivers wore masks to protect themselves from germs that wouldn't die. Infection control officers eventually traced the strain back to hospital linen and sinks. As a con-

sequence they recommended rigorous handwashing and the isolation of infected patients. The only antibiotic capable of
killing the super germ was vancomycin, a highly toxic and
expensive bacterial killer first discovered in 1956. Although
now used as the infection stopper of last resort in hospitals
around the world, until then it had been kept in the cupboard
for grim emergencies.

With the help of vancomycin, clean hands and stringent
antibiotic protocols Melbourne eventually contained the outbreak. But multi-resistant strains still account for 20 to 40 percent all of staph found in its hospitals. "Once a strain colonizes
a hospital, it's like bagging a cat," notes Donald Low, who battled a similar outbreak in an Ontario nursing home. "You get an
organism in one corner and then, bang, you've got one across
the room. It's like holding jello in your hands." This is why hospitals in Perth, Australia now monitor all incoming patients for
super strains of staph and segregate them. Individuals don't like
being singled out but the benefits for the general community in
terms of safer hospitals and reliable treatments have been
immense.

For reasons of limited finance, bad training and indifference,
the example of Perth stands as a largely isolated model. The
United States, for instance, is now adopting a health care
model that will shift patients around like sick cattle within an
"integrated" circuit of institutions. Gone are the days of visiting
one facility. Patients will now be bundled up or down the system, depending on the level of technological pricking they
need within "a given health-care entity." Driven by dubious
economics this shuffling has nothing to do with health and very
little to do with care. Health officials freely admit that the cir-
culation of patients "will in effect create a superhighway that
facilitates exchange of organisms between acute inpatient wards
and other settings of care." With enemies like these, resistant
bacteria have no need of friends.

To fully appreciate the horrors that hospitals and doctors have carelessly created for the public, consider the Frankenstein's monster of tuberculosis. Lax public health measures, increased homelessness and the emergence of HIV have all played a role in reviving "the Captain of all men of death." (As one of the world's most highly contagious and stubbornly persistent infections, TB has earned wide respect among nurses and doctors.) But it was the refusal of infected patients to complete a six- to twelve-month course of drugs in the 1970s that gave birth to strains of *Mycobacterium tuberculosis* that typically require not one but four antibiotics to treat. An individual with a super strain of TB costs $150,000 to heal (with no guarantee of immunity from reactivation), or tens times the cost of previous treatment. The chances of surviving such an infection are similar to those in the nineteenth century: 50/50.

A strain of TB resistant to seven drugs recently terrorized a teaching hospital in upstate New York. An HIV patient from a local prison entered the hospital with all the usual complaints: fever, cough and weight loss. With the patient's immune system shot to hell by HIV, M. *tuberculosis* had run amok. Confined to an isolation room, the consumptive wasn't allowed outside without a surgical mask. In spite of standard treatments with isoniazid, rifampin, ethambutol and clofazimine, he died twenty-seven days after admission. But not his TB.

Taking advantage of deteriorating air ducts in the isolation room, the microbe travelled. Swinging doors that moved air in and down the corridor outside his room swept contaminated air into other patients' rooms. Wall fans then circulated the germs.

In the end, forty-six health care workers tested positive with the same strain and received isoniazid as preventive therapy. Three patients exposed to the carrier developed active TB and died within a month. A hospital guard being treated for cancer of the larynx also developed a cough and fever after guarding the patient. He too died. "Continued urgent attention to TB infection control is needed," dryly concluded a medical account of this rampage in the *Journal of Infection Control and Hospital Epidemiology*. That such exchanges now take place routinely on the streets of New York, Cairo, New Delhi and Bangkok, without the benefit of any infection controls, is not noted.

The threats that bacterial resistance pose are so real and so serious that the new millennium will invite medieval if not Draconian measures. Travellers entering countries with low levels of drug resistance will be quarantined until their germ status has been determined. The medical profession will informally recognize two classes of people: those with low levels of resistance and those that are "biohazards" incubating super germs. Doctors will encounter more and more cases of ordinary yet untreatable infections. Many will die because they cannot afford $500-a-day antibiotics and others will be allowed to die because treatment might select strains hazardous to the greater community. Segregation of individuals with multi-resistant infections in hospitals will become routine. Citizens will no longer view hospitals or nursing homes as symbols of progress but as biological slums. They, too, will rate institutions on the likelihood of leaving them alive without catching an untreatable infection. And incineration will become the only method of burial.

Given the medical profession's abuse of antibiotics and the public's uncritical faith in technology, the epidemic of bacterial resistance will grow stronger and stronger. Everything, in fact, seems skewed for a bacterial victory. There is as yet no coherent public movement to end the use of antibiotics as growth promoters in animal husbandry. Without one, industrial agriculture will continue to select better and more efficient killers. Meanwhile doctors are still prescribing antibiotics willy-nilly without knowing which germs they are battling even though many simple tests are now available for identifying organisms and their resistant status. Instead of assuming responsibility for their own health, North Americans continue to behave like blind consumers, heedlessly expecting pills to fix their ills. And in the pursuit of profits pharmaceutical companies do what they have always done: flood the marketplace with drugs that come with costly biological consequences for the whole community. (Bacterial resistance costs the US alone nearly $8 billion a year.) Midnight, the hour of ghastly misfortunes and horrific pestilence, approaches but the clock ticks in an empty room.

This bacterial renaissance comes at a time when the world no longer considers bacteria very interesting or important. Viruses not only hog the headlines but monopolize scientific resources as well. The speed and chaotic make-up of viral plagues make them the perfect fetish of a technological society hooked on speed, immediacy and discord. So, in spite of their ancient history and unique genetic fluidity, bacteria have been underestimated and ignored. But until the human species learns to respect the superorganism and temper its technological intrusions, the world's public health will become increasingly vulnerable to guerrilla ambushes of the biological kind. There walk among us more Pablos than we know.

12

EBOLA'S APPRENTICES:

EMERGING VIRUSES

"A virus can be useful to a species by thinning it out."
Karl Johnson, health consultant

The death of Merrill Bahe and all the others was foretold. Since the beginning of the Navajo people, the elders have said that too much rain in a desert of piñon trees can unbalance life and cause bad things to happen.

In the spring of 1993 heavy skies split open and flooded the land with a murderous deluge the like of which hadn't been seen in decades. Then, in the second week of May, bad things began to happen. It started the day Bahe, a 19-year-old marathon runner, stopped breathing in his car on the way to the funeral of his beloved. He arrived unconscious and blue at the Gallup Indian Medical Center, where Dr Bruce Tempest, a resident clinician, tried but failed to revive the young man.

When a well-known cross country runner just stops breathing, a good clinician gets curious. Dr Tempest poked around; a routine chest X-ray found Bahe's lungs as soaked as desert sands after a heavy spring rain. Then the doctor remembered a colleague's patient who, on May 9, had also simply stopped breathing and died. Her name was Florena Woody and she was Bahe's fiancée. Alarmed by this coincidence Dr Tempest called his colleague and compared notes. They both made further calls. Within the space of a day they had uncovered the cases of five young people, all previously healthy, who had died suddenly of a flu-like illness.

The dead had all lived an hour away from Gallup, New Mexico. After ruling out the southwest's usual microbial suspect, pneumonic plague (the lungs just didn't seem wasted enough), the doctors realized they had a serious mystery on their hands. Dr Tempest called the New Mexico Office of the Medical Investigator.

Within two weeks of Tempest's call more than one hundred scientists and epidemiologists were racing about the state trying to solve "the desert mystery" or what the media dubbed "the Navajo plague." Doctors, meanwhile, dryly referred to the illness as "the unexplained acute respiratory distress syndrome." By the end of May, cases of the strange disease had popped up throughout the Four Corner states: Utah, Arizona, Colorado and New Mexico. But the epicentre of the epidemic remained the Navajo reservation, one of the largest Indian reserves in the U.S.

When the scientists approached the Navajo for an explanation the elders and the medicine men pointed to the piñon nuts. "Too many," they said. Only three times in this century had the nuts been available year round. That kind of abundance meant trouble, they said. The scientists, however, weren't looking for piñon clues but for viral and bacterial suspects.

On May 31 the state epidemiologist, Dr Ron Voorhees, was clearly exasperated. He announced, "We have not been able to identify any place where people have gone or any gathering in common. Nothing really fits."

As the illness continued to baffle doctors and alarm people in the southwest, Robert Parmenter, a local mammal expert, recorded a dramatic surge in the deer mouse population—a ten-fold increase in fact. He attributed the mice's great numbers to the heavy rains, abundant undergrowth, soft earth for burrowing and a rich food supply: plentiful piñons.

After ruling out bubonic plague, anthrax, Legionnaires' disease, mycoplasmas, herbicides and Navajo herbal remedies, flummoxed scientists started looking at a variety of viral possibilities. They had no other explanation for why the disease appeared to strike at random and didn't appear to be contagious. "There is a medical saying that when you hear hoof beats you think first of horses not zebras," confessed one epidemiologist to the *Albuquerque Journal*. "We're definitely in zebra country.... This is just a remarkable phenomenon."

Bad things, of course, continued to happen as June approached. They stole the breath from a 13-year-old dancing girl in Red Rock and buried 21-year-old Henry Henio Jr. just two weeks before his wedding. Over a five- to eight-day period the symptoms in twenty-four cases (twelve dead and counting) had stuck to a pattern: fever, back ache, vomiting, diarrhea, coughing and, finally, lungs that refused to work anymore.

In the first week of June scientists announced that blood taken from three survivors of the "desert mystery" tested positive for exposure to an unknown strain of hantavirus (there are five known ones). North American doctors had first encountered one member of this genus (Hantaan) during the war in Korea where it infected 3,000 troops, killing some 400 men. (Chinese physicians first described the symptoms of the disease a thousand years ago.) But until the New Mexico outbreak no hantavirus had caused disease in North America, nor had the virus ever been associated with pulmonary breakdown.

Rodents have long been the natural hosts of all the hantaviruses. A mouse or rat, once benignly infected, sheds and spreads the microbe via its urine and feces, which humans then unwittingly touch or inhale. Each year, for example, 100,000 Chinese peasants come down with hemorrhagic fever caused by the Hantaan virus, which is carried by a field mouse. During the rice harvest peasants routinely handle or inhale mice droppings, get sick and in most cases recover. The unlucky die. The same deadly play is performed with a related virus found outside Seoul, Korea.

Sixty percent of the rodents trapped in the homes of the Navajo dead or the illness's survivors were deer mice. One-third of these rodents, which live throughout North America except in the southeast, tested seropositive for hantavirus. Since New Mexico's "desert mystery" scientists have tracked more than seventy cases of respiratory failure caused by hantavirus as far afield as Alberta, California and Ohio. Fifty percent of the infected lost their ability to breathe and died. Old medical records revealed that hantavirus had been killing people anonymously for years. Scientists now call the new virus Muerto Canyon, after the dramatic locale where a virus serotype taken from the lungs of a mouse and those of a patient made a perfect genetic match.

In the end, the Navajo elders were right. An abundance of rain in the desert had disrupted the land's normal ecology creating an abundance of piñons. With this food bonanza the deer mouse population exploded, as did their virus-rich droppings. The result was increased human exposure and a sudden harvest of death.

Although scientists congratulated themselves on the swift identification of the virus, no one commented on the epidemic's uncanny resemblance to the plague of Justinian. That epidemic wiped out nearly two-thirds of the human race in the sixth and seventh centuries. Like Muerto Canyon, it began with a simple change in the weather in the arid foothills between India and China. Buckets of rain encouraged an explosion in rodent populations. As a consequence, a bacterial infection, *Y. pestis*, had a field day. The infection eventually spread to black rats, just as it would during the Black Death, and soon cleaned out human communities in Europe, North Africa, India and China. With the advent of cold weather the bacteria changed to its highly contagious pneumonic form. And so it went on. Fortunately for the species, Muerto Canyon wasn't contagious; not did it show any serious inclination towards becoming so. But "the desert mystery" certainly replayed a familiar tune that had been heard in deserts since the beginning of human history.

Most television watchers now know that the Muerto Canyon virus is just one player in a much larger ecological field where all kinds of death rattlers are now emerging like strange medieval heralds. These newly provoked viruses take their names, as scientific tradition insists, from the cities, jungles and rivers where they first showed themselves: Junin, Machupo, Sabia, Guranito, Hanann, Ebola, Marburg, Lassa, Rift Valley. What worries many viral experts is not only the often frightful character of these serial killers (scientists wear fully shielded spacesuits when handling most of these microbes) but the increasing frequency of their spontaneous visitations. In the chess games technological man is now playing with the natural world, viruses have recently placed the species in one deadly checkmate after another. As Richard Preston notes disturbingly in his international bestseller, *The Hot Zone*, a grim biography of Ebola, "the emerging viruses are surfacing from ecologically damaged parts of the earth.... In a sense the earth is mounting an immune response against the human species."

Stephen Morse, a virologist at Rockefeller University, first popularized the expression "emerging virus" in 1989. By selecting this adjective Morse was referring not to new mutants, such as the feared Andromeda strain, but to existing and even ancient viruses that "seemed to appear very quickly and suddenly in a population." In fact, many of the viruses now popping up in the headlines are the stuff of old nightmares: influenza, rabies, hepatitis A, B, C and D, dengue fever and the seven-member herpes clan. Others such as the hemorrhagic fevers or bleeders, including Ebola and Marburg, seem exotic and unfamiliar. But the viruses that keep Morse awake at night "are the ones not yet identified." (For the record, there are as many viruses as there are stars; scientists have so far identified only 5,000.)

The increased propensity of viruses to jump out of their native habitat and to kill humans is a byproduct of what Morse calls "viral traffic," the transfer of diseases that exist naturally in animal populations. By invading rain forests, building mega-cities, travelling incessantly and inducing climatic change (ultra-violet light can activate some viruses), modern people have accelerated viral traffic to such a degree that viral collisions such as AIDS are inevitable. Biological instability is perhaps the hallmark of technological advancement. "It is," says Morse with affable understatement, "a good time for viruses."

Just how good was illustrated as early as 1959 by the Machupo virus. It emerged, as many lethal killers do, in a scabrous frontier district—in this case in eastern Bolivia along the Machupo River. Hitchhiking on a small mouse, the virus slept largely unmolested until a malaria control program using DDT poisoned the local cat population. The cat killings coincided with Bolivia's social revolution of 1952, which turned frontier cowboys into landowners for the first time in their lives. To supplement their meagre diets the people planted corn and other vegetables on fertile plateaus rising above the river. They also moved their homes and gardens to the *alturas*. All of this hewing and ploughing upset one of the region's original inhabitants, a rare species of field mouse. Seeking some peace it scurried into people's *casas* and, with no feline predators, it flourished. And so too did Machupo.

By the time a team of three American scientists arrived in

the sick town of San Joaquin in 1962, Machupo was killing one out of every two infected people. A family of eleven lost nine of its members. The peasants called the scourge *el typho negro* or Black Typhus. After a week's incubation period, the virus caused people to burn up and bleed from the gums, nose and intestines. Convulsions and tremors followed. Then came hair loss and death. Before the Americans could figure out what the hell was happening all three had contracted the disease and nearly died. It took two years of exhaustive field work before Karl Johnson, now a viral detective of considerable fame, figured out that the rodents were shedding the virus in their urine.

To verify his finding Johnson employed a homely tool to end the epidemic. He divided the town of San Joaquin in half and provided every home on one side with mouse traps. Within a week the dying stopped in the mouse-free area; meanwhile Machupo kept on killing in the mouse-infested zone. Johnson concluded that the mice urinated in people's homes while munching on scraps of food during the night. The morning custom of sweeping dirt floors while preparing breakfast ensured that a good dose of Machupo was sprinkled in people's food and lungs. Thanks to the reintroduction of cats and a good supply of mouse traps Machupo has since maintained a low profile in Bolivia. But the virus illustrates just how innocently humans can set off a baffling series of viral events.

Machupo did not emerge alone in the tropics. At the same time Bolivians were dying, Argentinian agricultural workers were struggling with Junin, another hemorraghic fever. This arenavirus is also carried by an obscure field mouse. After World War II the expansion of well herbicided corn fields outside of Buenos Aires so thoroughly rearranged the wild grasses that a marginal rodent suddenly became top dog in the area. Every fall combine harvesters crush these monoculture lovers, creating aerosol bombs of Junin. A few human deaths accompany every harvest. In 1989 Venezuelan peasants uncovered another hemorraghic fever when they cleared a forest and dislodged the local cotton rat population—with mortal results. Then came Sabia in São Paulo, Brazil in 1990.

Another hemorraghic fever that has alarmed virologists popped up in West Africa among Nigerian diamond prospectors. In the late 1960s miners established garbage-filled towns in lands occupied by a wily rat whose urine and saliva shed Lassa particles. (The rats are notorious trap avoiders.) This frightful blood-borne infection causes muscle pain, body rashes, bleeding ulcers and hair loss. It has a 40 percent fatality rate and accounts for nearly 30 percent of all hospital deaths in West Africa. Surgeons fear the infection because it can be a hospital closer: an entire operating team died after performing a cesarean on a woman hemorrhaging from Lassa.

When the fever struck a Nigerian in Chicago in 1989, medical authorities, fearing the worst, carefully monitored all 102 contacts for signs of the disease, but fate and the virus gave them only one dead Nigerian. The man had gone home to bury his mother, a victim of Lassa, and brought back an emerging virus. The incident revealed the globe's biological insecurity and the simple pathway of epidemics in waiting: one ill traveller, one ambitious microbe, one hundred exposures and all in one twenty-four-hour period.

Another classic emerging virus is named after Africa's Rift Valley. Until the 1970s it was simply an annoying infection of European stock animals causing abortions and stillbirths in sheep, goats and cattle. Spread by the mosquito *Aëdes pseudoscutellaris*, the fever explodes in great epidemics after heavy rainfalls on Africa's grassy plains. Once it is established in domestic herds other mosquitoes pick up the virus and spread it around to other four-legged victims in what scientists call a "diabolical life cycle." Kenyan shepherds first reported an outbreak of the virus among European sheep in the Rift Valley during the 1930s. Until European animals started to invade its niche and Egypt's

Aswan dam was constructed, this ancient virus seems to have coexisted with African human and animal populations with little fanfare.

In 1977, six years after the completion of this technological monolith, an epidemic of the fever swept through the Nile Valley felling people and animals around the 800,000-hectare reservoir. The herders and herded who had been attracted to the water represented virgin terrain for the virus. The dam's still and shallow waters also created ideal breeding conditions for Aëdes. When travelling herdsmen or wind brought the virus to Egypt, an ecological holocaust took place. Some 200,000 people became seriously ill; 600 died of fever and failing livers. Many lost their sight and their mental faculties. The slaughter of livestock was on a Biblical scale, and Egyptians ate many a meatless meal that year. Subsequent dam building in Senegal, Mauritania and Madagascar triggered similar tragedies, causing hundreds of deaths. In fact, dam building in the tropics is now regarded as a hazardous activity that usually comes with unforeseen biological consequences. Scientists worry about this virus because many of the world's mosquitoes live near livestock and are quite capable of transporting the microbe. The United States, for example, harbours thirty native mosquitoes well suited for the virus's deployment. All that's necessary to move the virus to the United States would be a shipment of sick animals and a sleepy customs agent. This explains why Rift Valley may someday become as famous as Ebola.

Like Machupo and Lassa, Ebola is a bleeder and a real attention grabber. Any virus that can transform body organs into bloody pools of wasted flesh in a matter of days deservedly achieves a sort of fearful notoriety. Classified as a Level Four biohazard, Ebola kills nine out of ten victims, a record matched by few microbes (Richard Preston calls the virus "a slate wiper"). When scientists examine this filiovirus, a small family of microbes shaped like light bulb filaments, they do so from behind masks with high-energy particulate air filters in pressurized rooms. With Ebola carelessness means death.

The first recorded epidemics of Ebola occurred in two of the poorest parts of Africa, rural Sudan and Zaire in 1976. They probably weren't the first outbreaks of Ebola, but they marked the first time that Europeans as well as Africans were affected. The first victim was a teacher at the Belgian mission of Yambuku. He encountered the virus either in the rain forest while hunting or at the end of an unsterilized syringe containing anti-malarial drugs. African hospitals rely heavily on injectable drugs but rarely have the means or funds to sterilize the needles regularly. The hospital at Yambuku, which injected more than 300 patients a day with reusable needles, served as a convenient warehouse for the blood-borne virus.

Before the teacher died he "vomited dark brown bile that looked like coffee grounds," writes Dr William Close in his book *Ebola*. The next to die were those who washed the dead or who had visited the hospital, which soon became a house of horrors awash with vomit and blood. While Africans suspected bad spirits, Belgian nuns suspected fulminating yellow fever and wondered why none of their miracle drugs worked. The Europeans airlifted one infected nurse to Kinshasa, a city of fetid hovels, broken roads and teeming poverty. From Kinshasa the virus could have quickly travelled around the world had it been inclined to do so.

By the time Karl Johnson arrived on the scene, the epidemic had nearly peaked. "We knew it was bad in there and we knew we were dealing with something new," he recently told Preston. "We didn't know if the virus could be spread by droplets in the air, somewhat like influenza. If Ebola had spread easily through the air, the world would be a very different place today."

The epidemic stopped as suddenly as it had begun. To this day scientists don't know where Ebola hides in the rain forest or why it emerges when it does. In the last nineteen years Ebola has made two more bloody appearances in Zaire and Sudan and one in a monkey house outside Washington D.C. That strain, Ebola Reston, was only lethal to monkeys and originated in the Philippines. The Reston virus, however, had made a special genetic adaption: it could spread through the air. Ebola, it seems, is a microbe hell-bent on finding a more effective and conducive means of travelling than by blood.

The last Ebola epidemic to shake Zaire, one of the most dislocated countries in Africa, happened in Kikwit last year and became a world media event. True to form, it exploded in a hospital where a patient with a suspected appendectomy turned out to be a balloon of Ebola. Sprayed by gore, the contaminated surgical team helped spread the epidemic through the town. It eventually killed more than 300 people. (At first doctors suspected shigella as the cause of the epidemic.) Once villagers understood that handling the infected or washing the dead put them at Ebola's mercy, they abandoned these practices and the dying stopped. Then Ebola retreated into the shadows. When it emerges again, it may travel as easily as the flu and kill as ruthlessly as the plague.

While Ebola has dominated recent public attention, much older viral threats have worked quietly behind the scenes. Dengue or what the Africans call "breakdown fever" is celebrating a triumphant return around the world thanks to the spread of its mosquito carrier, *Aëdes aegypti*, the same fellow that transports yellow fever. Dengue does indeed break down humans, exhibiting miserable symptoms that range from severe headaches to disabling eye and joint pain. But what has unsettled public health experts is dengue's lethal new livery; hemorrhagic fever or shock syndrome. Ten to fifteen percent of the people who are infected by this strain of the disease, which first appeared in Manila in 1953, develop high fevers, and hemorrhage throughout their body before sinking into a coma and dying.

Prior to World War II dengue, a long-time resident of the tropics, had been on the retreat. But increased air travel helped this misery maker with its four different strains (infected globe-trotters don't show symptoms for a week) to see more of the world. As a consequence more than one strain now share the same geography. The preferred locale is a big tropical city with lots of refuse such as discarded cups, tires and other useful nurseries for *Aëdes aegypti*. For a person who has been infected and sensitized by one version of dengue and gets hit by another serotype, the odds of developing hemorrhagic fever become one in three hundred. According to one theory, multiple infections may have the effect of destablizing the immune system. Other scientists suspect that "dengue type 2" is quite capable of causing hemorrhagic fever all on its own.

In any case, dengue hemorrhagic fever first hit the Americas in 1981, when it struck 344,000 Cubans, hospitalizing 116,000 and killing 158. In the last ten years dengue has made a name for itself in Ecuador, Peru, Costa Rica and Venezuela. Now the major cause of child hospitalization in southern Asia promises to become the major cause of child hospitalization in Latin America and the Caribbean.

Free market economics have also given dengue a new edge: A. *albopictus* or the tiger mosquito. Once confined to Asia, this dengue spreader hitchhiked a ride in used tires shipped from Japan to America in 1985. These aggressive blood suckers, which have the capacity to carry many more viruses than A. *aegypti*, have now colonized twenty American states. Add to this scenario a little wet weather, sustained global warming, sloppy public health monitoring and increased urban crowding and you'll understand why dengue has become one of the world's most rapidly expanding diseases.

The same constellation of factors fostering fatal viral exchanges in the human world are also taking a toll among animals. Consider the parvovirus, the bane of every pet owner.

Some time in the late 1970s this virus jumped from cats to dogs, resulting in a worldwide epidemic of heart failure among puppies and severe diarrhea among their elders. Parvovirus, one of the smallest and simplest microbes, can only reproduce in rapidly dividing cells. This explains why it aims for a puppy's heart cells and targets the stomach cells of older dogs. Just how the cat virus jumped ship and whether it used another species as an intermediary host has yet to be determined. But there are now three types of parvo on the loose.

The Serengeti's lions have also witnessed hazardous viral traffic recently. After two behavioural researchers watched a third of their 250 study population start to twitch, convulse and die in 1995, investigators pegged the viral intruder as canine distemper. This finding has alarmed scientists because lions and infected dogs have mixed for hundreds of years in Africa; which leads them to conclude that either the virus has recently mutated or the immunological health of the lions in a stressed and troubled park has rendered them vulnerable to the plague. Scientists also noted that both dog and human populations have grown substantially along the parks borders in recent years thereby inviting a viral collision with feline casualties.

Dead dolphins and dead seals also have a tale to tell about viral exchange in unsettled seas. From 1987 to 1991 thousands of these mammals died throughout European waters. A massive seal die-off in Siberia was followed by more deaths in the North Sea and the Mediterranean. Scientists eventually identified four new viruses that looked a lot like human measles and canine distemper. In fact, the Siberian epidemic may well have been triggered by the dumping of dead sled dogs felled by distemper into Lake Baikal. But the viruses all seemed to have help of one kind or another. Many of the dead animals had massive amounts of pollutants such as PCBs in their livers and hence suffered from faltering immune systems. Warm weather, an aid to many viruses, had also heated up the seas in many places.

The formation of giant algal blooms, effective nurturers of viruses and bacteria, may also have played a role in the killing. But there is no doubt that viral traffic in the seas has become as intense as that on land.

The viral activity that is now scaring many humans to death and forcing scientists to think ecologically isn't really new. Viruses such as smallpox have a long history and will continue to appear when awakened by environmentally disruptive human activity. In this sense viruses haven't changed, but the size and number of human footprints in virus-rich jungles, savannahs and oceans definitely have. The idea that five billion people can manipulate the weather or exterminate other species without a biological response of one kind or another is beginning to strike a few scientists as shortsighted lunacy.

But unlike the superorganism, which seems capable of mounting a united defence, viruses behave more like twentieth-century terrorists. They tend to let off bombs with no warning. And it's just a matter of time before one of these biological missiles explodes with the force of a nuclear bomb.

EPILOGUE

The future of epidemics looks as lively as New World smallpox and as irrepressible as Renaissance syphilis. This observation shouldn't be cause for apocalyptic hair-pulling but for reflection.

The population of the world has now grown to the point where frequent collisions with the superorganism are as unavoidable as freeway accidents. Five billion human beings can't help but erode soils, build garbage piles and rouse the Horseman. Peasants started the die-offs ten thousand years ago by domesticating cows, cutting trees and ploughing up the land. Famine and war added to the lethal mix. In response, leprosy gave rise to the hospital, malaria sponsored racism, plague defeated feudalism and tuberculosis laid down linoleum. Future plagues will come and go, leaving stigmas as distinct as leprosy and social markers as potent as AIDS. Built on the energy of germs, civilizations still rise and fall according to bacterial rhythms.

In spite of all kinds of medical paraphernalia, the superorganism remains a workaholic. Malaria and tuberculosis once again top mortality tables because irrigation and homelessness are on the increase. The World Health Organization predicts that 30 million people will cough themselves to early graves by the end of the century. TB, it says, is now a "global health crisis." Adults of every colour are losing their antibodies to measles and diphtheria, which means these vaccines don't work well anymore, that our immune systems are becoming more compromised or that the germs are simply changing. Salmonella and campylobacter (a diarrhea-causing microbe) are appearing more often in human stomachs because chicken farms breed these germs with the same flourish that cities spawn epidemics. In Latin America and Asia dengue fever is enjoying renewed popularity because the virus's carrier, the mosquito, breeds well in the discarded styrofoam cups, old tires and other garbage that encircle slums.

Many of the so-called "emerging" pathogens stealing TV time are really "re-emerging" infections of old such as cholera. In the last two hundred years this quick and efficient water-borne killer has travelled the world at least seven times emptying the poor of their bodily fluids. *Vibrio cholerea* probably first sprang to life in the polluted Ganges River and has since inhabited algal blooms. Here the bacteria shrink in size, chatter with other microbes and wait for opportunities. Ocean warming, pollution and ultraviolet radiation probably all play a role in bringing this incredible agent back into action. The last cholera pandemic probably began in the watery stools of a Bangladeshi peasant that floated their way to an algal bloom, rested for a while and then stole away in a ship's bilge water finally to be released outside Lima, Peru.

Once swallowed, the bacterium multiplies in the human gut where it sends out a highly potent toxin. Violent diarrhea and vomiting eventually turn the face haggard and the lips blue. After a hundred-year absence cholera arrived in Peru in 1991 and stayed to tour the continent. More than a million Latin Americans found themselves rushing to the toilet (if they could find one in their neighbourhood) and thousands died. In 1993 the 139th strain of cholera popped up in India; it promises to be even hardier and more virulent than the last. Cholera's allies, poverty, poor sanitation and unsafe water supplies, are co-operating fully. The work of microbes has no beginning and no end.

While cholera continues to stack the dead among the poor like cord wood, the developed world has had nightmares about "the flesh-eating bug." Thanks to overheated imaginations in the media most people have heard of "galloping gangrene" or necrotizing fasciitis. Although it's hard to ignore a disease that reduces flesh or muscle to smelly pulp in hours while poisoning the body with noxious toxins, the flesh-eating bug is not new. Group A streptococcus, an omnipresent germ, was eating wounded sailors and soldiers alive two hundred years ago.

No one knows why this deadly skin infection filled military surgical wards then or why it has re-emerged now. But many biologists recognize a chameleon at work. In the nineteenth century strep A appeared among children as scarlet fever. Taking advantage of urban overcrowding, it came in small but fatal waves or larger floods that produced much illness but little death. With improved public health measures scarlet fever all but disappeared from the scene until re-emerging as "toxic shock syndrome" in the 1980s. It then hit all ages, crashing the immune system with bad toxins. It killed Jim Henson, creator of the Muppets, in just hours.

It, too, reappeared in its flesh-eating guise. In the last two years strep's most frightful persona has struck hundreds in Norway as well as one prominent Canadian politician (he lost his leg) and created lurid tabloid headlines in England. People infected with this germ have about a 20 percent chance of survival. The only sure thing that physicians can now say about Group A streptococcus is that it has a history of "changing stripes," and that all its permutations have caught them off guard. Some now speculate that the germ may be signalling its intent to break out in epidemic form as fatal scarlet fever in the world's mega-cities. If nothing else, strep proves that the superorganism has an unlimited capacity to surprise and adapt.

Each civilization absent-mindedly creates its own plague wonders, and global warming may be the next pestilential calling card. By spewing too much carbon dioxide into the atmosphere, human industry has directly challenged the superorganism's primary reason for being: the regulation of gases that make life possible. The consequences of this tinkering are already evident. When temperatures rise, farmland dries up, old people die, insects go on the march and pollutants concentrate in the cities creating pools of asthma, the world's fastest growing ailment. Malaria and a number of gut-loving amoebas are already taking advantage of these developments to travel well outside their former boundaries into higher altitudes and more northern climates. Rwanda, Africa's most densely populated country, has witnessed a 337 percent increase in the incidence of malaria since 1987 thanks to record high temperatures and rainfall. The world's new concern about skin cancer is also a reminder that humans can't erode the earth's protective ozone layer without exposing themselves to more ultraviolet radiation than the immune system can sustain.

Global and local environments are not the only terrains modern societies are rearranging. In the pursuit of progress and the good life, humans are shooting as many holes in their immune system as they are in the atmosphere. In the last hundred years, the species' natural defences against disease have suffered more battering than at any other time in history. Some of the suppressors are old standards such as water pollution, malnutrition and smog. Newer subversives include cocaine, pesticides, radiation, fast foods, ultraviolet rays, electromagnetic waves and allergies to plastics. The general abandonment of breast-feeding and the promiscuous popping of antibiotics also haven't helped T-cell counts. Thinking physicians (and there are a few) now suspect that each generation of the human species is getting progressively weaker as more and more unusual kinds of stress wear down our immune defences. AIDS won't be the last epidemic to illuminate our failing health.

As human defences have weakened, the superorganism has grown stronger. Modern medical technologies such as antibiotics have raised greater problems than they have solved. That bacteria inhabiting every known ecological niche in the world now carry genes resistant to tetracycline is simply astounding. That most physicians and citizens do not regard this development as a health problem is even more frightening. As a consequence, the manufacture of super germs is now a daily tragedy that threatens future generations with deadly hazards.

When the Fourth Horseman rides again, reshaping civilization in unforeseeable ways, modern medicine will take its traditional seat in the last row of history's bleachers. Doctors have never arrested or changed the course of a pandemic and likely never will. The fragmentary nature of technological societies guarantees that when the dying starts, there will be no consensus or communal response. AIDS proved that the most sophisticated and wealthy of people can be the most vulnerable to death in grand numbers. Cleaving to a misplaced faith in technology, modern cultures have lost their traditional wisdom and all humility before God. While rural Africans seal off their villages to strangers when the Fourth Horseman rides, tribes in New York and Paris argue about civil rights or demand medicines that don't exist. With their quiet fatalism the poor understand that life continues after death and that pestilence is but one of many history-makers. The rich in the developed world will reap what they have sown in the future.

So, too, will modern medicine. Although drugs, vaccines and the impressive fad of gene sequencing may create an illusion of competence, pestilence will continue to remind the masses that the youngest science is still wearing a diaper, and probably a dirty one at that. Modern medicine will remain a crippled force in the presence of plagues until it gives up the germ theory and views epidemics as crude ecolgical disturbances in human culture. A respect for limits and a skepticism of progress have always been the best defences against disease but the hardest medicines to sell. They, too, can be fallible, which only proves the tragic character of life and the calamitous texture of time.

For however hard modern people try, they can't beat the super-organism, bribe the Fourth Horseman or ignore the immutable presence of pestilence in history. Nor can they afford to ignore the eternal hoofbeats of the First Horseman, Hope.

ACKNOWLEDGEMENTS

Every book belongs to a literary tradition and this one was deeply influenced by an eminent cast of germ historians and bacterial watchers. William McNeill, Fernand Braudel, Alfred Crosby Jr., Hans Zinsser, Mirko Grmek, René Dubos, Sorin Sonea, Lynn Margulis, Robert Gottfried, Murdo MacLeod, Philip Curtin and Robert Desowitz first started taking germs seriously. This book respectfully builds on their microbial adventures.

My own interest in the bacterial way of life has had many beginnings. My parents, public health pioneers, laid the educational groundwork. Sally Jordan, Donald Pilgrim and Russ Chace nourished the language and ideas. Don Grant drummed in the importance of people in story-telling. Eduardo Galeano sharpened the pens.

The team at Penguin Books (Iris Skeoch, Jackie Rothstein and Lori Ledingham) produced this book with intelligence and grace.

Special thanks also go to Meg Masters, who ably handled all revisions, and Jem Bates, who cleaned the text, Heather Pringle, an enthusiastic reader over my shoulder and Mirielle Keeling who pursued the picture permissions.

The chapter on AIDS was completed while I worked under the auspices of the Atkinson Fellowship in Public Policy, a gift to journalists if there ever was one.

No book is ever complete or totally accurate, and I am responsible for any and all errors and many omissions.

Last but not least, my thanks to Doreen and Aidan, who were as patient as Job and as supportive as only kin can be.

Photo Credits

Selected Bibliography

1 BEASTS, GERMS AND THE SUPERORGANISM

Ackerknecht, Erwin H. *Rudolf Virchow: Doctor, Statesman, Anthropologist*. Madison: University of Wisconsin Press, 1953.

Burnet, Macfarlane, and David O. White. *Natural History of Infectious Disease*. Cambridge: Cambridge University Press, 1972. (A *Who's Who* of famous microbes.)

Cohen, Mark Nathan, and George J. Armelagos. *Paleopathology at the Origins of Agriculture*. New York: Academic Press, 1984. (Denser than a field of corn but interesting reading.)

Dubos, René. *Man Adapting*. New Haven: Yale University press, 1980.

—————. *Mirage of Health: Utopias, Progress and Biological Change*. New York: Harper colophon Books, 1979. (A classic study on the vitality and meaning of disease.)

Ellul, Jacques. *Apocalypse: The Book of Revelation*. Trans. George W. Schreiner. New York: Seabury Press, 1977.

Harris, Marvin. *Cannibals and Kings: The Origins of Cultures*. New York: Vintage Books, 1978.

Illich, Ivan. *Limits to Medicine: Medical Nemesis: The Expropriation of Health*. Middlesex: Penguin Books, 1976.

de Kruif, Paul. *Microbe Hunters*. New York: Pocket Books, 1964.

Margulis, Lynne, and Dorion Sagan. *Microcosmos: Four Billion Years of Microbial Evolution*. New York: Summit Books, 1986. (History from a bacterial perspective.)

May, Jacques. *The Ecology of Human Disease*. New York: MD Publications, Inc., 1958. (Any work by May is an ecological revelation.)

McKeown, Thomas. *The Modern Rise of Population*. London: Edward Arnold, 1976.

McNeill, William H. *Plagues and Peoples*. New York: Doubleday, 1976. (The bible on epidemics.)

Sigerist, Henry E. *Civilization and Disease*. Chicago: University of Chicago Press, 1943.

Sonea, Sorin, and Maurice Panisset. *A New Bacteriology*. Boston: Jones and Bartlett Publishers, 1983. (A short and revolutionary tract that popularized the superorganism. Should be required reading in medical schools.)

Winslow, Charles E. *The Conquest of Epidemic Disease*. Princeton: Princeton University Press, 1943.

2 MALARIA: THE GREAT WINNOWER

Desowitz, Robert S. *New Guinea Tapeworms and Jewish Grandmothers: Tales of Parasite and People*. New York: W.W. Norton & Company, 1987. (Quirky and lively reading.)

Harrison, Gordon. *Mosquitoes, Malaria and Man: A History of the Hostilities Since 1880*. London: John Murray, 1978.

Holden, Constance, "Entomologists Wane as Insects Wax." *Science* 246 (November 10, 1989): 754–756.

Kiple, Kenneth F. *The Caribbean Slave: A Biological History*. Cambridge: Cambridge University Press, 1985.

May, Jacques. "Influence of Environmental Transformation in Changing the Map of Disease." *The Careless Technology*. Eds. M. Taghi Farvar and John P. Milton. Garden City, N.Y.: Natural History Press, 1972: 19–34.

Russell, Raul F. *Man's Mastery of Malaria*. London: Oxford University Press, 1955.

Tangley, Laura. "Malaria: Fighting the African Scourge." *BioScience* 37.2 (February 1987) 94–98.

Warshaw, Leon J. *Malaria: Biography of a Killer*. New York: Rinehart and Company Inc., 1949.

Withington, E.T. *Malaria and Greek History*. Manchester: Manchester University Press, 1909.

3 LEPROSY: IMMORTAL BLEMISH

Brody, Saul N. *The Disease of the Soul: Leprosy in Medieval Literature*.

Ithaca: Cornell University Press, 1974. (A good read.)

Carlin, Martha. "Medieval English Hospitals." *The Hospital in History.* Eds. Lindsay Granshaw and Roy Porter. New York: Routledge, 1989: 21–29.

Dols, Michael W. "The Leper in Medieval Islamic Society." *Speculum* 58.4 (1983): 891–916.

Grmek, Mirko D. *Diseases in the Ancient Greek World.* Trans. Mireille Muellner and Leonard Muellner. Baltimore: Johns Hopkins University Press, 1989.

Mercier, Charles A. *Leper Houses and Medieval Hospitals.* London: Lewis, 1915.

Ober, William B. "Can the Leper Change His Spots? The Iconography of Leprosy." *Bottoms UP!: A Pathologist's Essays on Medicine and the Humanities.* New York: Harper & Row, 1987: 99–152.

Richards, Peter. *The Medieval Leper and His Northern Heirs.* Cambridge: Rowman and Littlefield, 1977.

4 THE BLACK DEATH: AN ECOLOGICAL DISASTER

Aries, Philippe. *The Hour of Our Death.* Trans. Helen Weaver. New York: Alfred A. Knopf, 1981.

Braudel, Fernand. *The Structures of Everyday Life: Civilization and Capitalism, 15th–18th Century.* Trans. Sian Reynolds. New York: Harper & Row, 1979.

Calvi, Giulia. *Histories of a Plague Year: The Social and the Imaginary in Baroque Florence.* Los Angeles: University of California Press, 1989.

Campbell, Anna Montgomery. *The Black Death and Men of Learning.* New York: Columbia University press, 1931.

Capra, Fritjof. *The Turning Point: Science, Society and the Rising Culture.* Toronto: Bantam Books, 1982.

Carmichael, Ann G. *Plague and the Poor in Renaissance Florence.* Cambridge: Cambridge University Press, 1986.

Cartwright, Frederick F. *Disease and History.* New York: New American Library, 1972.

Cipolla, Carlo M. *Cristofano and the Plague: A Study in the History of Public Health in the Age of Galileo.* Los Angeles: University of California

Press, 1973.

——————. *Faith, Reason and the Plague in Seventeenth-Century Tuscany.* Trans. Muriel Kittel. Ithaca: Cornell University Press, 1979.

Davies, Gerald. *Hans Holbein the Younger.* London: George Bell and Sons, 1903.

Gottfried, Robert S. *The Black Death: Natural and Human Disaster in Medieval Europe.* New York: The Free Press, 1983.

Hirshleifer, Jack. *Disaster and Recovery: The Black Death in Western Europe.* Santa Monica: The Rand Corporation, 1966.

Hirst, L. Fabian. *The Conquest of Plague: A Study of the Evolution of Epidemiology.* Oxford: Oxford University Press, 1953.

Huppert, George. *After the Black Death: A Social History of Early Modern Europe.* Bloomington: Indiana University Press, 1986.

LeGoff, Jacques. *Time, Work and Culture in the Middle Ages.* Chicago: University of Chicago Press, 1980.

Nohl, Johannes. *The Black Death.* London: Unwin Books, 1956.

Tuchman, Barbara. *A Distant Mirror: The Calamitous 14th Century.* New York: Alfred A. Knopf, 1978.

Ziegler, Philip. *The Black Death.* Markham: Penguin Books, 1982.

5 THE SMALLPOX CONQUEST: BIOLOGICAL IMPERIALISM

Borah, Woodrow, and Sherburn Cook. *Essays in Population History: Mexico and the Caribbean.* Berkeley: University of California Press, 1971.

Bratton, Timothy L. "The Identity of the New England Indian Epidemic of 1616–19." *Bulletin of the History of Medicine* 62 (1988): 351–383.

Butler, William Francis. *The Great Lone Land.* Toronto: Musson Book Co., 1924. (Butler was a maverick British officer—he was Irish—who reported on the ravages of smallpox among the Cree with much honesty and sympathy.)

Crosby, Alfred. *The Columbian Exchange: Biological and Cultural Consequences of 1492.* Westport: Greenwood Press, 1972.

——————. *Ecological Imperialism: The Biological Expansion of Europe, 900–1900.* New York: Cambridge University Press, 1986. (Hard to put down.)

Curtin, Philip. "Epidemiology and the Slave Trade." *Political Science Quarterly* (June 1968): 190–216.

Denevan, William, ed. *The Native Population of the Americas in 1492.* Madison: University of Wisconsin Press, 1976.

Dobyns, Henry F. *Their Number Become Thinned: Native American Population Dynamics in Eastern North America.* Knoxville: University of Tennessee Press, 1983.

Gibbons, Ann. "New View of Early Amazonia." *Science* 248 (June 1990): 1488–1490.

Heagerty, John J. *Four Centuries of Medical History in Canada.* Toronto: The Macmillan Company of Canada, 1928.

Hopkins, Donald R. *Princes and Peasants: Smallpox in History.* Chicago: University of Chicago Press, 1983.

Leon-Portilla, Miguel. *The Broken Spears: The Aztec Account of the Conquest of Mexico.* Boston: Beacon Press, 1962.

MacLeod, Murdo. *Spanish Central America: A Socioeconomic History 1520–1720.* Berkeley: University of California Press, 1973. (Dry but brilliant.)

Mannix, D.P., and Malcolm Cowley. *Black Cargoes.* New York: Viking Press, 1965.

Marriot, Alice, and Carol K. Rachlin. *American Indian Mythology.* New York: New American Library, 1972. (Source of the remarkable Kiowa smallpox tale, "The White Man's Gift.")

Martin, Calvin. *Keepers of the Game: Indian-Animal Relationship and the Fur Trade.* Berkeley: University of California Press, 1978.

Roberts, Leslie. "Disease and Death in the New World." *Science* 246 (December 8, 1989): 1245–1247.

Vogel, Virgil. *American Indian Medicine.* Norman: University of Oklahoma Press, 1970.

6 SYPHILIS: VENEREAL LIAISONS

Arya, O.P., A.O. Osoba and F.J. Bennett. *Tropical Venereology.* London: Churchill Livingstone, 1980.

Baker, Brenda J., and George J. Armelagos. "The Origin and Antiquity of Syphilis." *Current Anthropology* 29.5 (December 1988): 703–720.

Bibel, Debra Jan. "Santayana's Warning Unheeded: The Parallels of Syphilis and Acquired Immune Deficiency Syndrome (AIDS)." *Sexually Transmitted Diseases* (October/December, 1989): 201–209.

Brandt, Allan M. *No Magic Bullet: A Social History of Venereal Disease in the United States Since 1880.* Oxford: Oxford University Press, 1987.

Cleugh, James. *Secret Enemy: The Story of a Disease.* New York: Thomas Yoseloff, 1956.

Iversen, William. *O the Times! O the Manners!* New York: William Morrow & Co., 1965.

Kruck, William E. *Looking for Dr. Condom.* University of Alabama: American Dialect Society, 1981. (Full of condom lore.)

Lauritsen, John. *Poison by Prescription: The AZT Story.* New York: Asklepios, 1990.

Lawrence, D.H. "Introduction to These Paintings." *Selected Literary Criticism.* Ed. Anthony Beal. London: Heinemann, 1982. (Vintage Lawrence.)

Leishman, Katie. "AIDS and Syphilis," *The Atlantic* 21 (January 1988): 17–26.

Riddell, William Renwick. *Hieronymus Fracastorius and his Poetical and Prose Works on Syphilis.* Toronto: The Canadian Social Hygiene Council, 1928. (Dated but delightful.)

Rosebury, Theodor. *Microbes and Morals: The Strange Story of Venereal Disease.* New York: Ballantine Books, 1976.

Temkin, Owsei. *The Double Face of Janus and Other Essays in the History of Medicine.* Baltimore: Johns Hopkins University Press, 1977. (Chapters 32 and 37 are particularly insightful.)

Thorndike, Lynn. "Sanitation, Baths, and Street-Cleaning in the Middle Ages and Renaissance." *Speculum* 111 (1928): 192–203.

Waugh, Michael Anthony. "History of Clinical Developments in Sexually Transmitted Diseases." *Sexually Transmitted Diseases.* Ed. King K. Holmes et al. Toronto: McGraw-Hill, 1990: 3–16. (Essays such as this one remind us why doctors are so liberally ill-informed.)

Woodforde, John. *The Strange Story of False Hair.* London: Routledge, 1971.

7 THE IRISH FAMINE: A BLIGHTED FABLE

Crawford, Margaret E. "Dearth, Diet, and Disease in Ireland, 1850–: A Case Study of Nutritional Deficiency." *Medical History* 28 (1984): 151–161.

Evans, E. Estyn. *The Personality of Ireland: Habitat, Heritage and History.* Cambridge: Cambridge University Press, 1973.

Hardy, Anne. "Urban Famine or Urban Crisis? Typhus in the Victorian City." *Medical History* 32 (1988) 401–425.

MacKay, Donald. *Flight from Famine: The Coming of the Irish to Canada.* Toronto: McClelland & Stewart, 1990.

Matossian, Mary Kilbourne. *Poisons of the Past: Molds, Epidemics and History.* New Haven: Yale University Press, 1989.

McNeill, William. *Population and Politics Since 1750.* Charlottesville: University Press of Virginia, 1990.

Post, John D. *The Last Great Subsistence Crisis in the Western World.* Baltimore: Johns Hopkins University Press, 1977.

Salaman, Redcliffe. *The History and Social Influence of the Potato.* Cambridge: Cambridge University Press, 1949. (Recommended for spud lovers.)

Woodham-Smith, Cecil. *The Great Hunger: Ireland 1845–1849.* New York: Harper & Row, 1962. (A masterful piece of story-telling.)

Zinsser, Hans. *Rats, Lice and History.* New York: Bantam Books, 1971. (Typhus's unauthorized biography.)

8 TUBERCULOSIS: CONSUMPTIVE REVOLUTIONS

Clark, George, et al. "The Evolution of Mycobacterial Disease in Human Populations." *Current Anthropology* 28.1 (February 1987): 45–51.

Dubos, René, and Jean Dubos. *The White Plague: Tuberculosis, Man, and Society.* London: Rutgers University Press, 1987. (Not romantic reading.)

Imhof, Arthur. "From the Old Mortality Pattern to the New: Implications of a Radical Change from the Sixteenth to the Twentieth Century." *Bulletin of Medical History* 59 (1985): 1–29. (A creative analysis.)

Inglis, Brian. *The Diseases of Civilization.* London: Granada, 1983.

McKeown, Thomas. *The Origins of Disease.* New York: B. Blackwell, 1988.

Smith, F.B. *The Retreat of Tuberculosis: 1850–1950.* London: Croom Helm, 1988.

Waksman, Selman A. *The Conquest of Tuberculosis.* London: Robert Hale Limited, 1965.

Weinstein, Malcolm S. *Health in the City: Environmental and Behavioral Influences.* New York: Pergamon Press, 1980.

Wohl, Anthony. *Endangered Lives: Public Health in Victorian Britain.* London: J.M. Dent & Sons Inc., 1983.

9 INFLUENZA: VIRAL WAVES

Beveridge, William Ian. *Influenza: The Last Great Plague.* New York: Prodist, 1978.

Creighton, Charles. *A History of Epidemics in Britain, Vol. 2.* London: Frank Cass and Co. Ltd, 1965.

Crosby, Alfred, Jr. *Epidemic and Peace, 1918.* Westport, Connecticut: Greenwood Press, 1976. (History writing at its best.)

Fettner, Ann Giudici. *Viruses: Agents of Change.* New York: McGraw-Hill, 1990.

Finher, Jack. "America's Deadly Rendezvous with the 'Spanish Lady.'" *Smithsonian* 19 (1989): 130–.

Jordan, Edwin O. *Epidemic Influenza: A Survey.* Chicago: American Medical Association, 1927.

Kilbourne, Edwin D. *Influenza* New York: Plenum Press, 1987.

Miller, Julie Ann. "Diseases for Our Future." *BioScience* 39.8 (September 1989): 509–517.

Morse, Stephen S. "Stirring Up Trouble." *The Sciences* (September/October 1990): 16–21.

Patterson, David K. *Pandemic Influenza 1700–1900: A Study in Historical Epidemiology.* Totowa, N.J.: Rowman and Littlefield, 1983.

Pyle, Gerald F. *The Diffusion of Influenza: Patterns and Paradigms.* Totowa, N.J.: Rowman and Littlefield, 1986.

10 AIDS: FALTERING DEFENCES

Altman, Dennis. *AIDS and the New Puritanism*. London: Pluto Press, 1986.

——————. *The Homosexualization of America, the Americanization of the Homosexual*. New York: St Martin's Press, 1982.

Bayer, Ronald. *Private Acts, Social Consequences: AIDS and the Politics of Public Health*. New York: The Free Press, 1989.

Crewdson, John. "The Great AIDS Quest." *Chicago Tribune*, 19 November 1989.

Duesberg, Peter H., and Bryan J. Ellison. "Is HIV the Cause of AIDS?" *Policy Review* 54 (Fall 1990): 70–83.

——————. "Is the AIDS Virus a Science Fiction?" *Policy Review* 54 (Summer 1990): 40–51.

Fisher, Jeffrey. *The Plague Makers: How We Are Creating Catastrophic New Epidemics—And What We Must Do to Avert Them*, New York: Simon & Shuster, 1994: 53–69.

Fumento, Michael. *The Myth of Heterosexual AIDS*. New York: Basic Books Inc., 1990.

Grmek, Mirko D. *History of AIDS: Emergence and Origin of a Modern Pandemic*. Trans. Russell C. Maulitz and Jacalyn Duffin. Princeton: Princeton University Press, 1990.

——————. "Some Unorthodox Views and a Selection Hypothesis on the Origin of the AIDS Viruses." *The Journal of the History of Medicine and Allied Sciences*, 1995, Vol. 50, 253–273.

Larson, Ann. "The Social Epidemiology of Africa's AIDS Epidemic." *African Affairs* 89.354 (January 1990) 5–25.

Levine, Martin, ed. *Gay Men and the Sociology of Male Homosexuality*. New York: Harper & Row, 1979.

Miller, Norman, and Richard C. Rockwell, eds. *AIDS in Africa: The Social Impact and Policy Issue*. Lewiston: The Edwin Mellen Press, 1988.

Perlez, Jane. "Toll of AIDS on Uganda's Women Puts Their Roles and Rights in Question." *New York Times*, 28 October 1990, p. 16.

Root-Bernstein, R.S. "Do We Know the Cause(s) of AIDS?" *Perspectives in Biology and Medicine* 33.4 (Summer 1990): 480–500.

——————. "Non-HIV Immunosuppressive Factors in AIDS: A

Multifactorial, Synergistic Theory of AIDS Aetiology." *Research in Immunology* 141 (1990): 815–838.

Shilts, Randy. *And the Band Played On: Politics, People, and the AIDS Epidemic.* New York: St Martin's Press, 1987.

Sonnabend, J.A. "AIDS: An Explanation for Its Occurrence Among Homosexual Men." *AIDS and Opportunistic Infections of Homosexual Men.* Eds. P. Ma and D. Armstrong. Stoneham, Mass.: Butterworth, 1989. 449–465.

Thompson, Mark. *Gay Spirit: Myth and Meaning.* New York: St Martin's Press, 1987.

Van de Perre, Philippe. "The Epidemiology of HIV Infection and AIDS in Africa," *Trends in Microbiology*, June 1995, Vol. 3, No. 6, 217–221.

11 THE BACTERIAL RENAISSANCE: UNDYING GERMS

Fisher, Jeffrey. *The Plague Makers: How We Are Creating Catastrophic New Epidemics—And What We Must Do to Avert Them,* New York: Simon & Shuster, 1994.

Garrett, Laurie. *The Coming Plague: Newly Emerging Disease in a World Out of Balance.* New York: Farrar, Straus and Giroux, 1994. (An excellent resource book.)

Karlen, Arno. *Man and Microbes: Disease and Plagues in History and Modern Times.* New York: G.P. Putnam's Sons, 1995.

Krause, Richard. "Dynamics of Emergence," *Journal of Infectious Diseases,* 1994; 170: 265–71.

Lappe, Marc. *Germs That Won't Die: Medical Consequences of the Misuse of Antibiotics.* New York: Anchor Press, 1982. (A book way ahead of the times and the medical establishment.)

Lederberg, Joshua et al. *Emerging Infections: Microbial Threats to Health in the United States.* Washington, D.C.: National Academy Press, 1992.

Levy, Stuart. *The Antibiotic Paradox: How Miracle Drugs Are Destroying the Miracle.* New York: Plenum Press, 1992. (Should be on every physician's desk.)

12 EBOLA'S APPRENTICES: EMERGING VIRUSES

Close, William Dr. *Ebola.* New York: Ivy Books, 1995.

Garret, Laurie. "Plague Warriors," *Vanity Fair*, August 1995, No. 420: 85–93.

Henig, Robin. *A Dancing Matrix: How Science Confronts Emerging Viruses*, New York, Vintage Books, 1994.

Kilbourne, Edwin. "New Viral Diseases," *Journal of the American Medical Association*, July 4, 1990, Vol. 264, No. 1.

Le Guenno Bernard. "Emerging Viruses," *Scientific American*, October 1995, 56–64.

Miller, Julie Ann. "Diseases for Our Future," *BioScience* (September 1989), Vol. 39, No. 8, 509–517.

Morse, Stephen. "Stirring Up Trouble," *The Sciences* (September/October 1990): 16–21.

Murphy, Frederick. "New, Emerging and Reemerging Infectious Diseases," Monograph, School of Veterinary Medicine, University of California, 1992, 41 pages.

Preston, Richard. *The Hot Zone*. New York: Random House, 1994. (A spine-tingling book!)

INDEX